M000197878

224 MAIN STREET   BRATTLEBORO, VERMONT 05301

ENGLISH ESTATES OF AMERICAN COLONISTS

ENGLISH ESTATES
OF AMERICAN COLONISTS

American Wills and Administrations
in the Prerogative Court of Canterbury,
1700-1799

By Peter Wilson Coldham

Baltimore
GENEALOGICAL PUBLISHING CO., INC.
1980

INTRODUCTION

Until 1858 the proving of wills and the granting of administrations in England and Wales were matters dealt with by the ecclesiastical authorities in any one of some 300 probate courts. The principal such court was the Prerogative Court of Canterbury (PCC), so called because its jurisdiction was exercised on behalf of the Archbishop of Canterbury, the Primate. It was the PCC which handled matters of probate affecting the personal estates of English subjects dying overseas and its records are therefore of vital interest to the descendants of Englishmen who chose, or were compelled, to emigrate to the American colonies. It should be noted, however, that the ecclesiastical courts had no jurisdiction over bequests of real estate (land, houses, etc.), and though many wills included instructions for the disposal of such property, any such bequests that were disputed had to be tried at Common Law.

Over the past 150 years or so several abstracts or listings of American wills registered in the PCC have appeared in print, and some spasmodic attempts have been made to provide finding aids. Such attempts have been more successful for the period prior to 1700, for which consolidated printed indexes are available,[1] than for subsequent years for which the means of reference are so inadequate as to present an almost insuperable barrier for most people with limited time and funds at their disposal. The aim of this volume, therefore, is to present the genealogist and historian for the first time with a comprehensive guide to the American wills and grants of administration registered in the PCC between 1700 and 1799.[2] The collection of material for this purpose has required several years and detailed perusal of more than 200 contemporary Act Books, each crammed with hand-written entries of varying accuracy and legibility.[3]

A brief note on how this volume was compiled may be useful in indicating both the scope and some of the limitations of this series of abstracts. Summary notes of all grants of probate registered in the PCC were recorded month by month in the Probate Act Books (PROB 8), and of all grants of letters of administration in the Administration Act Books (PROB 6), now housed at the Public Record Office, Chancery Lane, London. Each Act Book covers a calendar year (reckoned according to the modern calendar) and is divided into sections, called *Seats* or *Walks*, according to the region in which the testator or intestate died. The so-called *Register Walk* catered for areas falling outside the Province of Canterbury (the southern half of Britain) and for grants made following litigation. Up to and including the year 1730 every entry in every Act Book has been examined but, because of the rapidly increasing number of entries after that date,[4] only the *Register Walk* sections have been scanned from 1731 to 1799. Until 1733 all entries were written in Latin.

The Probate Act Books usually record, in addition to the name of the testator and his executor(s), his marital status, the place where he died and, after 1796, the value of his personal estate. This information is not necessarily noted on the register copy of the will. The Administration Act Books note the name of the intestate, his marital status, his administrator(s), usually his place of death and, after 1796, the value of his personal estate. Throughout the period covered many entries in the Act Books refer to persons dying "in parts overseas": how many of them may have been American settlers will probably never be known. Certainly throughout the earlier part of the eighteenth century the PCC clerks betrayed a superficial knowledge of geography which leaves the researcher with plenty of room to guess whether the term West Indies might mean mainland America or, for that matter, whether when the scribe wrote of the Island of Virginia he had any idea of the place he was describing. Throughout the preparation of this volume entries from the

vi

Act Books have been transcribed only when, from the original wording, it has been possible to establish unambiguously that the deceased or his relatives had some connection with mainland America.

It is almost inevitable that a study involving many tens of thousands of separate entries should contain some omissions and inaccuracies, though every attempt has been made to minimize them. The compiler will be grateful rather than resentful to have such defects brought to his notice.

Peter Wilson Coldham
Purley, Surrey,
England.

Christmas 1979
AMDG.

Notes

1. Printed indexes to PCC records are available as follows: Wills 1385-1700; 1750-1800, A-Ce only (*in progress*). Administrations 1559-1619, 1649-1660.

2. The abstracts now consolidated into this volume originally appeared *seriatim* in the *National Genealogical Society Quarterly*.

3. The sources used were:
Administration Act Books: PROB 6/76 (1700) to 175 (1799).
Probate Act Books: PROB 8/93 (1700) to 192 (1799).
Limited Probate Act Book: PROB 9/1 (1781).

4. It has been estimated that by the end of the eighteenth century some 12,000 probate and administration acts were being recorded annually in the PCC.

Notes on Sources Used

The Acts listed in this book record grants made in the following categories:

FOR TESTATORS

a. *Probate* was normally granted after an executor had submitted the original will to the PCC and it had been found to be in order and subscribed by two witnesses. Executors could either attend the court in person or be sworn by two local clergymen.

b. *Administration with will* annexed. A grant was made in this form where, for some reason, probate could not be granted to the executor(s) named. Most frequently in the case of American wills such grants were made to attorneys or relatives in England because the named executors were unable to attend in person.

c. *Limited probate.*

d. *Limited administration with will* annexed. A limited grant of this kind empowered executors or their attorneys to act in the distribution of a testator's effects within defined conditions specified in the Act Books. An American will was often probated in one of the colonial courts and a copy transmitted to the PCC which would then empower a representative of the deceased to administer his effects in England and collect any debts owing to him.

Grants of probate and of administrations with wills annexed (a. and b.) have been abstracted in abbreviated form so as to include all relevant information in the Act Books; but limited grants (c. and d.), being often quite lengthy and filled with circumstantial detail, have been only partially abstracted. The text of grants made in limited form should, therefore, always be consulted in addition to the wills themselves. Register copies of all wills listed in this volume are available in class PROB 11 at the Public Record Office in Chancery Lane, London, complete references in each case being obtainable by consultation of the manuscript annual indexes, PROB 12. In addition, original or facsimile copies of wills (not always distinguishable) *may* be available in class PROB 10.

FOR INTESTATES

e. *Administration.* Letters of administration were usually granted to the widow, next of kin, or principal creditor of a person who died without making a will.

f. *Limited administration* was granted when some limitation of time or place was imposed. In the case of Americans dying intestate such grants were often limited to the administration of his effects in England. As with limited probates, the text of the grant in the appropriate Act Book should be consulted since only the salient points have been recorded in this volume.

Knowledge of the month and year in which a grant of administration was made will provide ready access to the affidavits sworn in the PCC by administrators (PROB 14), which indicate the approximate date of the intestate's death. In the case of American colonists, the grant can be several years delayed after the time of death as the following verbatim example will show:

"15th September 1717. On this day appeared personally John Bagge and alleged that Mary Bagg alias Butler, late of the parish of Washington in Westmoreland County, Virginia, in parts over the seas, died intestate in the month of April 1713; and he being the lawful husband of the said deceased prays that letters of administration of the goods and credits of the said deceased . . . may be granted to him."

The most valuable additional source of information about grants of administration is likely to be the Administration Bonds (PROB 46), which are still under arrangement and therefore not yet available for public inspection. They will be particularly significant in providing the names and addresses of the persons who entered into a bond with the administrator(s).

The PCC as a Court of Litigation

In recent years a mass of documents has become available in the Public Record Office, and many more are still being sorted and calendared, opening up extensive new areas for genealogical research. It would be impossible here to give an adequate description of these newly available resources, let alone recommend a methodology for their use. Sufficient to say that the PCC acted as a court of first instance for many disputed wills and grants of administration and as a court of appeal from other ecclesiastical probate courts, and that the procedures and types of document in use were those familiar to lay courts, e.g. Allegations, Answers, Depositions, Sentences, Exhibits. For those with the taste and enterprise recommended reading is "The Records of the Prerogative Court of Canterbury," a provisional guide published by the Public Record Office which gives an excellent summary of the classes of litigation papers available for consultation. Be warned, though, that the Great Fire of London in 1666 consumed the greater part of such records accumulated before that date.

Disputed Estates in Other Courts

As already noted, disputes over bequests of freehold were outside the jurisdiction of the PCC and had to be taken to Common Law. The volume of such business thus generated in the civil courts was considerable, and a substantial proportion of the whole, particularly in Chancery. The Chancery Court could, and often did, override the decisions of the PCC. Indexes to disputed estates in Chancery 1649-1714 are available on open shelves in the Long Room of the Public Record Office in Chancery Lane.

It would be as well to conclude this review with the observation that the pursuit of genealogical investigation through the medium of legal records is a wearisome and demanding task probably best left to the specialist in such matters.

Abbott, James, of Charles Town, South Carolina, who died at sea. Administration to sister Mary Abbott. (May 1720).

Abbott, Thomas, of H.M.S. *Russell*, bachelor. Administration to Jeremiah Jones, attorney for father Robert Abbott now at Massachusetts Bay. (Jan. 1747).

Abell, George, of Charles Town, South Carolina, widower. Probate to brother Thomas Abell. (Mar. 1742).

Abercrombie, James, of Philadelphia. Probate to William Neate, attorney for Charles and Alexander Stedman and Samuel McCall the younger in Philadelphia. (July 1761).

Abercrombie, James, Lieutenant-Colonel of 22nd Regiment who died at Boston, New England. Administration with will to Arthur Mair, attorney for Lieutenant-General James Abercrombie now at Glassaugh, Banffshire, Scotland. (Oct. 1775).

Ablett, Thomas, of Maryland, bachelor. Administration to Edward Parker, sole executor of the brother and next of kin William Ablett who died before administering. (Feb. 1755).

Acworth, John, of Philadelphia, merchant. Special administration with will to Abraham Acworth. (July 1746).

Adams, James, clerk of North Carolina, bachelor. Administration to Alexander Junes, attorney for sisters and next of kin Jannett and Elizabeth Adams now in Aberdeen, Scotland. (Sept. 1711).

Adams, Joseph, of York Town, Virginia, formerly of H.M.S. *Wolf* and late purser of H.M.S. *Fox*. Administration with will to Daniel Walton, attorney for relict Ann Adams at York Town. (June 1758).

Adams, Robert, of Pennsylvania. Administration to son and next heir William Adams. (Nov. 1700).

Adams, William, of St. Ann, Limehouse, Middlesex, who died in Philadelphia, bachelor. Administration to sister and only next of kin Sarah, wife of Absalom Wood. (July 1756).

Aderne - see Arderne.

Adler, Joseph, marine of H.M.S. *Glasgow* who died in South Carolina, bachelor. Administration to father Joseph Adler. (Aug. 1775).

Aglionby, William, of Savannah, Georgia. Probate to William Bradley. (May 1745).

Agnew, James, Brigadier-General, late of St. Andrew, Auckland, Co. Durham, Lieutenant-General of 44th Regiment who died at German Town, North America. Probate to relict Elizabeth Agnew. (Feb. 1778).

Aire, Robert, purser of H.M.S. *Deal* who died at New York, bachelor. Administration to sisters Jane, wife of Thomas Morland, and Mary, wife of Richard Thompson; the father Thomas Aire renouncing. (Dec. 1771).

Arey, John, of North Carolina, bachelor. Probate to Henry Trenchard Goodenough. (Nov. 1771).

Airey, Joseph, of Yorks Co., New York, Lieutenant of an Independent Company. Administration to James Goldtrap, attorney for relict Mary Airey now in New York. (May 1764).

Albro, Maturian, of West Greenwich, Kent Co., Rhode Island, of Lieutenant-Colonel Christopher Hargill's Company in the Rhode Island Regiment of Foot, who died at Havanna, bachelor. Administration by solemn declaration to Joseph Sherwood, attorney for brother and next of kin John Albro now at West Greenwich. (Dec. 1765).

Alexander, David, of Glasgow, Scotland, who died in Maryland, bachelor. Administration to brother James Alexander. (Apr. 1757).

Alexander, Thomas, formerly of Boston, Mass., but late of Shelburne, Nova Scotia, widower. Administration to Lewis Wolfe, attorney for son Charles Alexander now at Liverpool, Lancashire. (Apr. 1789).

Alexander, William, of St. Gregory, London, who died at Philadelphia. Probate to relict Mary Alexander. (Oct. 1727).

Alexon alias Ellixon, Jasper, of merchant ship *Preservation* who died in Virginia. Probate to relict Mary Alexon alias Ellixon. (Dec. 1706).

Aley, John, of Philadelphia, widower. Administration to brother and next of kin Robert Aley. (Dec. 1783).

Algeo - see Allgeo.

Allen, James, of Boston, New England. Administration to Barlow Trewthick, John Apthorp and John Thomlinson, attornies for relict Martha, now wife of William Brattle, residing at Cambridge, New England. (Apr. 1763).

Allen, John, of Colonel Holt's Regiment, bachelor. Administration by decree to principal creditor Elizabeth Jennings, widow. "Pauper." (July 1722).

Allen, John, of H.M.S. *Roebuck* who died at Philadelphia. Limited administration with will to Eleanor Brown, administratrix of the will of legatee John Allen. (July 1779).

Allen, Thomas, of merchant ship *Medway* who died in South Carolina. Administration to Diana, wife of father George Allen, now at sea. "Pauper." (Feb. 1729).

Allford, Dorothy, of Pennsylvania, spinster. Administration to sister and next of kin Mary, wife of Joseph Little. (Nov. 1718).

Allgeo, John, formerly of Quebec but late of North Carolina, bachelor. Administration to Peter Ogden, attorney for father David Allgeo at Quebec. (Dec. 1788).

Algeo, Margaret, of New York City, widow. Administration to Barnardus La Grange, attorney for only child David Algeo, now at Quebec. (Nov. 1792).

Amar, John, of Pensacola but late of New York City. Administration with will to James Dewey, attorney for relict Sarah Amar and Thomas Austen now at New York. (Oct. 1782).

Amory, Simon, of Pensacola, West Florida. Limited special probate to brother Thomas Amory, clerk. (Nov. 1766).

Amyand, Isaac, of Charles Town, South Carolina, gent. Special administration with will to Claudius Amyand. (Dec. 1739).

Anderson, Andrew, of H.M.S. *La Fortune* who died at Long Island, bachelor. Administration to brother and next of kin James Anderson. (Oct. 1785).

Anderson, George, of the Town of Georgia (sic), Captain of the packet *Georgia*, who died at sea. Administration to principal creditor James Gusthart; relict Deborah Anderson and only children John, Mary and George Anderson, being cited but not appearing. (Nov. 1777).

Anderson, Lauchlan, of Detroit, Canada, bachelor. Administration to John Anderson, attorney for mother Margaret Mongrief alias Moncrief, widow, now in Fifeshire, Scotland. (Mar. 1785).

Anderson, William, of merchant ship *Herbert* who died in Maryland, bachelor. Administration to principal creditor John Thompson. (Feb. 1734).

Anderson, William, formerly of Virginia but late of Vauxhall,
St. Mary, Lambeth, Surrey. Probate to relict Mary Anderson,
Samuel Gist, William Fowke and John Anderson, with similar
powers reserved to nephew Overton Anderson. (Jan. 1796).

Andre, John, Major and Adjutant-General of the Army in North
America, Captain of the 54th Regiment, who died at Tappan.
Probate to uncles David Andre, Andrew Girardot and John Lewis
with similar powers reserved to mother Mary Louisa Andre.
(Jan. 1781).

Andrews, William, of Cote, Bishops Canning, Wiltshire, who died
in Virginia, bachelor. Probate to Hester Brown alias Nash,
sole legatee of estate unadministered by executor Nicholas
Nash. (Aug. 1726).

Andrus, David, of Farmington, Hartford Co., Connecticut, Lieu-
tenant of First Connecticut Regiment who died at Havana.
Administration to Phineas Lyman, attorney for relict Mary
Andrus now at Farmington. (Nov. 1764).

Annely, Richard, of New York. Probate to Thomas Annely. (Oct.
1750).

Anthony, John, surgeon of H.M. Fireship *Strombole* who died at
New York. Administration with will to William Palmer,
attorney for mother and sole executrix Elinor Anthony, widow,
now at Ballimahon, Co. Longford, Ireland. (Mar. 1778)..
Revoked because of the death of William Palmer and granted
to the mother Elinor Anthony. (Nov. 1781).

Antill, Lewis, of New York, widower. Administration to brother
John Antill; mother Ann Antill having died before administering. (Feb. 1786).

Antram, William, of H.M.S. *Mermaid* who died at South Carolina,
bachelor. Probate to mother Mary, wife of Jacob Minor.
(Feb. 1752).

Applebee, Benjamin, of New York who died in Dorset. Admini-
station to William Bryant, attorney for relict Frances
Applebee now in New York. (Mar. 1744).

Appleton, John, of H.M.S. *Glasgow, Romney* and *Boston* who died
in Boston Hospital, bachelor. Administration to creditor
Roger Dawson; previous grant of February 1773 declared
void. (June 1775).

Appleton, Samuel, of Boston, New England, who died at St. Andrew
Undershaft, London. Limited administration to Jasper Waters,
Thompson Hayne and Samuel Southouse. (Jan 1729).

Appy, John, Secretary and Judge-Advocate to H.M. Forces in North
America. Administration with will to father Peter Appy.
(May 1763).

Apthorp, Charles, of Boston, Mass. Administration to aon Thomas
Apthorp; relict Grizzell Apthorp cited but not appearing.
(May 1784).

Apthorp, John, of Cambridge, Mass. Probate to brother George
Apthorp with similar powers reserved to relict Hannah Apthorp,
Barlow Trecothick, brother Thomas Apthorp and Martin Howard.
(Feb. 1733). Double probate to only surviving executor
brother Thomas Apthorp. (Nov. 1783).

Archdeacon, James, of Norfolk, Virginia. Administration to
creditor Robert Gilmour; relict Parnell Archdeacon and only
child John Archdeacon cited but not appearing. (Aug. 1784).

Aderne, John, of Carolina. Probate to Edward Warren. (Apr.
1715).

Arderne, John, of North Carolina. Probate to William Dunkin-
field. (Sept. 1720).

3

Arey - see Airey.

Arking,, Robert, of St. Botolph Aldgate, London, who died at
New York. Administration to relict Lilias alias Lillas
Arking alias Arken alias Brown. (Mar. 1735).

Arlington, Michael, of Stepney, Middlesex, who died on H.M.S.
Lyme in Virginia. Probate to Nathan Movelty with similar
powers reserved to his wife Sara Movelty. (Aug. 1719).

Armistead, Henry, of Caroline Co., Virginia, widower. Admini-
startion to Edward Hunt, attorney for son William Armistead
in Virginia. (Dec. 1748).

Armstrong, George, of merchant ship *Concord* who died in Maryland. Probate to Robert Pitt. (Dec. 1735).

Armstrong, Thomas, master of merchant ship *Peggy* who died
in Philadelphia, bachelor. Administration to George
Armstrong, attorney for father William Armstrong now at
Holy Island, Co. Durham. (July 1769).

Arnold, Sarah, formerly of Paddington Street, St. Marylebone,
Middlesex, but late of Philadelphia, spinster. Admini-
stration to sister Jemima, wife of Christopher Gartland.
(Apr. 1798).

Arnot, Robert, of merchant ship *Davy*, who died in Carolina,
bachelor. Administration to sister Jane, wife of James
Anderson. (May 1739).

Arthur, Christopher, of Sypryss Barony, South Carolina, who
died at St. Dunstan, Stepney, Middlesex. Probate to
Patrick Roche. (Dec. 1724).

Arthur, William, of H.M.S. *Apollo*, who died in New York Hospital. Probate to Elizabeth, wife of William Sutherland,
with similar powers reserved to said William Sutherland.
(Jan. 1781).

Arundell, Robert, of Ottery St. Mary, Devon, who died at
Annapolis Royal. Administration to James Channon, guardian
of niece by a daughter Rebecca Channon. (Nov. 1725).

Ash, Anne - see Livingston.

Ash, John, of Danho, Carolina. Probate to William Methuen,
attorney for relict Mary Ash in Carolina. (Jan. 1706).

Ash, John, of Westfield, Colleton Co., South Carolina, who
died in Wiltshire. Probate by decree to William Livingston,
husband and administrator of the relict Ann Livingston
alias Ash, who died before administering. (Aug. 1721).

Ashe alias Batt, Mary, widow, lately wife of John Ashe, of
Dahoe, Colliton Co., South Carolina. Administration by
decree to William Ashe; all others with an interest cited
but not appearing. (Feb. 1719).

Ashton, John, of New York, widower. Administration to son
George Ashton. (Nov. 1704).

Aspitall, William, soldier of 22nd Regiment of Foot in Captain
Rawlin Hillman's Company, who died at Movill, West Florida,
bachelor. Probate to Thomas Levingston. (Aug. 1766).

Astbury, Thomas, Major of 33rd Company of Marines on H.M.S.
Cornwall who died at New York, bachelor. Probate to Ann
Lane, spinster. (Mar. 1779).

Atchison, George, of Charles Town, South Carolina, who died
at Islington, Middlesex, bachelor. Probate to David
Atchison with similar powers reserved to James Pain.
(Sept. 1728).

Atkins, Sara, of New England, widow. Administration to principal creditor Sir Charles Hobby. (Sept. 1707).

Atkinson, George, of Charles Town, South Carolina, who died
at Islington, Middlesex, bachelor. Double probate to
James Pain. (Oct. 1729). *Appears to be the same as George
Atchison, q.v.*

Atkinson, Theodore, of Portsmouth, New Hampshire. Admini-
startion with will to Thomas Dickason, attorney for George
King, now George Atkinson, at Portsmouth, New Hampshire.
(Oct. 1783).

Atkinson, William, of West River, Maryland, Lieutenant on
half pay. Administration with will to John Clapham,
attorney for Frederick Green and Jonas Clapham, now in
Maryland. (July 1795).

Atwood, Anthony, of Newport, Rhode Island, sergeant in Lieute-
nant-Colonel Christopher Hargill's Company of the Rhode
Island Regiment of Foot, who died at Havana, bachelor.
Administration by the solemn declaration of Joseph Sher-
wood, attorney for father Joseph Atwood at Newport.
(Dec. 1765).

Attwood, Isaac, of Perth Amboy, North America, Captain in
Colonel Fanning's late Regiment of King's Americans.
Administration to David Thomas, attorney for relict
Elizabeth Attwood at Perth Amboy. (Aug. 1795).

Austell, Joseph, of Boston, New England. Special limited
probate to cousin Moses Austell. (Sept. 1748).

Austin, Matt, unchristened black slave of H.M.S. *Winchelsea*,
bachelor. Administration to William White, attorney for
owner Mary Austin, widow, at Charles Town, South Carolina.
(June 1762).

Austin, Sarah, of Philadelphia, widow. Administration to son
William Austin. (Aug. 1786).

Austin, William, surgeon's mate of H.M. Hospital in North
America, who died at Albany, New York, bachelor. Admini-
stration to Kenneth Mackenzie, attorney for father Joseph
Austin at Kilspindie, Perthshire, Scotland. (Dec. 1764).

Avery, Joseph, formerly of Connecticut, New England, but late
of City of Bristol. Probate to Jane Day, spinster. (July
1746).

Avory alias Avera, Mary, of Prince George Co., Virginia, widow.
Probate to son Charles Avera and daughter Molly, wife of
Amos Elliott. (Dec. 1769).

Avery, Richard, of Stepney, Middlesex, who died in New England,
widower. Administration to son Richard Avery. (Apr. 1743).

Ayscough, Richard, of New York City. Probate to Rev. Francis
Ayscough with similar powers reserved to relict Anne
Ayscough and Charles Williams. (Nov. 1760). Administration with will of goods unadministered by Francis Ayscough
deceased to William Moore, husband of relict Anne;
surviving executors Anne Moore and Charles Williams cited
but not appearing, and the minor children Richard Maximilian
Ayscough and Ann Ayscough, minors, also not appearing.
(Jan. 1768).

Bacon, Butts, of Piscataway, New England, bachelor. Administration to brother Sir Edward Bacon. (May 1726).

Badenhop, Jesse, of South Carolina, bachelor. Administration
to uncle and next of kin James Payzant. (Oct. 1740).

Bagg alias Butler, Mary, of Washington, Westmoreland Co.,
Virginia. Administration to husband John Bagg, clerk.
(Sept. 1717).

Bagshaw, Joseph, formerly of Newcastle, Staffordshire, but
late of Philadelphia. Probate to Samuel Worthington.
(Nov. 1797).

Bailley alias Bayley, John, of Philadelphia who died on H.M.S.
Jersey. Probate to Hugh Higins alias Hogan. (Oct. 1748).

Bayly, Melchizideck, of Boston, New England, bachelor.
Administration to brother and next of kin Benjamin Bayly.
(Sept. 1720).

Baily, Richard, of Stoughton, Suffolk Co., Mass. Probate to
son Henry Baily. (Nov. 1786).

Bailey, Sarah, of St. James, Westminster, who died in Maryland,
spinster. Administration to father Thomas Bailey. (Jan.
1751).

Baillie, William, of Maryland, bachelor. Probate to James
Pitts. (Jan. 1703).

Bayly, William, of Liberty of theTower, London, who died in
Virginia. Administration to relict Isabel Bayly. (Nov.
1727).

Baillie, William, Lieutenant of Royal Regiment of Highlanders
who died in North America, bachelor. Administration to
John Ogilvie, attorney for sister Mary, wife of William
Duff, in Scotland. (July 1759).

Baird, Archibald, of South Carolina who died at Plymouth, Devon.
Limited administration with will to William Greenwood.
(July 1777). Revoked and limited probate granted to James
Cassels with similar powers reserved to James Gordon;
relict Winifred having now married John Wilson. (Mar. 1788).

Baker, John, of Farlight, Sussex, who died in East Jersey.
Probate to Joseph Wakenham. (June 1709).

Baker, Nicholas, of St. George's, Maryland, widower. Administration with will to universal legatee Elizabeth, wife of
George Pell, formerly Elizabeth Baker; no executor being
named and brother John Baker having died before administering. (Jan. 1766).

Ball, formerly Chichester, Mary, of Stafford Co., Morth America.
Administration to Thomas Blane, attorney for husband Burgess
Ball now in Stafford Co. (Jan 1790).

Ballantyne, Hugh, of Henrico Co., James River, Virginia,
bachelor. Administration to brother George Ballantyne.
(Jan. 1736).

Ballew, Abraham, of merchant ship *Robert* who died in Virginia.
Probate to relict Mary Ballew alias Bellew. (Jan. 1709).

Balmain, William, of George Town, Potomac River, Maryland.
Probate to George Steele. (Sept. 1784).

Bamber, William, of merchant ship *Bugill* who died in New York,
bachelor. Probate to Thomas Scott. (Dec. 1731).

Banyar, William, of Albany City, North America, bachelor.
Administration to George Clarke, attorney for uncle
Goldsbroro (*sic*) Banyar at Albany. (May 1798).

Barbot, Francis, of South Carolina, bachelor. Administration
to mother Susanna Barbot, widow. (Dec. 1739).

Barbet, George, of Warton, Maryland, bachelor. Administration
to brother John Barbet. (Dec. 1743).

Barbot, James, of St. Margaret, Westminster, who died in Maryland. Probate to relict Mary Barbot.

Barbut, Theodore, of Boston, New England, Captain Lieutenant of 48th Regiment of Foot who died at Quebec. Administration to relict Sarah Barbut.

Barclay, John, of New York City, seaman of H.M.S. *Emerald*. Probate to relict Ann, now wife of James Thain. (July 1779).

Barker, Nathaniel, of H.M.S. *Glasgow*. Administration to James Gibson, attorney for brother Jacob Barker at Mass. (Aug. 1750).

Barker, Robert, Collector of Customs at West New Jersey. Probate to sister Mary, wife of Francis Hurdd; executors Nathaniel Hurdd and Jane Worthington renouncing and mother Mary Barker having died. (Dec. 1735).

Barlow, Jane, of Nottingham Co., Virginia. Administration to Samuel Gist, administrator to husband Thomas Barlow deceased, for use of the daughter Elizabeth, wife of Thomas Kendall, now in Nottingham Co. (Nov. 1797).

Barlow, Samuel, of H.M.S. *Shoreham* who died in Virginia. Probate to relict Elizabeth Barlow. (June 1716).

Barlow, Thomas, of Nottingham Co., Virginia, widower. Administration to Samuel Gist, attorney for daughter Elizabeth, wife of Thomas Kendall, now in Nottingham Co. (Nov. 1797).

Barnes, John, of Christ Church, Surrey, who died in Georgia, widower. Probate to William Graves. (Oct. 1740).

Barnier, Peter, of St. Ann, Westminster, who died at Philadelphia, bachelor. Administration with will to mother Ann Barnier now in Geneva. (June 1770).

Barnsley, Thomas, of Bensalem, Bucks Co., Pennsylvania. Probate by solemn affirmation of surviving executors William Redman and Gilbert Hicks. (Sept. 1774).

Barrack alias Benack, William, of Shadwell, Middlesex, who died at Staten Island. Administration with will to Adam Cromey; sole executor Robert Manley having died. (Jan. 1777).

Barrett, Ann - see Rimus.

Barrie, Robert, Assistant Surgeon to H.M. Hospital at St. Augustine, East Florida, who died at sea. Limited administration with will to relict Dolly alias Dorothy Barrie. (Aug. 1775).

Bartlett, formerly Pheasant, Rachel, formerly of Powis Place, Great Ormond Street, St. George the Martyr, Middlesex, but late of Maryland. Administration to husband John Bartlett. (Jan. 1798).

Bartlett, Sarah - see Batson.

Barton, Thomas, of Berkeley Co., South Carolina. Administration with will to Samuel Wragg, attorney for sons William and John Barton in South Carolina. (Jan. 1735).

Bassindine, Charles Boyle, of Virginia, bachelor. Administration to brother William Bassindine. (Jan. 1740).

Bateman, Robert, of Charles Town, South Carolina, bachelor. Administration by solemn affirmation to father George Bateman. (July 1728).

Bates, Joseph, Captain's clerk of H.M.S. *Mercury* who died at Boston, New England. Probate to Samuel Durham. (Nov. 1776).

Batson alias Bartlett, Sarah, of New England, widow. Administration to aunt and next of kin Benedicta, wife of William Nesbitt. (Nov. 1728).

Batt, Mary - see Ashe.

Battersbye, James, of Flushing, New York, bachelor. Administration to Thomas Prickman, guardian of niece by a sister, Hester Prickman. (Feb. 1717).

Baugh alias Bough, Thomas, of H.M.S. *Nonsuch* who died at
Rhode Island. Administration to daughter and next of kin
Jane Baugh. (Jan. 1781).

Bayley - see Bailey.

Bayliff, Featherston, surgeon's mate in General Oglethorpe's
Regiment in Georgia, bachelor. Probate to James Mackay
alias McKoy with similar powers reserved to Thomas Gold-
smith. (Sept. 1750).

Bayliss, Joseph, soldier of 15th Regiment of Foot who died at
Boston, New England. Administration to brother William
Bayliss. (Apr. 1776).

Bayly - see Bailey.

Baynes, Henry, of ship *Postilion*, bachelor, who died in
Virginia. Administration to brother James Baynes. (Apr.
1705).

Beale, Elizabeth, of East Florida, spinster. Administration
to brother Richard Beale; mother Elizabeth Beale renouncing. (Nov. 1772).

Beale, Richard, formerly of Newport, North America, but late
of Newark, Nottinghamshire. Administration to relict
Mary Beale. (Jan. 1789).

Bean, Caleb, of Boston, New England, who died in the Bay of
Honduras, widower. Administration to William Hodshon,
attorney for daughter Ann Bean in Boston. (Jan. 1753).

Beans, William, of Salem, New England H.M.S. *Otter*. Administration to Thomas Dixey, attorney for relict Rachel Beans
in Salem. (Aug. 1754).

Beasland, Alexander - see Bisley.

Beavour, John, of Stepney, Middlesex, master of merchant ship
Britannia who died in Maryland. Administration to relict
Mary Beavour. (July 1718).

Beckett, Simon, lately in America, bachelor. Administration
to aunt and next of kin Elizabeth Smith. (Mar. 1762).

Bedon, Stephen, of Charles Town, South Carolina, and of St.
Clement Danes and Chelsea, Middlesex, but who died in the
City of Bristol. Probate to cousin german George Bedon
with similar powers reserved to relict Ruth Bedon, Henry
and Benjamin Bedon and Isaac Nicholls. (Feb. 1752).

Bee, Henry, of Deptford, Kent, who died in Virginia on merchant
ship *South River*. Administration to relict Jane Bee.
(Nov. 1708).

Bere, Theodore, of Topsham, Devon, who died in Virginia,
widower. Administration to son George Bere. (Dec. 1757).

Beer, Thomas, of Virginia. Administration to mother Elizabeth
Beer, widow. (July 1700).

Beesley, Samuel, of Bristol who died in Virginia. Probate to
William Beesley. (Sept. 1727).

Beetham, William, of St. Mary le Bow, Middlesex, who died in
South Carolina. Probate to surviving executor father
Thomas Beetham. (Mar. 1783).

Belbin, Edward, of Rumsey, Hampshire, who died in South Carolina, bachelor. Administration to cousin german Richard
Belbin. (Feb. 1734).

Belcher, John, boatswain of merchant ship *Timothy and Jacob*
who died in Virginia, bachelor. Administration to principal
creditor James Powers. (Jan. 1740). Revoked and granted
by decree to father James Belcher. (May 1740).

Belin, Elizabeth, of Breewood, Stafforshire, but late of
Charles Town, South Carolina. Administration to husband
Peter Belin. (Feb. 1785).

Bell, David, of St. Giles in Fields, Middlesex, who died at
Albany Fort, America. Probate to relict Elizabeth Bell.
(Jan. 1713).

Bell, John, of Newport, Rhode Island, purser of H.M.S. *Apollo*.
Administration with will to William Roberts, attorney for
relict Mary Bell at Newport. (Feb. 1780).

Bell, William, formerly of Burr Street, St. Botolph Aldgate,
London, but late of Norfolk, Virginia. Probate to relict
Rebecca Bell and brother Henry Bell. (Mar. 1795).

Beman, Thomas, of Petersham, Worcester Co., Mass. Administration with will to Samuel Rogers, attorney for relict
Elizabeth Beman and sons Ebenezer and Joseph Beman;
executors Abijah Willard and Josiah Edson having died.
(June 1791).

Benack, William - see Barrack.

Bennett, Edmond, of Boston, New England, pensioner of Chatham
Chest. Probate to Edward Westall. (Oct. 1743).

Bennet, Elisha, of Rumney Marsh, Suffolk Co., New England.
Administration with will to Henry Palmer, attorney for
relict and principal legatee Dorothy Bennet at Rumney Marsh,
no executor having been named. (May 1727). Revoked and
granted to son John Bennet, relict now dead. (Jan. 1733).

Bennet, James, of merchant ship *James* who died in New York
Hospital, bachelor. Probate to John Oswald. (Apr. 1761).

Bennett, John, of Boston, New England, who died on H.M.S.
New Norwich. Administration to daughter Sara, wife of
Richard Deane. Former grant of September 1695 to relict
Aphram Bennett revoked. (Aug. 1709).

Bennett, Richard, of Queen Ann's Co., Maryland. Administration
with will to John Hanbury and William Anderson, attornies
for Edward Lloyd in Maryland. (Aug. 1750).

Bennett, Samuel, of St. Andrew, Holborn, Middlesex, who died
in South Carolina, bachelor. Administration to brother
and next of kin William Bennett by decree. (Apr. 1722).

Benson, Hanns, of Wapping, Middlesex, who died on merchant
ship *Henry* in Virginia, bachelor. Administration to principal creditor John Worme. (July 1703).

Benson, Henry, of New York City who died on H.M.S. *Princess
Mary*. Administration to William Bryant, attorney for
relict Judith Benson in New York. (Mar. 1747).

Benson, Hugh, of New York who died on H.M.S. *Princess Mary*.
Administration to William Bryant, attorney for relict
Judith Benson in New Yor. (Mar. 1750).

Bere - see Beer.

Berjeu, John, of New York, bachelor. Administration to father
Samuel Barjew *(sic)*. (Dec. 1783).

Berry, John, of New York City. Probate to surviving executor
Edward Cox. (June 1795). New grant June 1802.

Beswicke, Mary, formerly Mary Hill, of Charles Town, South
Carolina. Administration to husband John Beswicke. (July
1749).

Beswicke, Silence, of Charles Town, South Carolina. Administration to Thomas Fludyer, attorney for husband John
Beswicke in South Carolina. (Sept. 1740).

Beswicke, Charles, of South Carolina, bachelor. Administration
to brother John Beswicke. (Apr. 1734).

Bethune, Benjamin Faneuil, of Cambridge, Mass., bachelor.
Administration to Samuel Prince, attorney for mother Mary
Bethune at Cambridge. (Jan. 1796).

Bethune, George, of Cambridge, Middlesex Co., North America. Probate to nephew Samuel Prince with similar powers reserved to relict Mary Bethune and son Nathaniel Bethune. (July 1785).

Bevian, Mary, of George Town, South Carolina, widow. Administration to brother and next of kin Christopher Brocklebank. (Mar. 1785).

Bevis, William, of Topsham, Devon, master of merchant ship *Hope* who died in Virginia. Probate to relict Margaret Bevis. (Mar. 1717).

Bicknell, William, of Annapolis, Maryland, who died on H.M.S. *Richmond*, seaman. Probate to brother Andrew Bicknell. (June 1764).

Bigg, Samuel, of Maryland, bachelor, died at sea. Administration to sister Hannah, wife of Thomas Fox. (May 1703).

Biggs, Richard, of New York, bachelor. Administration to father Joseph Biggs. (Dec. 1794).

Biles, Thomas, of New York. Administration to son Thomas Biles. (Feb. 1702).

Billings, William, surgeon of H.M.S. *Eolus* who died at Pensacola, West Florida. Probate to uncle George Billings. (June 1767).

Billop, Christopher, of Fleet Prison, London, with lands in New York. Probate to James Fitter alias Fittar and Thomas Billop. (Apr. 1725).

Billopp, Joseph, of New York, widower. Administration to brother and principal creditor Christopher Billopp; only child Middleton Billopp being incapable. (Nov. 1712).

Binsteed, Henry, wheelwright in General Burgoyne's Army, bachelor. Administration to father Henry Binsteed. (Nov. 1778).

Birch, Chamberlain, formerly of St. Bride's, London, after of Augustine, Georgia, but died at New York. Limited administration with will to relict Elizabeth Birch. (Jan. 1799).

Birch, Elizabeth, of Pennsylvania. Probate to daughter Alice Birch. (Jan. 1701).

Birch, Matthew, of Newcastle, Pennsylvania. Administration to daughter Alice Birch; relict Elizabeth Birch renouncing. (Feb. 1701).

Bird, John, Lieutenant-Colonel of 15th Regiment of Foot who died in Philadelphia. Probate to Lough Carleton. (May 1778).

Bisaker, Ambrose, corporal of 22nd Regiment of Foot in Captain Farmer's Company who died at West Florida, bachelor. Probate to William Chipman. (June 1766).

Bishop, Joseph, of New York City, master's mate of H.M.S. *St. Alban's* and after First Lieutenant of private warship *Experiment*. Administration with will to relict Elizabeth Bishop formerly Groshon; executors James King and John Le Couteur cited but not appearing. (Dec. 1784).

Bishop, Nathaniel, master of ship *Princess Wales Fort* who died in Hudson's Bay. Probate to Thomas Bird. (Oct. 1723).

Bisland alias Beasland alias Bisley, Alexander, of H.M.S. *Shoreham* who died in New York. Administration to principal creditor Charles Lodwick in New York. (Jan. 1714).

Bisset, Rev. George, Rector of St. John's, New Brunswick, who died at Rhode Island. Administration to relict Penelope Bisset. (Aug. 1791).

Bissill, William, of St. Margaret, Westminster, Middlesex, who
died in Virginia. Probate to relict Anne Bissill. (Sept.
1713).

Bittle, Richard, mariner under Captain John Williams who died
at Annapolis Royal. Administration to principal creditor
John Irving. (Sept. 1719).

Blaau, Waldron, of New York City. Administration with will
to Charles Cooke, attorney for relict Eleanor Blaau and
son Uriah Blaau at New York. (Nov. 1787).

Black, Richard, Controller of Customs at Port Royal, South
Carolina, bachelor. Administration to principal creditor
Edmund Smith. (Jan. 1768).

Blackall, Abraham, of North Carolina, bachelor. Administration
to Mary Harris alias Blackall, relict and executrix of
brother Thomas Blackall who died before administering.
(Jan. 1749).

Blackett, William, Captain of 14th Regiment of Foot who died
in Virginia, bachelor. Administration to brother John
Blackett. (June 1777).

Blacklock, Christopher, of Boston, New England, and H.M.S.
Mermaid. Administration with will to John Coles, attorney
for relict Ruth Blacklock at Boston. (Dec. 1750).

Blackman, Anthony, of Shadwell, Middlesex, who died in Spotswood, Virginia. Administration to Anne Munt, attorney for
principal creditor Daniel Munt now at sea; relict Dorothy
Blackman renouncing. (June 1728).

Bladen, William, of Maryland. Administration to son Thomas
Bladen, attorney for relict Anne Bladen in Maryland. (Dec.
1718). Revoked and granted to relict Anne Bladen. (Sept.
1720).

Blagdon, Sweeting, of North Carolina, bachelor. Administration
to sister and next of kin Susanna, wife of Edward Kershaw.
(Sept. 1761).

Blague, Newcombe, of New England, master of merchant ship
Victory. Limited administration to son and executor Newcombe
Blague. (Oct. 1718).

Blake, Charles, of Maryland. Probate to son Philemon Blake
with similar powers reserved to son John Blake. (Jan. 1734).

Blake, John Sayer, of Queen Ann's Co., Maryland. Administration
to William ---nderson, attorney for son John Sayer Blake in
Maryland. (Jan. 1760).

Blake, Joseph, of South Carolina who died on merchant ship
Wilmington, widower.. Administration to John Nicholson,
guardian of sons Daniel and William Blake. (Sept. 1751).
Revoked and administration with will granted to son Daniel
Blake with similar powers reserved to Ralph and Rebecca
Izard. (Feb. 1752).

Blake, Philemon Charles, of Queen Ann Co., Maryland. Administration with will to William Anderson, attorney for
relict Sarah Blake now in Queen Ann Co. (May 1766).

Bland, Elias, formerly of All Hallows, Barking, London, and
late of New York. Administration to relict Hannah Bland.
(Oct. 1781).

Blunt, John, of Shadwell, Middlesex, who died on ship *Samuel*
in New England. Probate to Amy Blunt, mother and executrix
of named executrix Amy Blunt who died before administering.
(Feb. 1712).

Boggas, John, Lieutenant of an Independent Company in Carolina, bachelor. Administration to brother George Boggas. (Dec. 1762).

Boldry, Philip, of merchant ship *Patsey* who died in Virginia, bachelor. Probate to William Green. (Sept. 1731).

Bond, Barnet, formerly of Maryland but late of Limehouse, Middlesex. Probate to relict Alice, now wife of William Grimes. (Apr. 1749).

Bonus, William - see Bownass.

Boorman, John, formerly of Hollingbourne, Kent, but late of New York. Probate to David Colgate with similar powers reserved to Benjamin Boorman. (Dec. 1796).

Bordley, Thomas, of Annapolis, Maryland, who died at Greenwich, Kent. Probate to Martin Smith. (Sept. 1747).

Borland, Francis, of Boston, Mass. Administration with will to William Mills, Edward Brice and Edward Wheeler, attornies for son John Borland and relict Phebe Borland at Boston. (Oct. 1768).

Borland, John, of Boston, Mass. Probate to relict Ann Borland. (Feb. 1779).

Borre, John, of Boston, New England. Administration to relict Elizabeth Borre. (Sept. 1701).

Boss, Ann, of New York, spinster. Probate to Edward Baker. (June 1779).

Bostock, Wilcock, of Virginia. Administration to principal creditor Amor Blythman. (Jan. 1709).

Botetourt, Norborne, Lord, of Virginia. Probate to nephew Henry Duke of Beaufort. (Jan. 1771).

Bouchier, Edward Bass, sergeant of Portsmouth Division of Marines who died at New York. Probate to sister Ann Bouchier. (May 1783).

Bough, Thomas - see Baugh.

Bouquet, Henry, Brigadier-General of H.M. Forces and Lieutenant Colonel of Royal American Regiment who died in North America. Probate to Frederick Haldimand. (Nov. 1766).

Bourne, George Stuart, Captain of Coldstream Regiment of Foot Guards who died in New York City. Probate to Goalston Bruere with similar powers reserved to Elizabeth Edgeley Hewer, widow, and Charles Spooner. (Jan. 1777). Further grants in April 1793 to Mark Stuart Harris, child of Sophia Stuart Brown (formerly Harris), relict of Charles Brown; and in November 1863.

Bourne, Thomas, citizen and perfumer of London who died in Maryland. Probate to Benjamin Bourne, attorney for Richard Johns of Maryland, executor of relict and executrix Mary Bourne. (Nov. 1711).

Bowdoin, Hon. James, of Boston, Mass. Limited administration with will to Thomas Dickason the elder. (Dec. 1791).

Bowen, Charles, of merchant ship *Catherine* who died at New York, bachelor. Administration to sisters Jane and Margaret Bowen. (Oct. 1777).

Bowen, Goodin, of Mount Pleasant, North Carolina. Probate to John Younger. (Nov. 1799).

Bowen, Sarah, of Bladon Co., North Carolina, widow. Administration with will to son Goodin Bowen; surviving executor Richard Watt renouncing. (Feb. 1793).

Bowles, James, of Maryland. Probate to relict Rebecca Bowles. (June 1729).

12

Bowles, John, of Poole, Dorset, Captain of merchant ship
Prince who died in Carolina, bachelor. Administration to
brother Samuel Bowles. (Dec. 1739).

Bowness, George, of Virginia, bachelor. Administration to
brother Francis Bowness; mother Ann Bowness renouncing.
(Dec. 1787).

Bownass alias Bonus, William, of New York. Probate to relict
Martha Bownass with similar powers reserved to John Cockburn. (Apr. 1784).

Bowyer, William, of Jamaica who died in New York, merchant.
Probate to William Turner with similar powers reserved to
David Jamison and Richard Mills. (May 1707).

Boylan, Patrick, Captain's clerk of H.M.S. *Jamaica* who died at
Charles Town, South Carolina. Administration to creditor
Robert Field; relict and others cited but not appearing.
(Sept. 1767).

Boyles, Philip, of New York who died on H.M.S. *Ludlow Castle*.
Administration to William Bryant, attorney for relict
Catherine Boyles in New York. (Feb. 1744).

Boylston, John, formerly of Boston, Mass., but late of the City
of Bath. Limited administration with will to Harry Daniel
Mander. (May 1795).

Boylston, Thomas, formerly of Boston, Mass., but late of St.
Martin Vintry, London. Administration with will to nephew
Ward Nicholas Boylston; executors Thomas Woodroffe Smith,
Thomas Coles and Robert Slade cited but not appearing.
(Apr. 1799). Further grant July 1828.

Boyse, John, of South River, Virginia, bachelor. Administration to principal creditor Edmund Hunt. (Jan. 1710).

Bradburne, Richard, of merchant ship *Susanna* who died at Boston,
New England. Administration to father Joseph Bradburne.
(Apr. 1740).

Braddock, Edward, Major-General of H.M. Forces in America.
Probate to John Calcraft with similar powers reserved to
Mary, wife of John Yorke. (Sept. 1755).

Bradley, Ann, of Wilmington, North Carolina, spinster. Administration to Hagger Allis, attorney for mother Elizabeth
Bradley at Wilmington. (Nov. 1789). Further grant August
1802.

Bradley, Edward, of Philadelphia. Special administration with
will to Edward Shepherd. (Nov. 1746).

Bradley, Lewis, of H.M.S. *Happy* who died in South Carolina.
Probate to John Bryan and Paul Debell, attornies for John
Owen and William Mallard in South Carolina. (Aug. 1735).

Bradstreet, Simon, of Portsmouth, New Hampshire, bachelor.
Administration to father Lyonel Bradstreet. (Apr. 1783).

Brailsford, Edward, of South Carolina. Administration with
will to Samuel Wragg, attorney for Arthur and Sarah Middleton in South Carolina. (Apr. 1733). Further grant to
Samuel Brailsford, attorney for surviving executor Sarah
Middleton, widow; other executor Arthur Middleton and
attorney Samuel Wragg now dead. (May 1762).

Brand, Jonathan, of Philadelphia, widower. Administration to
son Thomas Brand. (Feb. 1749).

Branwood, John, of merchant ship *Providence* who died in Carolina,
bachelor. Administration to brother Abraham Branwood.
(Dec. 1706).

Brasseur alias Splatt, Ann, of South Carolina, widow. Administration to Johanna, wife of William Cripps, aunt and guardian of daughters Mary Splatt and Ann Brasseur. (Nov. 1742).

Brathwaite, John, of South Carolina. Probate to relict Silvia Brathwaite and Elizabeth Tichborne, spinster, with similar powers reserved to Margaret Pultney, widow, and Thomas Revell. (Aug. 1740).

Bray, Thomas, of Bristol who died in New England. Administration to father Henry Bray. (Nov. 1726).

Brayfield, John, formerly of Newington, Surrey, but late of Philadelphia, bachelor. Administration to sister and next of kin Hester Brayfield. (Sept. 1789).

Bressey, John, of St. Clement Danes, Middlesex, who died in Maryland, bachelor. Probate to Eleanor Lloyd. (Apr. 1723).

Brett, Robert, of Pennsylvania. Administration to brother Roger Brett, attorney for relict Mary Tudor alias Brett in New York. (Sept. 1701).

Brew, Arthur, formerly of St. Sepulchre, London, and after of Philadelphia but who died at Jamaica. Probate to sister Jane Brew with similar powers reserved to sister Ann, wife of John Teir. (Feb. 1788).

Brewen, Hubbard, of Maryland. Probate to John Philpot. (July 1756).

Brewton, Miles, of Charles Town, South Carolina. Limited administration by decree to creditor Joseph Nutt until the will is brought in. (Apr. 1785).

Bridges, John, of New York. Administration to principal creditor Godfrey Lee, attorney for relict Anne Bridges and daughter Elizabeth Bridges during their absence. (July 1712).

Briggs, Richard, of City of Northampton who died at sea on merchant ship returning from Virginia, widower. Administration to sister Elizabeth, wife of Christopher Oliver. (June 1701).

Brinkley, William, of H.M.S. *Sultan* who died at Rhode Island Hospital, widower. Administration to John Day, attorney for brother John Brinkley at Manningtree, Essex. (Apr. 1781).

Brinley, Elizabeth, formerly of Boston, Mass., but late of Edgware Road, St. Marylebone, Middlesex, widow. Probate to George Lyde and nephew Wentworth Brinley. (Apr. 1793).

Brinley, Francis, of Boston, New England. Probate to grandson Francis Brinley with similar powers reserved to William Hutchinson. (July 1721).

Briscoe, John, of H.M.S. *Success* who died in Virginia, bachelor. Administration to father John Briscoe. (Sept. 1716).

Bristol, Joseph, of transport ship *Marlborough* who died in New York, bachelor. Administration to Ann Fernley, widow; father and others cited but not appearing. (Feb. 1764).

Bristow, Robert, of Virginia, bachelor. Administration to sister Rachel Bristow; father James Bristow renouncing. (Oct. 1755).

Broadhurst, John, of Virginia. Probate to relict Elizabeth Broadhurst. (Dec. 1701).

Brocas, Richard, of Wilmington, North America, bachelor. Administration to sister Elizabeth Brocas. (May 1788).

Brocas, Thomas, of Littleton, New England, bachelor. Probate to Christopher Kilby. (July 1751).

Brockhall, John, of South Carolina, bachelor. Administration to brother Joseph Brockhall. (May 1742).

Brockwell, Nathaniel, corporal of 20th Regiment of Foot who died in Pennsylvania, bachelor. Limited administration with will to John Noseworthy. (Nov. 1783).

Bromfield, James, of Shadwell, Middlesex, who died on H.M.S.
Somersett in Boston, New England. Administration to
principal creditor Richard Merry; relict Sarah Bromfield
renouncing. (Feb. 1724).

Bromfield, Thomas, of Boston, Mass. Administration with will
to Gilbert Harrison, John Ansley and George Bainbridge,
attornies for William Philips at Boston. (Sept. 1787).

Bromfield, William, of Stepney, Middlesex, who died on ship
London Merchant in Virginia. Administration to relict
Frances Bromfield. (Oct. 1702).

Bromley, Henry, Captain of a Company of Sir Peter Hulkett's
Company who died in America, bachelor. Administration
to father William Bromley. (Dec. 1756).

Brooke, Henry, of Port Lewes, Pennsylvania, bachelor. Limited
administration with will to John Plumtree. (Dec. 1737).

Brooke, Paulin, of York River, Virginia, bachelor. Administration with will by special grant to William Watts.
(Feb. 1748).

Brooke, Ricey, master of merchant ship *Neptune* who died in
Virginia, bachelor. Administration to sister Deborah
Brooke; mother Margaret Brooke renouncing. (Apr. 1740).

Brooker, Joanna, of Boston, New England, widow. Limited
special administration with will to Edward Pearson,
attorney for Silvester Gardiner, Joshua Henshaw and John
Winslow in Boston. (Aug. 1763).

Brookes, Mildred, of Gloucester Co., Virginia, spinster.
Administration to brother Thomas Brookes. (Nov. 1748).

Brooks, Philip, soldier of 22nd Regiment of Foot who died
at Mobile, West Florida, bachelor. Administration with
will to Jane, wife of John Drummon, formerly Jane Irvine,
administratrix to universal legatee Robert Carson who
died before administering. (Apr. 1766).

Brookes, Samuel, of Dorchester, Mass. Limited administration
with will to Henry Norris. (Oct. 1758).

Browne, Benjamin, of Salem, Essex Co., New England. Administration with will to John Ive, attorney for nephews
Samuel and John Browne in New England. (Jan. 1712).

Brown, Charles, of Williamsburgh, Virginia, bachelor. Administration to brother Robert Brown.

Brown, Francis, of Madeira who died at Philadelphia, bachelor.
Administration with will to creditor Robert French; father
Andrew Brown, brother Andrew Brown, and sister Mary Brown
being cited and not appearing, and executor Robert Kirwan
being dead. (Mar. 1738).

Browne, Isaac, chaplain of New York Volunteers who died at
Windsor, Nova Scotia. Administration with will to David
Thomas, attorney for Daniel Isaac Browne at Annapolis Royal.
(Sept. 1789).

Brown, James, of Wapping, Stepney, Middlesex, then of Rotherhithe, Surrey, but who died on merchant ship *Champion* in
Maryland. Probate to relict Abigail Brown. (Sept 1725).

Brown, James, of ship *Priscilla* who died in Philadelphia.
Administration to relict Rachel Brown. (Sept. 1725).

Browne, James, of Philadelphia. Administration with will to
William Lea, administrator to relict Sarah Lea. (Oct. 1749).

Brown, James, Lieutenant of First Connecticut Regiment of
Foot who died at Havana, bachelor. Administration to
Phineas Lyman, attorney for father Nathaniel Brown at
Preston, New London Co., Connecticut. (Nov. 1764).

Browne, John, master of ship *Happy Union*, of Whitechapel, Middlesex, who died in Maryland. Administration to father John Browne. (Mar. 1700).

Browne, Jonathan, of Philadelphia. Probate to relict Elizabeth Browne. (Oct. 1784).

Browne, Peregrine, of Maryland, bachelor. Administration to father Peregrine Browne. (Sept. 1712) Revoked and granted to Margaret Browne, relict and executrix of father. (Oct. 1713).

Brown, Peter, formerly of East Florida but late of New Providence. Administration to James Phyn, attorney for relict Sarah Brown at New Providence. (May 1791).

Brown, Richard, of H.M.S. *Hector* who died in Virginia, bachelor. Administration to Elizabeth Brown, attorney for brother John Brown; mother Marjery Brown, widow, having died before administering. (Dec. 1740).

Brown, Robert, of Savannah, Georgia, bachelor. Administration to brother Richard Brown; father Richard Brown renouncing. (Jan. 1798).

Brown, Thomas, of New York City who died at St. Sepulchre, London. Probate to William Hardwick with similar powers reserved to Elias Desbrosses and Richard Light. (July 1769). Revoked and administration granted to William Browning, attorney for Edward Laight at New York; executors William Hardwick and Elias Desbrosses now dead. (Apr. 1779).

Browning, John, of ship *Old Pendennis* who died in New England. Administration to principal creditor Jane Hilling, widow. (Feb. 1702).

Brownejohn, Mary, of New York City, widow. Administration to Robert Richard Randall, attorney for son Samuel Brownejohn at Flushing, Queen's Co., North America. (May 1786).

Brownjohn, William, of New York City. Administration with will to Robert Richard Randall, attorney for relict Mary Brownjohn at New York; executors Gabriel William Ludlow, Cornelius Clopper, James Beckman and Henry Remsen cited but not appearing. (June 1785).

Bryan, Richard, of Milford, New England. Administration to grandson Alexander Bryan; relict Elizabeth Bryan dying before administering. (July 1720).

Buchanan, Archibald, of Baltimore, Maryland. Administration to principal creditor Joshua Johnson; relict Sarah Buchanan, brothers and sisters George, Andrew, William, Elizabeth wife of James Gittins, and Elizabeth *(sic)* Brocall, widow, cited but not appearing. (Feb. 1786).

Bulkley, Peter, of Boston, New England, bachelor. Administration to creditor John Baynham. (Mar. 1761).

Bull, Absalom, of Savannah, Georgia. Administration with will to Effingham Lawrence, attorney for Thomas Bull in Ulster Co., but late of New York. (July 1797).

Bull, Jonathan, of Boston, New England. Probate to relict Elizabeth Bull; Samuel Greenleaf renouncing. (Jan. 1729).

Bullin, Thomas, of Boston, New England, bachelor. Administration to brother and next of kin John Bullin. (Oct. 1717).

Burger, Peter, of H.M.S. *Worcester*. Administration to Joseph Mico, attorney for relict Elizabeth Burger in New York. (Aug. 1750).

Burgis, John, of Virginia, widower. Administration to son
William Burgis. (July 1712).

Burgis, Joseph, of St. Giles in Fields, Middlesex, who died
in Virginia, bachelor. Administration to brother and next
of kin Richard Burgis. (Aug. 1749). Revoked and granted
by decree to Thomas Card, guardian of only child Joseph
Burgis. (Aug. 1752).

Burley, Susannah - see Kearny.

Burley, William, of New York and H.M.S. *Torbay*, *Tartan* and
Kent. Probate to Peter Seignoret and Marc Anthony Ravaud.
(Aug. 1727).

Burnett, John, of New England who died abroad or at sea.
Probate to Thomas Amiger. (Jan. 1716).

Burnett, Hon. William, Governor of New York and New Jersey.
Probate to Abraham and Mary Vanhorn. (July 1730).

Burnley, John, of York River, Hanover Co., Virginia. Probate
to brother Hardin Burnley with similar powers reserved to
brother Richard Burnley. (Feb. 1780).

Burr, Emma, of New England, widow. Administration to Benjamin
Franklin, attorney for son Daniel Burr in New England.
(May 1701).

Burrell, Edward, of Wapping, Middlesex, who died in Virginia
on merchant ship *John*. Administration to relict Abigael
Burrell. (Aug. 1701).

Burridge, Robert, boatswain of H.M.S. *Launceston* who died in
Virginia. Probate to relict Sarah Burridge. (July 1769).

Burrows, John, of Williamsburgh, Virginia, bachelor. Administration to sister Mary, wife of John Burrows. (June 1785).

Burrowes, William, of Maryland. Administration to brother
Thomas Burrowes, attorney for relict Anne Burrowes in
Maryland. (Feb. 1707).

Burt, Benjamin, of East New Jersey, bachelor. Administration
to brother Maynard Burt. (Feb. 1733).

Burton, Isaac, of Charles Town, South Carolina, who died at
Granada, West Indies. Administration to brother George
Burton; relict Ann Burton having died before administering.
(Apr. 1788).

Burton, Richard, master of merchant ship *Richard and Ann* who
died at Charles Town, South Carolina, bachelor. Administration to George Burton, attorney for father Richard
Burton at Staiths, Yorkshire. (Oct. 1763).

Busby, James, of Over Norton, Oxfordshire, who died in Maryland, bachelor. Administration to brother William Busby.
(July 1709).

Butcher, James, of Maryland, bachelor. Administration to
brother Francis Butcher. (July 1733).

Butler, Henry, of Montgomery, Maryland. Administration to
relict Mary Butler. (Dec. 1789).

Butler, Mary - see Bagg.

Buxton, John, of New York City. Limited administration with
will to Robert Rolleston, attorney for relict Ann Buxton
in New York City. (Apr. 1795).

Byrn, Barnaby, of Jamaica, Long Island, New York. Limited
administration with will to James Rivington, attorney for
William and Robert Bayard and Terence Kerin. (May 1776).

17

Cairnes, Alexander, of Islington, Middlesex, who died in
Virginia, widower. Probate to John Lidderdale. (Feb. 1761).

Caldwell, Thomas, of Maryland, bachelor. Administration to
sister Mary Caldwell. (July 1703).

Cailloyell, Isaac, of Boston, New England. Administration
to relict Rebecca Cailloyell. (Mar. 1721).

Caldwell, James - see Calwell.

Calvert, Benedict Leonard, of Epsom, Surrey, bachelor.
Limited administration with will to Hon. Cornelius Calvert.
(Aug. 1733).

Calvert, Edward Henry, of Annapolis, Maryland. Probate to
relict Margaret Calvert. (Nov. 1730).

Calvet, Peter, of Charles Town, South Carolina, widower.
Administration to brother and next of kin Raimond Calvet.
(May 1765).

Calvert, Reynard alias Raymond, of South Carolina. Probate
to Emanuel Reller. (Aug. 1767).

Calwell alias Caldwell, James, seaman of H.M.S. *Captain* who
died at Boston Hospital. Probate to Andrew Rice, attorney
for relict Agnes Calwell at Falkirk, Scotland. (Sept.
1774).

Cameron, Alexander, of Savannah, Georgia. Probate to William
Ogilvy with similar powers reserved to Donald Cameron.
(Feb. 1784).

Cameron, Allan, corporal of 2nd Regiment of Foot who died in
New Jersey, bachelor. Special limited administration to
cousin german Colin Cameron who is to produce the will
when found. (June 1765).

Cameron, Charles, Captain of 71st Regiment who died at
Savannah, Georgia, bachelor. Administration to father
Donald Cameron at Kilmally, Scotland. (Jan. 1782).

Cammel, Philipp, of H.M.S. *Jersey* who died in New York.
Administration to relict Rose Cammel. (May 1703).

Campbell, Archibald, Captain of Marines who died at Boston,
bachelor. Administration to Neil Malcolm, attorney for
father Colin Campbell at Roseneath, Dumbartonshire,
Scotland. (Dec. 1775).

Campbell, Archibald, of Fredericksburgh, New York, Captain
of New York Company of Volunteers, who died at Long Island,
bachelor. Administration with will to brothers Duncan
and John Campbell. (Aug. 1781).

Campbell, Collin, of Charles Town, South Carolina. Probate
to brother Hugh Campbell and Daniel Campbell with similar
powers reserved to Hugh Mackay. (Jan. 1783).

Campbell, Collin, of Charles Town, South Carolina. Administration with will to Charles Vicaris Hunter, attorney
for sister Elizabeth Campbell at Straban, Argyleshire,
Scotland; Hugh Mackay renouncing. (June 1794).

Campbell, Hugh, of St. Helena, Granville Co., South Carolina,
but late of North Carolina. Administration to Abraham Le
Messurier, attorney for relict Katherine Campbell at St.
Helena. (May 1770).

Campbell, James, surgeon's mate of hospital under late General
Braddock in America, bachelor. Administration to mother
Dorothy Campbell, widow. (June 1757).

Campbell, James, master of ship *Maria* who died at Charles
Town, South Carolina, widower. Administration to creditors Dr. John Hall and Thomas Emerson Headlam; sister
and only next of kin Agnes Campbell renouncing. (Aug. 1780).

Campbell, Patrick, of New York City, Major of 71st Regiment.
Limited probate to father Duncan Campbell and brother
Alexander Campbell with similar powers reserved to brother
Collin Campbell. (June 1784).

Campbell, William, of Glasgow, Scotland, who died in a mer-
chant ship off Maryland, bachelor. Administration to Hugh
Campbell, attorney for mother Elizabeth Adair in Scotland.
(Sept. 1718).

Candler, Anne, of Virginia, spinster. Administration to
brother John Candler. (Dec. 1733).

Caner, Rev. Henry, of Boston, New England, who died at Long
Ashton, Somerset. Probate to surviving executor William
Bacon. (Jan. 1793).

Cappel, George Lewis, of Westminster, Middlesex, who died in
Virginia, bachelor. Administration to aunt and only next
of kin Mary, wife of George Mullins. (Nov. 1768).

Capper, Henry, of Philadelphia. Administration to brother
John Capper; relict Hannah Capper cited but not appearing. (Nov. 1794).

Carbonell, Thomas, Ensign and Quartermaster of 46th Regiment
of Foot under Lieutenant-General Thomas Murray who died
in North America, bachelor. Administration to father
Stephen Carbonell. (Mar. 1759).

Carpenter, John, of Annapolis, Maryland. Limited administration with will to William Hunt, attorney for relict
Elizabeth Carpenter. (Feb. 1749).

Carpenter, Nathaniel, of King and Queen Co., Virginia.
Administration to son William Fauntleroy Carpenter; relict
Ann Bushrod Carpenter having died. (Mar. 1796).

Carpenter, Thomas, of Rhode Island, who died at sea on a
merchant ship, bachelor. Administration to sisters and
next of kin Anne, wife of Henry Atwells, and Mary, wife
of Francis Seburt, of the City of Canterbury. (Aug. 1715).

Carr, Ralph, of Great Bridge, Virginia, bachelor. Administration to brother and next of kin Henry Carr. (May 1772).

Carr alias Kerr, Thomas, of Portsmouth, Hampshire, who died
in New York. Probate to relict Jane Carr. (Apr. 1730).

Carroll, Dorothy, of Maryland. Administration to William
Anderson, attorney for son Charles Carroll in Maryland;
husband having died. (Jan. 1760).

Carroll, Edward, Lieutenant of 16th Regiment who died at
Pensacola, bachelor. Administration to brother James
Carroll. (June 1787).

Carsan, James, formerly of Charles Town, South Carolina, but
late of Troquire, Scotland. Administration to relict Agnes
Carsan. (Sept. 1787).

Carson, Robert, sergeant of 22nd Regiment of Foot who died at
Mobile, West Florida, bachelor. Administration with will
to Jane, wife of John Drummon, (formerly Jane Irvine),
administratrix to sole executor Jerret Irvine now dead.
(Apr. 1766).

Carter, Anne - see Ludlam.

Carter, Richard, of Maryland. Administration to Micajah Perry,
attorney for relict Elizabeth Carter. (Dec. 1708).

Cartwright, Timothy, of Boston, North Britain *(sic)*, seaman
of H.M.S. *Renown*. Administration with will to Richard
Prowse, attorney for relict Sarah Cartwright at Halifax,
North America. (Nov. 1787).

Cary, Richard, of Bristol who died in Virginia, bachelor.
Probate to niece by a brother and next of kin Jane Cary;
sole executor having died in testator's lifetime. (Nov.
1730).

Cary, Samuel, of Chelsea, Suffolk Co., Mass. Administration
with will to Abraham Dettorne by his solemn affirmation,
attorney for Richard and Nathaniel Cary in Mass. (Nov.
1770).

Castles alias Castle, William, of H.M.S. *Bedford* who died at
Long Island, bachelor. Administration to Abraham Harman,
attorney for sister and only next of kin Nelly Castle in
Scotland. (Oct. 1780).

Caswall, Henry, of Boston, New England. Probate to sister
Susanna, wife of Thomas Allison, and cousin John Caswall,
with similar powers reserved to Charles Shearman. (June
1748).

Catherwood, Robert, of St. Augustine, East Florida. Probate
to relict Jane Catherwood with similar powers reserved to
Hon. John Moultrie, John Adam, Frederick Hesse and William
Colville. (Sept. 1787). Administration of goods not
administered by relict Jane Catherwood now deceased to
Jane Ann, wife of Richard Draper, daughter of Lucy
Caldewood deceased, who was sister of testator; John Adam
and Frederick Hesse having died and Hon. John Moultrie
renouncing. (June 1797).

Cato, John, negro slave of H.M.S. *Launceston* and *Superbe*,
bachelor. Administration to Lawrence Reade, son and attorney of proprietor Joseph Reade in New York. (Oct. 1749).

Causton, Thomas, of Savannah, Georgia, who died on merchant
ship *Loyal Judith*, widower. Administration to principal
creditor William Williamson. (June 1746).

Cavallier, John, surgeon of Livingstone's Hospital at Long
Island. Probate to Fergus Forster. (Oct. 1783).

Cay, David, of Philadelphia. Probate to William Cramond,
John Leg--- and Hugh Holms. (May 1797).

Cay, Rev. Jonathan, Rector of Christ Church, Calvert Co.,
Maryland. Probate to relict Dorothy Cay. (Oct. 1738).

Chabert, Anthony, of Baltimore, North America. Administration with will to David Maitland, attorney for relict
Renie Charlotte Chabert at New York City. (Jan. 1797).

Chambers, Joseph, of Charles Town, South Carolina, widower.
Administration to brother Chadwick Chambers. (May 1737).

Chambers, Richard, of Maryland. Probate to mother Mary Chambers.
(July 1701).

Chamier, Daniel, of Baltimore, Maryland. Limited administra-
tion with will to brother Anthony Chamier. (Oct. 1780).
Limited administration to John Chamier formerly Deschamps.
(Apr. 1781).

Chance, Thomas, soldier of 31st Regiment of Foot who died at
St. Augustine, East Florida, bachelor. Administration to
brother and next of kin Joseph Chance. (May 1771).

Chandler, William, formerly of St. Marylebone, Middlesex, but
Captain in North Carolina Volunteers, bachelor. Admini-
stration to Charles Cooke, attorney for father Thomas
Bradbury Chandler at sea. (May 1785).

Chandler, William, of New Haven, North America, bachelor.
Administration to Charles Cooke, attorney for Thomas
Chandler at Westmoreland, North America, son of intestate's
father Joshua Chandler who died before administering.
(Aug. 1790).

Chandliss, Charles, Captain in Portsmouth Division of Marines
    who died at Boston, bachelor. Administration to half-
    sister Mary Monckton, spinster. (Dec. 1775).
Chapman, Anne, of Virginia. Administration to John Weeton,
    attorney for son John Chapman in Virginia. (Aug. 1716).
Chardon, Henry, of Charles Town, South Carolina, bachelor.
    Administration to sister Mary Ann Mareschal, widow. (May
    1739).
Charlton, Daniel, of H.M.S. *Garland* who died at Maryland in
    Virginia *(sic)*. Probate to Elizabeth, wife of Richard
    Dawley, formerly Elizabeth Libbard. (Dec. 1757).
Cheesman, Joseph, master of H.M.S. *Galatea* who died at St.
    Augustine, East Florida. Probate to John Huntingdon.
    (Dec. 1778).
Cheston, Francina Augustina, of Kent Co., Maryland, widow.
    Probate to son William Stephenson. (Feb. 1767).
Chichester, Ellen - see Downman and Robertson.
Chichester, John, of Virginia, bachelor. Probate to brother
    Richard Chichester with similar powers reserved to James
    Ball the younger. (May 1763). Further grant June 1803.
Chichester, Mary - see Ball.
Chichester, Richard, of Virginia. Administration with will to
    John Tucker and Richard Tucker, attornies for mother Ellen
    Chichester, widow, guardian of minor son John Chichester;
    relict Ellen Chichester renouncing. (Mar. 1746). Revoked
    and granted to Richard Chichester, brother and executor of
    John Chichester, son of the testator; said John Chichester
    having died without executing. (May 1763).
Child, Margaret, of Boston, New England. Administration to
    husband Thomas Child by decree. (May 1721).
Chrystie, John, of merchant ship *Rumsey* who died at York River,
    Virginia, bachelor. Probate to Elizabeth Grimes alias
    Cheshire, wife of William Grimes. (Nov. 1718).
Church, George, of H.M.S. *Hawk*. Administration to John Brad-
    ford, attorney for relict Mary Church in New Hampshire.
    (Jan. 1746).
Claiborne - see Clayborne.
Clare, Joseph, of South Carolina. Administration to principal
    creditor William Adye; other interested parties cited but
    not appearing. (July 1731).
Clark, Daniel, of Augusta, Georgia, bachelor. Administration
    to William Hanson, attorney for brother and sister, Alexan-
    der Clark and Elizabeth, wife of Donald Fraser, in Perth,
    Scotland. (Aug. 1757).
Clarke, Frederick, of Carolina who died in Barbadoes, bachelor.
    Administration with will to John Trott, attorney for Robert
    Stevens alias Stephens in Carolina. (Aug. 1700).
Clarke, George, of Milford, New England. Administration to
    Daniel Clarke, attorney for Abigail Peirson in New England.
    (Apr. 1700).
Clark, Henry, of Shadwell, Middlesex, who died in Pennsylvania.
    Probate to Elizabeth Clark. (Mar. 1727).
Clarke, Hutchinson, of North Kingstown, King's Co., Rhode
    Island, one of Captain Thomas Fry's Company in Rhode Island
    Regiment of Foot, who died at Havana, bachelor. Administra-
    tion by solemn declaration to Joseph Sherwood, attorney
    for brother and next of kin Joseph Clarke at North Kings-
    town. (Dec. 1765).

Clarke, John, of ship *Maryland Factor* who died in Virginia,
bachelor. Administration to William Harbottle, surgeon
of Galeside near Newcastle upon Tyne, attorney for sister
Abigael Harbottle. (Jan. 1710).

Clarke, John, formerly of London but late of Gloucester Co.,
Virginia, bachelor. Probate to father John Clarke. (Nov.
1757).

Clarke, Joseph, of Mile End, Stepney, Middlesex, who died in
Virginia, bachelor. Administration to sisters Mary
Whistler, widow, and Anne, wife of Henry Lee. (May 1738).

Clark, Joseph, of New York, bachelor. Administration to
mother Elizabeth, relict and executrix of George Clark.
(July 1766).

Clarke, Richard, formerly of Boston, New England, but late of
St. George, Hanover Square, Middlesex. Probate to John
Singleton Copley with similar powers reserved to son
Isaac Winslow Clarke and Henry Bromfield. (June 1795).
Double probate May 1797.

Clarke, Thomas, of East Sheen, Surrey, who died in Maryland.
Administration to sister Joane, wife of Edward Absey.
(June 1709).

Clarke, William, of St. Bride's, London, mariner on ship
George of Lyn, who died in Virginia. Administration to
principal creditor Rubart Vincksteijn. (Aug. 1701).

Clark, William, of Pennsylvania, sergeant of 20th Regiment.
Administration with will to residual legatee Henry Rowland,
no executor named. (Nov. 1783).

Clarvise alias Clarvis, Robert, of H.M.S. *Bedford*, who died
at Long Island Hospital, bachelor. Administration to
Nathaniel Betton, attorney for father Thomas Clarvise at
Normanby, Lincolnshire. (Feb. 1780).

Clay, Stephen, of merchant ship *Anne* who died in Virginia,
bachelor. Probate to William Norwood. (Oct. 1734).

Claiborne, William, of Virginia who died at Hackney, Middlesex. Limited probate of codicil to John Hanbury. (July
1746).

Clayton, John, of Ware, Virginia. Probate to son William
Clayton. (Apr. 1791).

Clegg, James Wilson, formerly of St. Thomas's, Southwark,
Surrey, but late of Georgia, bachelor. Administration to
sister and only next of kin Mary, wife of Edmund Beck.
(Nov. 1796).

Clephan, George, of H.M.S. *Asia* who died at New York, bachelor.
Administration to Henry Creed, attorney for brother James
Clephan at New York. (Oct. 1777).

Clephan, James, physician of the Royal Hospital at New York.
Probate to William Marsh and Henry Creed with similar
powers reserved to John Hills. (Apr. 1783).

Clever, Thomas, of Virginia, bachelor. Probate to sister
Mary Clever. (July 1700).

Clifford, Peter, of Whitechapel, Middlesex, who died at Annapolis in West Indies. Probate to relict Mary Clifford.
(July 1715).

Clifton, William, Chief Justice of West Florida. Administration to niece and next of kin Ann Raincock. (Mar. 1783).

Clinton, Anne, of New York, spinster. Administration to
Maynard Guerin, attorney for father Hon. George Clinton in
New York. (Feb. 1746). Revoked on death of Maynard Guerin
and granted to John Catherwood, attorney for Hon. George
Clinton. (June 1751).

Clowes, John, of Long Island, North America, bachelor.
Administration to David Thomas, attorney for brother and
next of kin Gerhardus Clowes at St. Johns, New Brunswick.
(Aug. 1795).

Coates, Sarah, of Baltimore, Maryland, spinster. Administration to father Francis Peachey Coates. (Mar. 1772).

Cobb, Woolley, of Virginia. Administration to father John
Cobb. (Dec. 1732).

Cochran, James, steward of H.M. transport ship *Betsey* who
died at Savannah, Georgia, bachelor. Administration to
Thomas Gibson, attorney for mother Isabell Gairn at Errol,
Scotland. (Jan. 1781).

Cocke, Catesby, of Prince William Co., Virginia. Administration with will to William Perkins and William Brown,
attornies for sons Williams and John Catesby Cocke in
Virginia; executors William Henry Lee, Richard Lee, Thomas
Everard and Thomas Jett renouncing. (Mar. 1773).

Cocke, Christopher, of New York. Administration to brother
John Cocke. (Oct. 1714).

Cocke, Thomas, of Virginia, bachelor. Administration to
father John Cocke. (Feb. 1712).

Cockburn, John, of All Saints the Great, London, who died in
New England. Limited administration with will to relict
Mary Cockburn. (Dec. 1700).

Cockburne, Thomas, of Pennsylvania who died on merchant ship
Newberry, bachelor. Probate to John Cockburne. (Jan.
1725).

Cockin, Stephen, of St. George, Southwark, Surrey, who died
on merchant frigate *Bibins* in Boyston *(sic)*, New England.
Administration to relict Anne Cockin. (Oct. 1701).

Cockshutt, Geoffrey, of Virginia, bachelor. Probate to brother
Thomas Cockshutt. (Jan. 1710).

Codenham, Robert, of Shadwell, Middlesex, who died in New
York. Administration with will to John Chapman, guardian
of children Jane, Robert and William Codenham; executor
Richard Jones having died. (Feb. 1700).

Cogell, William, of New York, bachelor. Administration to
sister and only next of kin Ann, wife of David Mackintosh.
(Jan. 1792).

Coggeshall, Giles, of Portsmouth, Newport Co., Rhode Island,
sergeant in Lieutenant-Colonel Christopher Hargill's
Company of Rhode Island Regiment of Foot who died at
Havana, bachelor. Administration by solemn declaration
to Joseph Sherwood, attorney for brother and next of kin
Baulston Coggeshall at Portsmouth. (Dec. 1765).

Coggeshall, James, formerly of Newport, Rhode Island, but late
of Brunswick, Nova Scotia, bachelor. Administration to
John Andrews, attorney for mother Lucy Ann Coggeshall at
Newport. (Sept. 1790).

Coker, William Lawrence, Captain of 38th Regiment of Foot who
died at Boston, bachelor. Administration to brother Robert
Coker; mother Susanna Coker having died before administering. (Sept. 1777).

Colchester, Thomas, of H.M.S. *Southampton*, bachelor, who died
in Virginia. Administration to principal creditor Mary
Starland, widow. (June 1703).

Colden, Alexander, of New York City. Probate to brother John
Antill. (Aug. 1784).

Coldstream, William, master of transport ship *Friendship* who died at Savannah, Georgia, widower. Administration to son Charles Coldstream. (Mar. 1781).

Cole, Charles, of Annapolis, Maryland, bachelor. Administration to creditor Amey Yarp, widow. (Feb. 1759).

Collart, William, of H.M.S. *Otter* who died at Norfolk, Virginia. Probate to mother Rebecca Collart, widow. (Dec. 1776).

Colles, Thomas, of Deptford, Kent, who died in Virginia on ship *Nicholson*. Probate to relict Mary Colles. (Feb. 1706).

Colleton, John, of Fair Lawns, St. John's, Berkely Co., South Carolina. Probate to father and surviving executor Sir John Colleton. (Apr. 1751). Administration with will and two codicils of goods unadministered by Sir John Colleton to Robert Colleton, executor of the will of said Sir John; other executors Susannah, relict of testator, and Peter Colleton, son of testator, having died. (Nov. 1754). Administration with will of goods unadministered to William Field, guardian of children Sir John, Elizabeth, Mary Ann and Susanna Snell Colleton; Ann Collins, surviving executor of Sir John Colleton renouncing; Peter Colleton, testator's son dying without issue; and with consent of guardian of cousins and that of relations. (Mar. 1756).

Colleton, Sir John, of St. John's, South Carolina. Probate to Elizabeth Janverin, spinster, during the minority of daughter Louisa Carolina Colleton, with similar powers reserved to James Parsons. (Dec. 1779). Revoked and granted to Louisa Carolina Colleton on her coming of age. (Apr. 1785).

Colleton, Peter, of Fair Lawns, St. John's, Berkeley Co., South Carolina, who died at sea. Probate to brother and surviving executor Robert Colleton. (Nov. 1754).

Colleton, Peter, of Fair Lawns, South Carolina. Administration to William Field, administrator with will to father John Colleton for benefit of minor children Sir John, Elizabeth, Mary Ann, and Susanna Snell Colleton. (Mar. 1756).

Collier, Alexander, of H.M.S. *Wolf* who died in Virginia, bachelor. Probate to William Culling. (Nov. 1739).

Collier, Daniel, of H.M.S. *Devonshire* who died in New York, bachelor. Probate to Susannah Long, spinster. (June 1763).

Collier, Joseph, of South Carolina, bachelor. Administration to mother Rebecca Collier, widow. (July 1730).

Collier, Thomas, of New York, sergeant of Marines on H.M.S. *Coventry*. Administration to relict Joanna Collier. (Oct. 1766).

Collingwood, Gerard, of merchant ship *Three Brothers* who died in Virginia, bachelor. Probate to Eleanor Slater, widow. (Oct. 1732).

Collins, John, of New York Province. Administration to Samuel Beven, attorney for relict Margaret Collins. (Nov. 1729).

Collins, John, of Cape Fear, North Carolina, bachelor. Administration to creditor James Rae. (July 1753).

Collins, Palfrey, of Boston, Mass., seaman of H.M.S. *Liverpool*. Administration to John Callahan, attorney for relict Alice Collins in Boston. (Dec. 1787).

24

Collins, Thomas, of Lingstead, Kent, who died in Maryland, bachelor. Administration to father Christopher Collins. (July 1725). Administration of goods unadministered by said Christopher Collins now deceased to sisters Anne and Mary Collins. (Nov. 1726).

Colson, Elizabeth, of Bethnal Green, Middlesex, who died in Charles Town, South Carolina, widow. Probate to James Crockatt, attorney for William Roper in Charles Town. (Aug. 1751).

Colsworthy, George, of Maryland, bachelor. Administration to father John Colsworthy. (Oct. 1704).

Colvill, Matthew alias Maturin, of Cape Fear, North America, bachelor. Administration to sister Mary, wife of Rev. Isaac Patrick. (Aug. 1790).

Comer, John, of New York, bachelor. Administration to brother Walter Comer. (Apr. 1736).

Comer, George, of Fort Anjango, East Indies. Administration to brother Walter Comer; mother Mary Comer having died. (Apr. 1736).

Comrin, John, of Boston, New England, master of merchant ship *Princessa*. Limited administration to William Green of Grosvenor Square, Middlesex, haberdasher; relict Sarah Comrin and only child Sarah, wife of James Lloyd, renouncing. (Oct. 1765).

Comyn, Frederick Duke, of West Florida, bachelor. Administration to father Thomas Comyn. (Apr. 1778).

Comyn, Valence Stephen, of West Florida. Administration to father Thomas Comyn; relict Mary Comyn and children Thomas and Samuel Comyn renouncing. (Apr. 1778).

Con, Thomas, of Scarborough, Yorkshire, seaman of H.M.S. *Eagle* who died in New York. Administration to relict Mary Con. (May 1779).

Concannon, James, of St. Magnus, London, who died in Virginia, widower. Administration to Christopher Hooke, attorney for sister Elinor, wife of John Grant, at Back Lane, Dublin, Ireland. (Sept. 1764).

Connop, John, of merchant ship *Olive Tree* who died in Virginia. Probate to Edmund Castle. (Dec. 1706).

Connor, John, formerly surgeon of H.M.S. *Cygnett* but late of Charles Town, South Carolina, bachelor. Administration to mother Jane Connor, widow. (May 1768).

Constable, Alexander, of Charles Town, South Carolina. Probate to William Redmon and relict Jane Constable. (Mar. 1781).

Constable, John, of St. Christopher who died at Philadelphia, bachelor. Administration to sister Helen, wife of Rev. William Moir. (Mar. 1791).

Constant, Thomas, of H.M.S. *Apollo* who died in New York Hospital, bachelor. Administration to father William Constant. (Mar. 1779).

Conyers, Richard, of Boston, New England. Administration to John Howes, guardian of son James Conyers; relict Mary Conyers renouncing. (Sept. 1709).

Cook, Edmund, of Norwich, Norfolk, who died at St. John's, St. Mary Co., Maryland, bachelor. Probate to Charles Martin with similar powers reserved to his wife Susanna Martin. (May 1747).

25

Cooke, George, of South Carolina, bachelor. Administration
  to Elizabeth Cooke, spinster, attorney for sister Rebecca
  Cooke in South Carolina. (Feb. 1755).
Cooke, John, of St. James Santee, Craven Co., South Carolina.
  Administration with will to Elizabeth Cooke, spinster,
  attorney for daughter Rebecca Cooke in South Carolina;
  executors James Maxwell cited but not appearing and son
  George Cooke having died. (June 1755).
Cooke, John the younger, of 20th Regiment of Foot who died
  at Stillwater, North America, bachelor. Administration
  to father John Cooke. (Apr. 1778).
Cook, John, formerly of Ninety Six but late of Richmond
  District, Quebec. Administration to James Phyn, attorney
  for relict Elizabeth Cook at Mecklenberg, Quebec. (Nov.
  1790).
Cooke, Nicholas, of St. Botolph Aldgate, London, who died
  on merchant ship *Perry and Lane* in Virginia. Admini-
  stration to relict Margaret Cooke. (Apr. 1700).
Cooke, Sarah, of New York City. Administration to Quintin
  Dick, attorney for husband Edward Cooke at Tortola.
  (Dec. 1797).
Cookson, George, of St. Augustine, East Florida. Administra-
  tion with will to Thomas Harrison, attorney for brother
  John Cookson in East Florida. (Feb. 1777). Probate to
  said John Cookson. (Feb. 1786).
Cooper, James, of H.M.S. *Boyne*. Administration to Thomas Lui,
  attorney for relict Susan Cooper in New England. (Jan.
  1705).
Cooper, Mary, formerly of Charles Town, South Carolina, but
  late of Bristol, widow. Probate to John Page and Elias
  Vanderhorst with similar powers reserved to Arnoldus
  Vanderhorst. (May 1797).
Cope, Henry, of New York, Lieutenant-Colonel of H.M. American
  Regiment. Administration with will to Richard Jeneway,
  attorney for Stephen Byard in New York. (Feb. 1744).
Cope, John, of Maryland, bachelor. Administration to mother
  Blanch Hulen alias Whittington alias Cope, widow of John
  Hulen alias Whittington, at Brevell, Gloucestershire.
  (Apr. 1724).
Copson alias Weaver, John, of St. Paul, Bedford, who died
  in Maryland. Administration to only child Mary, wife of
  Rev. Jacob Rogers. (Dec. 1740).
Corbisley, Samuel, of Liverpool, Lancashire, bachelor, who
  died in Maryland or Virginia. Administration to brother
  George Corbisley. (Mar. 1720).
Cordis, Hannah, formerly of Boston, New England, but late
  of St. Andrew by Wardrobe, London, widow. Limited probate
  to Thomas Fraser. (Dec. 1779).
Corker, Thomas, of Charles Town, South Carolina. Administra-
  tion with will to James Poyas, attorney for Josiah Smith
  the younger at Charles Town. (Aug. 1772).
Cormity, Adam - see Cromartie.
Cornell, Samuel, formerly of New Bern, North Carolina, but
  late of New York. Probate to daughter Susanna, wife of
  Henry Chads; surviving executors William Low renouncing
  and Jacob Blount cited but not appearing. (May 1787).
Cornock, Samuel, master of ship *Molly* who died in South
  Carolina, bachelor. Probate to Thomas Plumstead by solemn
  affirmation. (Aug. 1733).

Cornwall, Alexander, of ship *Maryland Factor* who died in Maryland. Probate to William Finlason. (Aug. 1704).

Cosby, Henry, commander of H.M.S. *Centaur* who died at New York. Probate to mother Hon. Grace Cosby, widow. (Aug. 1754).

Cotton, Rev. Nathaniel, formerly of New Inn, Middlesex, but late chaplain of H.M. Garrison at Pensacola, bachelor. Administration to Elizabeth Hendy, relict and administratrix of creditor Samuel Hendy deceased; others concerned cited but not appearing. (Jan. 1789).

Cotton, Richard, Captain of 33rd Regiment who died at Camden, North America. Probate to brother Henry Calveley Cotton with similar powers reserved to brother Thomas and Sir Robert Cotton. (May 1789).

Couttes, Henry, of City of London, merchant, who died in Newcastle, Pennsylvania. Probate to brother James Couttes. (Aug. 1709).

Couzens, John, of Oswego, New York, Ensign in Sir William Pepperel's Regiment of Foot, bachelor. Administration with will to Henry Kidgell, attorney for father Samuel Couzens in Dublin; executrix Anne Hopper, now wife of Edward Barron, renouncing. (Jan. 1757).

Coventry, George, of Fairhill, Hamilton, Lanarkshire, Scotland, Captain of a New York Independent Company. Administration with will to John Bryson, guardian of children Alexander, Elizabeth and James Coventry. (Aug. 1777).

Cowan, Joseph, formerly of New York City but late of Prosperous near Dublin, Ireland. Probate to relict Jane Cowan. (Nov. 1791). Further grant February 1814.

Cowand, John, of Edenton, North Carolina, bachelor. Administration to brother and next of kin James Cowand. (Oct. 1772).

Cowden, John, of Frederick Co., Virginia, bachelor. Administration to sister Mary, wife of George Garrard; mother Elizabeth Cowden, widow, having died before administering. (Aug. 1777).

Cowell, Elizabeth, of Greenwich, Kent, who died at Charles Town, South Carolina, spinster. Administration to father Martin Cowell. (May 1797).

Cox, Andrew, of Suffolk, Nansemond Co., Virginia, who died in merchant ship *Happy Return*. Probate to Peter Hodgson, attorney for William Shepherd and James Holt in Virginia. (Feb. 1764).

Cox, Isaac, of Philadelphia. Probate to son Isaac Cox and Isaac Wickoff with similar powers reserved to Peter Wickoff; other surviving executor John Cox renouncing. (July 1784).

Cox, John, of Whitechapel, Middlesex, who died in Maryland. Administration to relict Mary Cox. (Nov. 1702).

Cox, John, of St. Thomas Apostle, London, Ensign of 17th Regiment of Foot, who died on River Elk in North America, bachelor. Administration to father Rev. Hadley Cox. (May 1778).

Cox, Hon. Samuel, of Barbados who died in Maryland. Administration with will to Henry Palmer, attorney for relict Elizabeth Cox in Barbados. (June 1726).

Cox, Sem, of St. Mary's, Richmond, Virginia. Probate to Benjamin Doverill with similar powers reserved to George Downing. (Oct. 1711).

Cox, William, of Holborn, Middlesex, who died in Georgia. Administration to relict Frances Watt alias Cox. (Jan. 1735).

Cracklow, January, of Lambeth, Surrey, who died in Pennsylvania, New England *(sic)*, bachelor. Administration to mother Mary Cracklow. (Apr. 1727).

Cradock, Sarah, formerly of Edgware Road, Middlesex, but late of Boston, Mass. Administration with will to George Brinley, attorney for Edward Brinley at Boston. (Feb. 1799).

Crain, Jotham, of H.M.S. *Duke*, bachelor. Administration to William Bryant, attorney for father Robert Crain at East New Jersey. (Mar. 1747).

Cramond, James, formerly of Philadelphia but late of New York City. Probate to Joshua Smith and Simmons Smith with similar powers reserved to relict Ann Cramond and brother William Cramond. (Nov. 1799).

Craske, John, of St. Giles Cripplegate, London, who died on a merchant ship in Virginia. Administration to brother Andrew Craske; father Andrew Craske renouncing. (May 1705).

Craven, John, of Philadelphia, widower. Administration to Edward Ridsdale, guardian of grandchildren and next of kin Mary, Jane and William Inman; granddaughter Dorothy Inman renouncing. (Feb. 1705).

Craven, Lawrence, of H.M.S. *York* who died at Baltimore, Maryland, bachelor. Administration to brother Thomas Craven. (Jan. 1772). Administration of goods unadministered by Thomas Craven deceased to brother John Craven. (Mar. 1778).

Creake, Samuel, of Stepney, Middlesex, master of ship *Britannia* who died in Maryland. Probate to relict Mary Creake. (Oct. 1716).

Crispe, Thomas, of ship *Isaac and Sarah* who died in Virginia, bachelor. Administration to brother Henry Crispe, clerk. (Nov. 1704).

Crofts, Henry, of Boston, New England. Administration to brother James Crofts, attorney for mother Elianor Crofts alias South in Ireland. (Mar. 1703).

Crockett, William, of H.M.S. *Alborough* who died at Providence Island, South Carolina, bachelor. Probate to Thomas Vinter. (June 1730).

Cromartie alias Cormity, Adam, of H.M.S. *Colchester* who died in Virginia. Probate to Elizabeth, wife of John Crafts, with similar powers reserved to said John Crafts. (Jan. 1741).

Crommelin, Charles, of New York. Probate to son Daniel Cox with similar powers reserved to Samuel Butler, John and Joseph Read. (Apr. 1740).

Crosby, William, superintendent of armed ship who died at New York. Probate to Edward Ommanney. (Dec. 1780).

Crossley, Leonard, Lieutenant in Colonel Burton's Regiment in America, bachelor. Administration to sister Ann, wife of John Cory; mother Elizabeth Crossley having died. (Oct. 1773).

Crossley, William, of New York, widower. Administration to nephew and next of kin Nicholas Datton. (Sept. 1788).

Crouch, Thomas, of Philadelphia. Administration to relict
Elizabeth Ann Crouch. (Apr. 1779).

Croucher, Henry, of New York City, sailmaker of H.M.S.
Coventry. Administration to William Sawer alias Sawyer,
attorney for relict Ann Croucher in New York. (Feb. 1768).
New grant to same April 1768, following Ann Croucher's
appearance.

Crow, John, of merchant ship *Providence* who died in Virginia.
Probate to Thomas Jackson. (Jan. 1710).

Cruden, Rev. Alexander, formerly Rector of Farnham, Virginia,
but late of Aberdeen, Scotland. Probate to Rev. Roderick
MacLeod with similar powers reserved to Alexander Leslie.
(June 1792).

Cruger, Henry the elder, formerly of New York City but late
of Bristol. Limited probate to Thomas Hayes and Jeremiah
Osborne. (Mar. 1780).

Crutchfield, John, Lieutenant of 35th Regiment of Foot who
died at Pensacola, widower. Administration to William
Sawtrey, guardian of only child Mary Crutchfield. (Apr.
1766).

Cuming, Rev. Robert, of South Carolina, bachelor. Administration to creditrix Isabella Campbell, widow; brothers and
sisters Patrick, Walter and William Cuming, Janett wife
of Thomas Donald, and Christopher wife of John Ritchie,
cited but not appearing. (Feb. 1754).

Cummings, Archibald, of Philadelphia, clerk. Limited administration with will to Thomas Moore. (Aug. 1741).

Cunningham, James, Lieutenant of Royal North British Fusiliers
who died in Florida, bachelor. Administration to James
Russell, attorney for mother Ann Cunningham, widow, at
Carrickgergus, Co. Antrim, Ireland. (Feb. 1769).

Cuninghame, William, formerly surgeon of H.M.S. *Windsor* but
late of New York City. Administration with will to Thomas
Maude, attorney for relict Margaret Cuninghame at New York.
(May 1789).

Cunningham, William, formerly of St. Augustine, East Florida,
but late of Nassau, Bahamas. Administration to Charles
Edwards, attorney for relict Mary Cunningham at New Providence. (Sept. 1791).

Cure, Charles, of Rotherhithe, Surrey, who died at Rappahannock, Virginia, widower. Administration to son Charles
Cure. (Jan. 1734).

Currie, Ebenezer, of Pennsylvania. Probate to John Sexton
with similar powers reserved to Samuel McAll the elder.
(Dec. 1747).

Curry, John, of Pennsylvania, bachelor. Administration to
principal creditor John Adams. (May 1703).

Curry, Samuel, of St. Martin in Fields, Middlesex, who died
at Boston, New England. Probate to sister Ester, wife of
Henry Herbert; executor John Le Sage renouncing. (Jan.
1737).

Curtis, Uriah, of Thedford, Gloucester Co., New York. Administration to James Phyn, attorney for relict Abigail Curtis
in Quebec. (Dec. 1790).

Custis, Daniel Parke, of New Kent Co., Virginia. Limited
administration to John Morrey. (June 1758). Revoked and
granted to relict Martha, now wife of George Washington.
(Junly 1774).

Custis, Hon. John, of Williamsburgh, James City Co., Virginia. Probate to son Daniel Parke Custis. (Nov. 1753). Administration of goods unadministered by Daniel Parke Custis now deceased to Wakelin Welch, attorney for relict of said Daniel Parke Custis, Martha, now wife of Hon. George Washington.

Cuthbertson, John, of St. Botolph Aldgate, London, who died in Virginia on ship *Sea Horse*, bachelor. Administration to mother Margaret Bromwich, widow. (Feb. 1727).

Dacres, Robert, of Carolina, bachelor. Administration to Robert Johnson, attorney for principal creditor Thomas Broughton, Vice-Governor of Carolina; mother Lady Mary Dacres renouncing. (Apr. 1707).

Daft, Thomas, of New York City. Administration to relict Elizabeth, now wife of James Williams. (May 1792).

Dagworthy, Ely, of Trenton, New Jersey, Captain of 48th Regiment of Foot. Limited administration with will to Robert Barclay, attorney for John and Sarah De Hart at Elizabeth Town, New Jersey. (June 1780).

Dalrumple alias Dalrumble alias Dalrymple, Alexander, of H.M.S. *Woolwich* but formerly of Salem, New England, bachelor. Probate to Paul Moor with similar powers reserved to Mary Moor. (Feb. 1747).

Dalrymple, John, of Brunswick Co., North Carolina, reduced Captain of Sir William Pepperel's Regiment of Foot. Limited administration with will to Alexander Duncan of Wilmington, North Carolina. (Oct. 1767).

Dalrymple, Martha, of Brunswick Co., North Carolina, widow. Administration with will to residuary legatee Elizabeth Dalrymple alias Hamilton Macgill, widow; brother Samuel Watters, sister Sarah wife of Alexander Lillington, said Alexander Lillington, and John Rutherford having died, and Joseph Watters, executor of said Samuel Watters, cited but not appearing. (Dec. 1787).

Dalton, Joseph, of Virginia, bachelor. Administration to brother and next of kin Benjamin Dalton. (July 1720).

Daly, John - see Dayly.

Daniel, James, of Jersey Hospital and Jersey Prison Ships at New York, seaman. Probate to sister Jane Daniel. (Sept. 1782).

Darby, Josiah, of St. Stephen, Coleman Street, London, who died in South Carolina. Administration to relict Hannah Darby. (May 1715).

Daubuz, Henry James, formerly of George Town, South Carolina but late of Falmouth, Cornwall. Probate to relict Christiana Daubuz. (May 1777).

Davenport, Addington, of Boston, New England, clerk. Administration with will to William Baker, Alderman of London, attorney for Joseph Dowse and William Price in Boston. (Aug. 1747). Revoked and probate granted to son Addington Davenport on his coming of age. (Mar. 1756).

Davenport, Ann, of Boston, Mass. Administration to husband Addington Davenport, clerk. (Aug. 1745).

Davenport, Thomas, of New York. Probate to William Horspoole.
  (Aug. 1716).
Davenport, William, of Williamsburgh, Virginia, bachelor.
  Administration to Sampson Hanbury, attorney for aunts
  Mary Davenport and Peachey, wife of Elias Wills, of
  Williamsburg, by solemn affirmation. (Jan. 1796).
Davers, Henry, Lieutenant of H.M.S. *Neptune* who died in
  America, bachelor. Probate to Thomas Bilcliffe. (Sept.
  1759).
Davers, Jermyn, of Rushbrooke, Suffolk, and later of Virginia
  who died at sea, bachelor. Probate to mother Lady
  Margaretta Davers, widow. (Mar. 1751).
David, Ezekiel, of Charles Town, South Carolina. Probate to
  Edward Brice with similar powers reserved to Francis Magnus.
  (Feb. 1769).
Davies, James, of Yarpole, Herefordshire, who died in New
  York, bachelor. Administration to cousin german and next
  of kin John Nash. (Nov. 1773).
Davis, John, of H.M.S. *Sea Horse* who died in Boston, New
  England. Probate to Evan Jones with similar powers
  reserved to Mary Jones his wife. (Feb. 1725).
Davis, John, of Philadelphia, mariner of H.M.S. *Roebuck*,
  bachelor. Administration to father John Davis. (Jan. 1779).
Davies, John, of H.M.S. *Rainbow* and *Culloden* who died at
  Gardener's Island, New York. Probate to James Mathews.
  (Apr. 1783).
Davis, Lewis, of H.M.S. *Advice* who died in New England.
  Probate to relict Hannah Davis. (Dec. 1702).
Davies, Stephen, of St. Saviour, Southwark, Surrey, who died
  on merchant ship *Mermaid* in Virginia. Administration to
  relict Anne Davies. (Dec. 1704).
Davies, Thomas, of North Carolina. Administration to daughter
  Sarah Davies; relict Rebecca Davies having died before
  administering. (Sept. 1707).
Davies, Thomas, of Bermondsey, Surrey, who died on H.M.S.
  Winchelsea in Virginia, bachelor. Administration to
  principal creditor Joyce Drake. (Feb. 1735).
Davis, Wells, of Blisland, New Kent Co., Virginia, bachelor.
  Administration to Phillip Jones, attorney for mother
  Temperance Gillmett alias Davis, wife of Richard Gillmett
  in Virginia. (Nov. 1732).
Davies, William, of King George Co., Virginia, who died on
  merchant ship *Jett* in River Thames, bachelor. Probate
  to John Hopkins. (Oct. 1775).
Davison, William, Captain of 52nd Regiment of Foot who died
  at Boston. Administration with will to Robert Douglas,
  attorney for sister Lily Braidfitt, widow, at Biggar,
  Peeblesshire, Scotland; no executor named. (July 1776).
Dawney, Bryan, who died in Virginia, widower. Administration
  by decree to son John Dawney. (Jan. 1722).
Dawson, Patrick, formerly of Bermondsey, Surrey, but late of
  Philadelphia. Administration with will to nephew Patrick
  Dawson; executors in trust sisters Jane and Ann Dawson
  having died in testator's lifetime. (June 1785).
Day, Mary - see Gledhill.
Day, Thomas, of merchant ship *Dove* who died in Maryland,
  bachelor. Administration to principal creditor Hon. Colonel
  Thomas Lascelles; father John Day renouncing. (Oct. 1728).

Day, Thomas, of Charles Town, South Carolina, bachelor.
Administration to brother James Day; mother Elizabeth
Day, widow, renouncing. (Mar. 1765).

Day, William, of Oxford City who died in New Jersey.
Administration to nephew by a sister John Cross; sister
and next of kin Jane, wife of Thomas Shreeve, renouncing.
(May 1706).

Dayly alias Daly, John, of H.M.S. *Sardoine* who died at Charles
Town, South Carolina. Administration with will to William
Ellis, executor to named executor Domnick Copinger deceased.
(Mar. 1768).

De Beaufain, Hector Beringer, of Charles Town, South Carolina.
Limited probate to George Schutz. (Feb. 1767).

Debuke, Thomas, of Boston, New England. Administration to
son Thomas Debuke; relict Jamima Debuke having died
before administering. (Dec. 1748).

Dedicott, John, of South Carolina, bachelor. Administration
to mother Elizabeth Dedicott, widow. (Apr. 1718).

Delagal, John, of South Carolina, bachelor. Administration
to Abraham Le Messurier, attorney for brother and next of
kin Philip Delagal in North America. (Feb. 1769).

Delagal, Philip, formerly of Guernsey but late Captain in
General Parsons' Regiment of Invalids. Administration
with will to Abraham Le Mesurier, attorney for relict
Eleanor Delegal and son Philip Delegal in Georgia. (Sept.
1764).

De La March, John, of merchant ship *Prince Royal* who died in
Virginia, bachelor. Administration to Charles De La March,
attorney for father Daniel De La March. (Sept. 1723).

De Lancy, Oliver, of New York City. Probate to son Stephen
De Lancy with similar powers reserved to relict Phila De
Lancy, son Oliver De Lancy, Ann wife of John Harris Cruger,
and Charlotte De Lancy. (Jan 1786).

De Lanne alias De Launce, John, of South Carolina who died in
Stepney, Middlesex. Probate to Robert Aubert alias Auber
and Anne De Launce, spinster. (May 1728).

Demere, Paul, Captain of Indepnedent Company of Foot who died
at Fort Loudon, South Carolina, bachelor. Administration
to creditor Dr. David Nisbett; brother and only next of
kin Raymond Demere cited but not appearing. (Nov. 1765).

Dennis, William, of Colonel Holt's Regiment, bachelor.
Administration by decree to principal creditor Elizabeth
Jennings, widow. (July 1722).

Denny, Alexander, of Charles Town, South Carolina, who died in
Stepney, Middlesex. Probate to relict Lucy Denny; named
executor John Bro--- renouncing. (Aug. 1730).

Dent, George, formerly of Bristol but late of Bunkers Hill,
North America, bachelor. Administration to cousin german
once removed and only next of kin Jane, wife of Thomas
Tyas. (Apr. 1791).

Dent, John, formerly of Bristol but late of Bunkers Hill,
North America, bachelor. Administration to Jane, wife of
Thomas Tyas, administratrix to George Dent the brother and
only next of kin. (Apr. 1791).

Denwood, Mary, of Somerset Co., Maryland. Administration to
Anthony Bacon, attorney for husband Thomas Denwood in
Maryland. (Apr. 1753).

Depont, James, of New York, bachelor. Administration to principal creditor Robert Myre; aunt and next of kin Ester Bernon renouncing. (July 1706).

De Rossett, Lewis Henry, formerly of North Carolina but late of Holborn, Middlesex. Administration with will to Thomas Younger, attorney for James Walker Armand and nephews John De Rossett and John Armand Du Bois at Wilmington, North Carolina. (Nov. 1787).

Desbrisay, Albert, Captain in General Oglethorpe's Regiment in Georgia, bachelor. Administration to creditor George Simpson. (Dec. 1751).

Desbrosses, Magdalen, of New York City. Administration with will to William Thwaytes, attorney for James Desbrosses in New York City; executors James Desbrosses the younger and David Clarkson having died and Samuel Jones renouncing. (June 1796).

Descury, Simon, Captain in General Pepperell's Regiment of Foot who died at the Ohio in America. Administration to creditor Christopher Baron; mother Elizabeth Descury and brother Henry Descury renouncing. (June 1763).

De Silvie, Manuel, of New York City who died on H.M.S. *Gaspie*. Administration to relict Jane De Silvie. (Oct. 1771).

Deupey, Sarah, of Carolina. Administration to sister Catharine Coatsworth, widow. (Aug. 1715).

Deverall alias Deverell, Benjamin, of Virginia. Probate to relict Rachel Deverall and to Jeremy Deverall with similar powers reserved to other executors. (Feb. 1720). Revoked and granted to daughter Rachel, wife of John Russell, with similar powers reserved to William Bronaugh and Samuel Matthews. Testator now described as late of Bristol. (Aug. 1730).

Devine alias Devin, Magdalen, formerly of Philadelphia but late of Holborn, Middlesex, relict of George Devine. Sentence pronounced for validity of will and probate granted to sister Elizabeth Wade, spinster. (Nov. 1785).

Devisme, Peter, of New York City, bachelor. Administration to sister Elizabeth Beaufile Duval; mother Ann Devisme cited but not appearing. (Apr. 1781).

Devonald, Thomas, of Philadelphia. Probate to William Rees and John Napier with similar powers reserved to brother George Devonald. (Feb. 1794).

Dick, Alexander, of South Carolina, widower. Administration to George Mackenzie, attorney for father George Dick at Airth, Stirling, Scotland. (Jan. 1742).

Dick, Mathew, of Stepney, Middlesex, who died in Virginia. Administration to relict Mary Dick. (Nov. 1726).

Dickins, Grace - see Tunstall.

Dickinson, Nathaniel, formerly of Deerfield, Mass., but late of King's Co., New Brunswick. Limited administration with will to Robert Shedden, attorney for Benjamin Minison Woolsey and relict Hannah Dickinson. (July 1789).

Dinwiddie, Robert, formerly of Virginia but late of City of Bath. Probate to John Hyndman and John Hunter with similar powers reserved to Robert Scott. (Oct. 1770).

Dixon, Richard, of Potoxon, merchant, bachelor. Probate to younger brother William Dixon. (Jan. 1711).

Dixon, Thomas, formerly of Orphan House, Christ Church parish, Georgia, but late of St. Botolph Aldgate, London, widower. Probate to sister and only next of kin Ann Adams, widow; wife Mary Dixon having died in testator's lifetime. (Oct. 1773).

Dobbs, Arthur, Governor of North Carolina. Probate to son Conway Richard Dobbs with similar powers reserved to relict Justina Dobbs and son Edward Brice Dobbs. (June 1766).

Dobbyn, Richard, of Carrick, Co. Tipperary, Ireland, who died at Savannah, Georgia. Administration with will to relict Anastasia Dobbyn; named executor Edward Somerville having died. (May 1770).

Dodd, James, master of merchant ships *Nancy* and *Holbeach*, late of Boston, North America, widower. Administration to Robert Wild, administrator to father William Dodd, attorney for mother Margaret Dodd at Berwick upon Tweed. (Mar. 1774).

Doherty, Constantine, of New York, surgeon on half pay of Major Goram's Regiment of Rangers, bachelor. Administration to mother Mary Doherty, widow. (Dec. 1766).

Dolding, Richard, of H.M.S. *Monmouth* who died at Boston, New England. Administration to sister and next of kin Africa Chare, widow. (July 1712).

Dolphin, John, of Frederick, Georgia, bachelor. Probate to Martha, wife of Alexander Heron. (Aug. 1745).

Doncett, John, of Annapolis Royal, America, widower. Administration to Frances Weedon, widow, guardian of children Henry, Mary, John, Hugh and Frances Doncett. (Apr. 1727).

Donkester, William, of merchant ship *Henrietta* who died at Boston, New England, bachelor. Probate to Judith, wife of William Cooke. (Dec. 1730).

Douglas, Joseph alias Joseph Hamilton, of St. Paul's parish, Baltimore, Maryland. Administration to Rachel Crispin, widow, attorney for relict Rachel Douglas alias Reachel Dugles in Baltimore Co. (Mar. 1774). Revoked and granted by solemn affirmation to John Blake, attorney for only child George Crispin Douglas in Maryland. (Nov. 1791).

Douglas, Sholto, of merchant ship *St. George* who died in North America. Administration with will to Robert Mackoun, attorney for John Dalglish in New York. (Apr. 1759).

Douglas, William, of Boston, New England, doctor of physick, bachelor. Administration to sister Catherine Kerr. (Apr. 1753).

Dover, John, of St. Olave, Southwark, Surrey, who died in New England. Administration to relict Hannah Dover. "Pauper." (Feb. 1718).

Dover, William, of merchant ship *Old Neptune* who died in Virginia, bachelor. Probate to sister Anne Dover; father Thomas Dover having died. (Dec. 1706).

Dow, Alexander, of Plymouth, Mass., who died on H.M.S. *Montague*. Administration to William Fletcher, attorney for relict Sarah Dow in Plymouth. (Mar. 1750).

Downe, William, of Boston, New England. Administration to Thomas Downe, attorney for relict Sarah Downe in Boston. (Sept. 1753).

Downman, formerly Chichester, Ellen, of Lancaster Co.,
Virginia. Administration to husband William Downman.
(Nov. 1763).

Downman, Frances, of Lancaster Co., Virginia, widow.
Administration to son Joseph Ball Downman. (Sept. 1782).

Downman, Rawleigh, of Christ Church, Lancaster Co., Virginia.
Limited probate to son Joseph Ball Downman. (Sept. 1782).

Doyley, Cope Senior, of Virginia, widower. Administration
to Robert Doyley, guardian of sons Charles and Cope Doyley.
(Jan. 1706). Revoked and granted to son Charles Doyley.
(June 1713).

Doyley, Cope Junior, of Virginia, bachelor. Administration
to brother Charles Doyley. (June 1713). Revoked and
granted to uncle and next of kin Sekeford Cage; Charles
Doyley having died. (Nov. 1714).

Driffill, John, of Pon Pon, South Carolina. Administration
with will to Moyer Thomas, attorney for Sarah Ross,
child of Elizabeth, wife of George Burks, sister of
testator, at Hull, Yorkshire; executors Lewis Morris
and Henry Mulholland cited but not appearing. (June 1797).

Drummond, Robert, of New York. Administration to relict
Elizabeth Drummond. (Feb. 1718).

Drury, Edward, Captain of 63rd Regiment of Foot who died at
Philadelphia, bachelor. Administration with will to
James Callaghan, attorney for brother James Drury at New
York. (Jan. 1779).

Drysdale, Hon Hugh, Lieutenant-Governor of Virginia who died
in Virginia. Probate to relict Hester Drysdale. (Dec.
1726).

Drysdall, William, of Boston, New England, and of H.M.S. *Rye*
and *Stafford*. Administration to Robert Hewes, attorney
for relict Eleanor Drysdall in Boston. (July 1750).

Duane, Dennis, of St. Benet Finck, London, who died in Maryland. Administration to relict Winifred Duane. (Nov.
1739).

Du Bois, Walter, of New York. Administration with will to
William Jackson and Henry Jackson, attornies for nephew
and niece Gualtherus Du Bois and Margaret, wife of John
Du Bois, in New York City. (Apr. 1793).

Duche, Jacob, formerly of Philadelphia but late of Lambeth,
Surrey. Probate to son Rev. Jacob Duche and grandson
Thomas Spence Duche with similar powers reserved to Andrew
Doz, Joseph Swift and Myers Fisher. (Oct. 1788).

Duck, Thomas, clerk of H.M. Stores at New York. Probate to
surviving executor Duncan Drummond. (Feb. 1778).

Dudgeon, Patrick - see Townsend.

Dugdale, John, of Boston, New England, bachelor. Administration to brother Thomas Dugdale. (Feb. 1702).

Dummer, Elizabeth, of Littleton, New England, spinster.
Administration to Thomas Hutchinson, attorney for mother
Elizabeth, wife of Rev. Daniel Rogers, in New England.
(Aug. 1741).

Dunbar, James, Captain of 3rd Batallion of Royal Regiment of
Artillery who died at New York. Probate to brother William
Dunbar. (Oct. 1783).

Duncan, George, of Charles Town, South Carolina, bachelor.
Administration to creditor Robert Steell; mother Mary
Duncan, widow, and sister Margaret Bradly, widow, renoun-
cing. (May 1784).

Dunkan, John, of merchant ship *Society* who died in Virginia.
Probate to Elizabeth, wife of David Browne. (Aug. 1714).
Dunkin, Roberts, of Philadelphia, Lieutenant of H.M.S.
Milford . Administration to relict Ann Dunkin. (Dec.
1784).
Dunn, Charles, of Captain John Williams' Independent Company
who died at Annapolis Royal. Administration to principal
creditor Richard Roberts by decree. (Feb. 1722).
Dunn, Joseph, of St. Olave, Southwark, Surrey, who died in
Maryland. Probate to relict Elizabeth Dunn. (Apr. 1718).
Dunster, Charles, of New Jersey, bachelor. Probate to John
MacCulloch alias Maculah and John Boughton with similar
powers reserved to James Alexander and Michael Kearney.
(Apr. 1732).
Dupont, Gideon, of Charles Town, South Carolina, widower.
Administration to daughter and next of kin Mary, wife of
John Collett. (Sept. 1788).
Durant, Thomas, of Captain Richard Bradshaigh's Company of
Marines commanded by Colonel Cornwall but late of H.M.S.
Rye who died in South Carolina, bachelor. Administra-
tion to brother Anthony Durant. (Apr. 1744).
Durly, William, of Nansemond, Virginia, who died at St. Martin
in Fields, Middlesex. Administration to William Parker,
attorney for relict Mary Durly at Nansemond. (Nov. 1741).
Revoked on death of William Parker and granted to James
Stockdale, attorney for said Mary Durly. (Dec. 1753).
Durrance, John, of St. Anne's, Westminster, Middlesex, who
died in Virginia, surgeon on a merchant ship. Administration to principal creditor Sarah Landman; relict Mary
Durrance renouncing. (Jan. 1705).
Dyer, Robert, of Mock Jack Bay, Virginia, bachelor. Administration to sister and next of kin Sarah, wife of John
Mercer. (Sept. 1718).
Dyson, Rev. Edward, late Fellow of Peterhouse College, Cam-
bridge, who died at Savannah, Georgia, bachelor. Administration to brother John Dyson. (July 1740).

Eackman, Martin, of H.M.S. *Bredah*, bachelor. Administration
to Elizabeth, wife of principal creditor Peter Rowlandson,
in Virginia. ((Dec. 1704).
Earle, Joseph, formerly midshipman of H.M. sloop *Swift* and
after Lieutenant of a Regiment of Foot who died at New
York, bachelor. Administration to Thomas Courtney, attorney
for creditor James Courtney at Shelburne, Nova Scotia;
sister and only next of kin Mary Earle renouncing. (Oct.
1785). Revoked and regranted, deceased now described as
formerly Ensign of 44th Regiment of Foot at New York.
(May 1786).
Edds, William, of Colonel Holt's Regiment, bachelor. Administration by decree to principal creditor Robert Hood.
"Pauper." (July 1722).
Ede, John, of North Carolina who died at Cork, Ireland.
Administration with will to Paul Henry Robinson, creditor;
brother Richard Ede renouncing. (Sept. 1760).

Eden, Thomas, of H.M.S. *Stork* who died in West Florida,
bachelor. Administration to Samuel Inman, attorney for
sister and next of kin Elizabeth, wife of John Stovey,
at Acklam, Yorkshire. (July 1788).

Edgar, John, of Maryland. Administration to John Eglesham,
attorney for relict Mary, now wife of John Hampton.
(Jan. 1711).

Edge, John, of Holborn, Middlesex, who died at Boston, New
England. Probate to sister Martha Darby alias Comby.
(Feb. 1724).

Edie, George, of Virginia, Ensign on half pay of 96th Regiment of Foot, widower. Administration to brother John
Edie. (May 1781).

Edmonds, Benjamin the younger, of Boston, Mass. Probate to
Albert Dennie, attorney for relict Rebecca, now wife of
Moses Penniman, at Braintree, New England. (June 1741).

Edmonds, John, of Philadelphia, bachelor. Administration
to brother Joseph Edmonds. (Jan. 1776).

Edwards, Ann, of Charles Town, South Carolina, spinster.
Administration to brother and next of kin Alexander
Edwards. (July 1789).

Edwards, Richard, formerly of Bradforton, Worcestershire,
and late of Eaton Town, North Carolina. Probate to Henry
Murcott with similar powers reserved to William Daniel.
(Dec. 1757).

Edwards, Sweet, of New England who died at sea, bachelor.
Administration to Thomas Blettso, attorney for mother
Mary Edwards in New England. (Oct. 1705).

Eells, Hannah, of Hanover, Mass., widow. Administration to
Joseph Paice, attorney for sons Robert Lenthall Eells
and William Witherall Eells at Hanover. (June 1792).

Egan, Stephen, formerly of St. John's River, East Florida,
but late of Dominica, widower. Administration to Robert
Payne, attorney for son Stephen Egan at Dominica. (Aug.
1789).

Eggleston, Hezekiah, of Boston, New England, widower. Administration to son Samuel Eggleston. (Aug. 1744).

Elam, Joseph, of Philadelphia, bachelor. Administration to
brother and only next of kin Emanuel Elam. (Jan. 1794).

Elbrow, John, of Maryland who died on merchant ship *Dover*.
Administration to relict Anne, now wife of Richmond Eaton.
(Dec. 1709).

Elkin, Elizabeth, of Barbados who died in Virginia, spinster.
Administration to brother John Elkin. (Aug. 1752).

Ellerston, James - see Elliott.

Elletson, Goodin, of North Carolina. Probate to Edward Fuhr
and George Hibbert with similar powers reserved to Thomas
Hibbert. (Mar. 1790).

Ellice, George - see Ellis.

Elliott, Andrew, of Senegambia, Africa, but late of Savannah,
Georgia. Probate to John Ross and Thomas Davies. (Jan.
1775).

Elliot, Andrew, Major of Marines who died at Rhode Island,
bachelor. Administration to brother Gavin Elliot; mother
Katharine Elliot renouncing. (Sept. 1778).

Elliott, Gray, formerly of Georgia but late of St. Margaret,
Westminster, Middlesex. Probate to relict Mary Elliott.
(July 1787).

Elliott alias Ellerston, James, of H.M.S. *Russell*, bachelor.
Administration to Jane, wife and attorney of brother
Niels Ellerston, at Philadelphia.
Elliott, John, of North Carolina. Administration to son
Bartholomew Elliott. (June 1738).
Eliot, John, Governor of West Florida, bachelor. Administra-
tion to brother and next of kin Edward Eliot. (July 1769).
Elliott, William, of St. James, Westminster, Middlesex, who
died at Annapolis Royal. Administration to relict Mary
Elliott. (Mar. 1712).
Ellice, George, of Philadelphia, bachelor. Administration
to John Black, clerk, attorney for brother William Ellice
in Scotland. (Jan. 1753).
Ellis, Griffith, of Clynnog, Caernarvon, who died in America,
bachelor. Administration to John Owen, guardian of
nephew Thomas Ellis. (Jan. 1732).
Ellis, James, Lieutenant in General Francis Nicholson's
Regiment, formerly of St. Margaret, Westminster, Middlesex, who died near New York. Administration to relict
Anne Ellis. (Jan. 1717).
Ellis, John, paymaster-sergeant of 10th Regiment who died
at Bunkers Hill, North America, bachelor. Administration
to sister and next of kin Margaret Ellis. (Jan. 1785).
Ellison, Robert, Lieutenant-Colonel of a Regiment of Foot
who died at Albany, North America. Probate to brother
Hon. Major-General Cuthbert Ellison with similar powers
reserved to brother Henry Ellison. (June 1756).
Elliston, Robert, Controller of Customs in New York Province.
Administration to Abraham Maddock, clerk, attorney for
relict Mary Elliston in New York. (Apr. 1759).
Ellixon - see Alexon.
Elson, Samuel, of H.M.S. *Greyhound* who died at Blackpoint,
New England. Probate to Robert Harding. (Sept. 1707).
Emerson, Mary, of Bristol, Rhode Island, New England, widow.
Probate by solemn declaration to Richard Partridge with
similar powers reserved to Mary Vonheinen, widow. (Nov.
1748).
England, John, of Maryland. Probate by solemn declaration
to sons Allen and Joseph England. (Mar. 1739).
Escott, Gabriel, of St. Katherine, Coleman Street, London,
who died in South Carolina, widower. Administration to
aunt Anna Loyd, widow. (Aug. 1741).
Ettricke, John, of Charles Town, Jamaica *(sic)*. Probate
to sister Rachael Ettricke; administration granted
February 1766 to mother Isabella Ettricke declared void.
(Feb. 1767).
Eva, Hannah, of Charles Town, South Carolina, spinster.
Administration to mother and next of kin Mary Eva, widow.
(Oct. 1771).
Evans, Evan, of Satterton, Lincolnshire, who died on Island
of Maryland. Probate to John Brace. (Aug. 1729).
Evans, Mary, of Bertie Co., North Carolina, spinster.
Administration to brother John Evans. (May 1794).
Eveleigh, Samuel, of Charles Town, South Carolina, but late
of Bristol. Administration with will to son Nicholas
Eveleigh; executors Sir William Baker, George Austin,
Benjamin Stead and George Eveleigh renouncing. (Oct. 1766).

Everest alias Everist, Richard, of Georgia. Administration
to relict Sarah, now wife of Laurence Dolan. (Feb. 1789).
Evett alias Evit, Mary, of Boston, New England, widow.
Administration to Joseph Jekyll, attorney for mother
Joanna, wife of John Cutler, in New England. (Mar. 1744).
Evetts, James, of New York. Administration to son Nathaniel
Evetts. (Apr. 1707).

Faesh, John, Captain of 60th or Royal American Regiment.
Administration to James Schweighauser, attorney for relict
Elizabeth Faesh in New York. (July 1767).
Fairfax, George William, formerly of Truro, Fairfax Co.,
Virginia, but late of City of Bath. Special probate to
relict Sarah Fairfax, Samuel Athewes, Robert Burton, John
Maud, Joseph Beevers and Martin Bladen, Lord Hawke. (July
1787).
Falconer, Thomas, of Philadelphia, Captain of 44th Regiment
of Foot. Administration to William Neate, attorney for
relict Sarah Falconer in Philadelphia. (June 1767).
Faldo, Charles, of Yately, Hampshire, who died in Carolina.
Probate to William Palmer; wife Mary Faldo having died
in her husband's lifetime. (Apr. 1729).
Fananbrouse, John, of H.M.S. *Pembroke*, bachelor. Administra-
tion with will to Joseph Argent, attorney for Elizabeth
Partridge at Boston, New England. (May 1750).
Fane, George, Captain of H.M.S. *Lowstaff* who died in New York.
Limited probate to brother Charles Fane. (Oct. 1709).
Faneuil, Andrew, of Boston, New England. Probate to nephew
Peter Faneuil. (Sept. 1738).
Faneuil, Benjamin, formerly of Boston, New England, but late
of Bristol. Probate to Brook Watson and Robert Bashleigh.
(May 1787).
Faneuil, Peter, of Boston, New England, bachelor. Administra-
tion to brother Benjamin Faneuil. (Dec. 1743).
Farmar, Robert, of Mobile, West Florida. Limited administra-
tion with will to mother Mary Farmar, widow, guardian of
children Elizabeth Mary, Catharine Louisa and John Theo-
dore Farmar. (Aug. 1784).
Farmar, Samuel, of Norfolk, Virginia. Limited administration
to William Innes, attorney for relict Susanna Farmar in
Norfolk. (Apr. 1791).
Farmer, William, of Lambeth, Surrey, who died in South Caro-
lina on H.M.S. *Seaford*. Administration to relict Eliza-
beth Farmer. (Sept. 1739).
Farquharson, John, doctor of physick, formerly of Charles
Town, South Carolina, after of Broad Street Buildings,
London, and late of Aberdeen, Scotland. Probate to
nephew John Brown and to Robert Irvine. (Jan. 1791).
Farrant, Henry, formerly of Lanton, Northumberland, Lieute-
nant of a New York Independent Company under Captain John
Gordon, and late of Schenectady, Albany Co., New York.
Probate to John Steel with similar powers reserved to
John Sanders. (July 1768).
Farrell, Kennedy, barrack master to Forts of Detroit and
Machillimachinac in North America, widower. Admini-
stration to son John Farrell at Schenectady. (May 1771).

Farrell, Patrick, of H.M.S. *Jupiter* who died at Long Island
Hospital. Probate to James Mountgaritt. (Oct. 1783).
Farrow, James, of St. Botolph Bishopsgate, London, recruit
for General Oglethorpe's Regiment of Foot at Georgia.
Administration to brother William Farrow. (May 1748).
Fauquier, Hon. Francis, Lieutenant-Governor of Virginia.
Limited probate to son Francis Fauquier. (Dec. 1771).
Fear, Thomas, of H.M.S. *Sultan* and *Renown* who died at Rhode
Island Hospital. Administration with will to John Broom,
administrator to mother Mary Brown. (Mar. 1781).
Fell, James, of merchant ship *Dolphin* who died in Virginia,
bachelor. Administration to Mary Williams, wife and
attorney of principal creditor Griffith Williams. (Aug.
1704).
Fenn, James, formerly of Isle of Thanet but late of Norfolk,
Virginia, bachelor. Administration to father James Fenn.
(Aug. 1794).
Fenwicke, John, formerly of South Carolina but late of St.
George, Hanover Square, Middlesex. Probate to daughter
Countess Dowager Delaraine with similar powers reserved
to Isaac Whittington and Edward Fenwicke. (July 1747).
Fenwick, Robert, Captain-Lieutenant of Royal Regiment of
Artillery who died at New York. Administration with will
to relict Ann Fenwick; executors Erasmus John Philipps
and Robert George Bruce having died before executing.
(Mar. 1780). Further grant to Robert Douglas, guardian
of only children Robert George, William and Thomas Howard
Fenwick. (Jan. 1786).
Fenwick, William, of Boston, New England. Probate to sur-
viving executor brother Michael Fenwick. (May 1763).
Ferguson, Patrick, formerly Captain of 17th Regiment but late
Major of 71st Regiment who died in Carolina. Probate to
brother George Ferguson. (Aug. 1782).
Fernsley, John, of H.M.S. *Lowestoff* and *Worcester* who died
at Boston Hospital, New England, bachelor. Probate to
sisters Sarah Fernsley and Mary Crouchefer, widow.
(Jan. 1749).
Fidler, James, of Stepney, Middlesex, who died on ship
Dispatch in Pennsylvania. Administration with will to
principal creditor Thomas Coutts; relict Deborah Fidler
renouncing. (Jan. 1700).
Fielding, Cornelius, of 20th Regiment who died at Lancaster,
Maryland. Administration with will to James Tidswell;
no executor named. (Oct. 1783).
Fielding, Henry, of King and Queen Co., Virginia. Probate
to Francis Thompson with similar powers reserved to Gawin
Corbin and John Story. (Nov. 1712).
Files, John, of St. Augustine, East Florida, Lieutenant of
armed ship *Lord George Germaine*, bachelor. Administra-
tion to brother and next of kin Stephen Files. (Feb.
1780).
Finnie, William, Lieutenant of 61st Company of 2nd Division
of Marines who died at Boston. Administration with will
to John Ogilvie, attorney for George Skene at Rubislaw,
Aberdeen, Scotland. (Nov. 1775).
Fisher, Edward, of Euhaws St. Luke, Granville Co., South
Carolina, widower. Administration to son Robert Scrooby
Fisher. (Sept. 1783).

Fisher, John, of Conhow, Lorton, Cumberland, who died in Virginia, bachelor. Administration to Richard Barnes, attorney for sister Anne Langton, widow, at Cockermouth, Cumberland. (Nov. 1723).

Fisher, William, formerly of Sweetings Alley, London, but late of Philadelphia. Administration to John Pasley, attorney for only child Mary, wife of Thomas Ruston, in Philadelphia. (June 1791).

Fitch, Patrick, of New York Province who died on H.M.S. *Launceston*. Probate to John Dupre, attorney for relict Abigal Fitch at New York. (Dec. 1751).

Fitch, Thomas, of Boston, New England. Administration with will to Thomas Gainsborough, attorney for Andrew Oliver and relict Abiel Fitch and James Allen in Boston. (Sept. 1737).

Fleet, William, of Martin Worthy, Hampshire, and after of Chopthank, Talball Co., Maryland, who died at sea on ship *Peach Blossome*, bachelor. Probate to Mary Tanner alias Fleet, wife of Robert Tanner. (Apr. 1733).

Fletcher, William, of Boston, New England, late commander of H.M. armed vessel *Boston Pacquet*. Administration to William Bollay, attorney for relict Margaret Fletcher in Boston. (Aug. 1746).

Flint, Thomas, of New England, who died on H.M.S. *Severn*, bachelor. Administration with will to Elizabeth King, widow, administratrix to named executor William King deceased. (Feb. 1706).

Flower, Walter, of Virginia, bachelor. Administration to Noblett Ruddock, attorney for mother Lucy Flower, widow, in Ireland. (Feb. 1726).

Forbes, George, of St. Mary's Co., Maryland. Administration with will to William Black, attorney for George Gordon and Kenelm Greenfield Jowles in Maryland. (June 1742).

Forbes, James, of H.M.S. *Savage* who died in Long Island Hospital, bachelor. Administration to father James Forbes. (Aug. 1782).

Forbes, Thomas, of St. James, Westminster, Middlesex, Collector of Customs at Lewis, Pennsylvania. Limited administration to John Keith of St. Margaret Patten, London. (Aug. 1739).

Foord, Gabriel, mariner of South Carolina, bachelor. Administration to father Isaac Foord. (Mar. 1719).

Fordyce, Charles, Captain of 14th Regiment of Foot who died in Virginia, bachelor. Administration to John Seton, attorney for brother and sisters, John Fordyce, Allan wife of Andrew Grant, and Ann wife of Charles Ferguson at Edinburgh. (Nov. 1777).

Forman, William, Commissary and Paymaster of Artillery at New York. Probate to brother and surviving executor Richard Forman. (June 1775).

Forten alias Fortune, Thomas, of North Kingston, Rhode Island, negro man. Administration by solemn affirmation to Joseph Sherwood, attorney for negro woman Abigail Mingo at North Kingston. (Dec. 1765).

Foster, Isaac, of Christ Church, Middlesex, who died at Philadelphia. Probate to Simon Bailey by his solemn affirmation. (Mar. 1781).

Foster, John, of Boston, New England. Administration to
Thomas Blettsoe of St. Swithin, London, merchant, attorney
for Thomas Hutchinson in Boston. (Aug. 1711).
Fottrell, Edward, of Baltimore Co., Maryland, widower.
Administration with will to William Black, attorney for
creditor William Chapman in Maryland; executors Basil
Dorsey and Alexander Lawson and only children Edward,
Thomas and Achsah Fottrell cited but not appearing. (Nov.
1748).
Foulace, Sarah - see Nourse.
Foulks, John Lawrence of H.M.S. *Sea Horse* who died in Virginia,
bachelor. Administration to mother Elizabeth Foulks,
widow. (Feb. 1737).
Fowl, Peter, of H.M.S. *Shoreham* who died in Virginia. Admini-
stration to relict Mary Fowl. (Aug. 1700).
Fowler, James, of Virginia who died at Mile Rnd, Stepney,
Middlesex. Probate to John Goodwin with similar powers
reserved to relict Elizabeth Fowler. (May 1709).
Fox, John, of H.M.S. *Chester* who died in Boston, New England.
Probate to Anne Perry. (Jan. 1713).
Foxcroft, John, formerly of James Street, St. James, West-
minster, Middlesex, but late of New York City. Admini-
stration to relict Judith Foxcroft. (Nov. 1791).
Foxhall, John, of Westmoreland Co., Virginia. Probate to
Caleb Butler. (Aug. 1704).
Francis, Tarbutt, reduced Lieutenant of 44th Regiment, of
Philadelphia. Probate to surviving executrix and relict,
Sarah, now wife of John Connelly. (Aug. 1782).
Francomb, George, of General Holt's Regiment, bachelor.
Administration by decree to principal creditor Elizabeth
Jennings, widow. (July 1722).
Francklyn, Henry, of Boston, New England. Administration to
George Chabot, attorney for relict Hannah Francklyn in
Boston. (Nov. 1725).
Franklyn, Jonathan, of Boston, New England, seaman of H.M.S.
Magnanime. Administration to Nathaniel Green, attorney
for relict Sarah Franklyn in Boston. (May 1759).
Franks, David, of Philadelphia. Probate to son Jacob Franks
with similar powers reserved to son Moses Franks and to
Tench Coxe. (July 1794).
Fraser, Alexander, Lieutenant and Adjutant of 71st Regiment
who died at Savannah, Georgia, bachelor. Administration
with will to Robert Waddell, attorney for brother Thomas
Fraser at Dalcaitick, Scotland. (Dec. 1783).
Fraser, Patrick, of Long Island, Bahamas *(sic)*, bachelor.
Administration to David Robertson, attorney for brother
and next of kin John Fraser at Perth, Scotland. (Mar.
1795).
Fraser alias Frazer, Thomas, Lieutenant of 71st Regiment of
Foot who died in Virginia, bachelor. Administration to
creditor Alexander Alison; father Hugh Fraser renouncing.
(July 1782).
Fraser, Thomas, Captain of 14th Regiment who died at Norfolk,
Virginia, bachelor. Administration to John Ogilvie,
attorney for father Simon Fraser at Fannallan, Scotland.
(Jan. 1790).
Frazier, Edward - see Frizell.

Frazon, Samuel, of Boston, New England, who died in Barbados, bachelor. Administration to cousin and next of kin Francis de Caseres. (Sept. 1705).

Freame, Thomas, of Philadelphia, Captain of a Company in Colonel Gooch's Regiment. Probate to Thomas Penn by his solemn affirmation with similar powers reserved to Margaretta Freame and Richard Hockley. (Sept. 1744).

Frederick, Anthony, Ensign of 15th Regiment of Foot who died at German Town near Philadelphia, bachelor. Administration to father Felix Frederick. (May 1778).

Freeman, John, of Cohansey, New Jersey, Pennsylvania. Administration to John Blackwell, guardian of only child Anthony Freeman; relict Mary Freeman renouncing. (Jan. 1717).

Freeman, John, of Virginia, bachelor. Administration to sister Charity Freeman. (July 1739).

French, Thomas, formerly of Holborn, Middlesex, but late Captain of 1st Batallion in De Lancy's late Corps, bachelor. Administration to David Thomas, attorney for brother and only next of kin George French at George Town, South Carolina. (Aug. 1795).

Freshwater, William, citizen and haberdasher of London who died in Virginia. Probate to relict Elizabeth Freshwater. (May 1706). Revoked and granted to sister Elizabeth, wife of Richard Freshwater, on death of relict Elizabeth Freshwater. Testator now described as of St. James, Clerkenwell, Middlesex. (Apr. 1714).

Frisby, James, of Cecil Co., Maryland. Probate to son James Frisby with similar powers reserved to Thomas and Peregrine Frisby. (Dec. 1703). Double probate to sons Thomas and Peregrine Frisby. (Dec. 1706).

Frizell alias Frazier, Edward, of H.M.S. *Boyne* and *Harwich*, bachelor. Administration to Isabel, wife of nearest kin Hugh Poulson, in Lincoln, Virginia. (Aug. 1701).

Frost, Augustine, of York Fort, North America. Probate to James Isham. (Jan. 1759).

Frwid, James, of Liverpool, Lancashire, who died in Maryland, bachelor. Administration to William Jeffreys, attorney for father James Frwid in Scotland. (Oct. 1725).

Fry, James the younger, of Nottingham, Maryland. Probate to William Molleson and Ninian Pinckney. (Mar. 1771).

Fulham, John, of Carolina. Probate to relict Ursula Fulham. (Sept. 1715).

Fullerton, George, of Carolina. Probate to William Rhett with similar powers reserved to Sarah Rhett. (Sept. 1709).

Fullwood, Thomas, of Birmingham, Warwickshire, who died at sea between New England and Carolina. Administration to relict Elizabeth Fullwood. (May 1725).

Fuser, Louis Valentine, Lieutenant-Colonel of 60th or Royal American Regiment who died in North America. Probate to James Wright with similar powers reserved to Alexander Shaw, George McInzie, Andrew Turnbull, James Penman and Spencer Mann. (Dec. 1783). Revoked on death of James Wright and administration granted to daughter Louisa Dorothy, wife of Thomas Grierson; executors William Wulff, Alexander Shaw, George McInzie, Andrew Turnbull amd James Penman having died and Spencer Mann cited but not appearing. (Feb. 1797).

Gabourel, Joshua, of Cape Fear, North Carolina, bachelor.
Probate to brother Amos alias Amice Gabourel; brother
Thomas Gabourel having died. (Apr. 1737).

Gaisford, John, formerly of Beckington, Wiltshire, but late
of Charles Town, South Carolina, bachelor. Administration to sister and next of kin Lydia Gaisford. (June 1796).

Galey, Thomas, soldier of 22nd Regiment of Foot who died in
West Florida, bachelor. Administration to sister and next
of kin Jane, wife of Thomas Payne. (Apr. 1766).

Galpin, Joseph, of King Street, Wortchester *(sic)* Co., North
America, bachelor. Administration to Charles Cooke, attorney
for nephew and next of kin Gabriel Strang at St. Johns,
New Brunswick. (July 1790).

Gardner, Robert, of merchant ship *Society* who died in Virginia,
bachelor. Administration to Anne Browne, wife and attorney
of principal creditor William Browne of merchant ship
Robert and John. (Apr. 1710).

Gardiner, Silvester, doctor of physick, formerly of Boston,
North America, after of Poole, but late of Newport, Rhode
Island. Probate to Robert Hallowell alias Hollowell with
similar powers reserved to Oliver Whipple. (Apr. 1787).

Gardiner, Thomas, of Kingston upon Hull, Yorkshire, master
of transport ship *Juno* who died at Boston, New England,
bachelor. Administration to Ann Gardiner, widow, mother
of niece and only next of kin Ann Loft. (Dec. 1776).

Garrett, Amos, of Maryland, bachelor. Administration with will
to sisters Elizabeth Ginn and Mary Woodard, widows. (July
1728). Revoked and granted to Elizabeth Ginn on death of
Mary Woodard. (Jan. 1735). Revoked and granted to William
Woodard, son and executor of Mary Woodard now deceased;
mother Sarah Garrett having died in testator's lifetime.
(Dec. 1739).

Garrett, George, formerly of Christ Church, Spitalfields,
Middlesex, but late of Charles Town, South Carolina, bachelor. Administration to father William Garrett. (Apr. 1769).
Revoked and granted to Dorothy Garrett, relict and executrix of said William Garrett. (May1771).

Gatehouse, Edward, of New York Province, bachelor. Administration to nephew Richard Gatehouse; brother John Gatehouse
renouncing. (Feb. 1746).

Gatehouse, Richard, of New York, bachelor. Administration to
father John Gatehouse. (Apr. 1761).

Gaych, James, of Shadwell, Middlesex, who died on merchant
ship *Mary* in Virginia. Administration to relict Mary Gaych.
(Aug. 1709).

Gayner, Henry, of merchant ship *Dove* and then of H.M.S. *Shoreham* who died in South Carolina, bachelor. Administration
to principal creditor Charles Disney. (May 1733).

Geekie, Daniel, of St. Martin in Fields, Middlesex, surgeon
of H.M.S. *Phoenix* who died in South Carolina, bachelor.
Administration to Robert Ogilvie, attorney for father
Alexander Geekie in Scotland. (July 1740).

Gellie, George, Ensign of 46th Regiment who died at Niagara,
bachelor. Administration to brother Lewis Gellie. (Apr.
1763).

Gibbins, John, of Newport, Rhode Island, corporal in Lieutenant-Colonel Christopher Hargill's Company of Rhode Island
Regiment of Foot who died at Havana. Administration by
solemn declaration to Joseph Sherwood, attorney for relict
Hannah Gibbins at Newport. (Dec. 1765).

44

Gibbs, Thomas, of H.M.S. *Centurion* who died at Long Island
Hospital, bachelor. Administration to father John Gibbs.
(Feb. 1784).

Giberson, Gilbert, of Sunbury, Northumberland Co., Pennsylvania, widower. Administration to William Taylor, attorney for son Thomas Giberson in Pennsylvania. (July 1791).

Gibson, of Newport, Rhode Island and H.M.S. *Maidstone*.
Administration with will to James Sykes, attorney for
William Parker at sea. (May 1782).

Gibson, Use, of St. Anne and St. Agnes, Aldersgate, London,
who died in York Town, Virginia. Administration to relict
Hannah Gibson. (Aug. 1709).

Gildemaster, Christopher, of London who died in East New Jersey,
bachelor. Probate to brothers John Frederick and Henry
Daniel Gildemaster. (July 1736).

Giles, Isaac, of Virginia, bachelor. Administration to sister
and next of kin Rebecca, wife of John Lowe. (Nov. 1730).

Giles, Jean alias Jane, of Charles Town, South Carolina.
Administration with will to James Farquhar, attorney for
daughter Elizabeth Warley, widow, and James Munro at
Charles Town. (June 1797).

Giles, John, of Charles Town, South Carolina. Administration
with will to James Farquhar, attorney for daughter Elizabeth Warley, widow, at Charles Town; relict Jane Giles
and son Othniel Giles having died before executing. (Nov.
1798).

Giles, William, of New York. Probate to father George Giles
and to Roger and Charles Rhodes, with similar powers
reserved to John Burroughs. (Jan. 1703).

Gyles, William, of Fredericksburg, Virginia, bachelor. Administration to sister Elizabeth, wife of John Adams. (Aug.
1769).

Gillespie, George, of Tinwall, Dumfriesshire, Scotland, who
died in St. Mary's parish, Maryland, merchant, bachelor.
Administration to Andrew Drummond, attorney for sisters
and next of kin Janett Haliday, widow, Elizabeth wife of
John Lawson, and Jane wife of Alexander Ackin. (Mar. 1724).

Gillespie, George, formerly of Jamaica but late of Bristol,
Bucks Co., Pennsylvania. Limited probate to John Abraham
de Normandie. (Mar. 1782).

Gilligan, Ferdinand, of Virginia who died in Jamaica, widower.
Administration to brother Thomas Gilligan. (Apr. 1705).

Gilson, John, of St. Bride, London, who died in South Carolina.
Administration to relict Joane Gilson. (Aug. 1719).

Girard, Peter, of New York, Chatham pensioner. Administration
to Robert Crucifix, attorney for relict Jane Girard in New
York. (Jan. 1717).

Glassford, John, of Susquehannah, North America. Administration to John Inglis, attorney for relict Sarah Glassford
at Matilda, Quebec. (Oct. 1790).

Gledhill alias Day, Mary, of Isle of Wight, Virginia, widow.
Administration with will by decree to Micajah Perry,
attorney for James Day and Nathaniel Ridley in Virginia.
(June 1721).

Glencross, William, of New York. Probate to Broughton Wright.
(Dec. 1713).

Glover, Thomas, of Bermondsey, Surrey, who died at Charles
Town, South Carolina. Administration to relict Mary Glover.
(Oct. 1730).

Goddard, William, of St. Margaret Moses, London, who died in
South Carolina. Probate to aunt Mary Darby, spinster.
(May 1740).

Godson, Richard, of Stepney, Middlesex, who died on H.M.S.
Advice in New York. Administration with will to principal
creditor Henry Willoughby; relict Agnes Godson renouncing. (Dec. 1702).

Goffe - see Gough.

Gold - see Gould.

Goldie, William, of H.M.S. *Rose* who died in Carolina, bachelor.
Administration to Samuel Barlow, attorney for sisters
Janet and Jean Goldie in Scotland. (Dec. 1736).

Goldsborough, William, of Talbot Co., Maryland. Administration with will to William Anderson, attorney for relict
Henrietta Maria Goldsborough in Maryland. (Jan. 1766).

Goldthwaite, Joseph the elder, of New York City. Administration to son Philip Goldthwaite; relict Martha Goldthwaite cited but not appearing. (Oct. 1780) Revoked
and re-granted as probate on presentation of will. (Nov.
1780).

Goldthwaite, Joseph the younger, of New York City, bachelor.
Administration to Thomas Goldthwaite, attorney for father
Joseph Goldthwaite in New York. (Mar. 1780). Revoked and
granted to Philip Goldthwaite, son and administrator to
Joseph Goldthwaite the elder. (Oct. 1780). Revoked and
granted to Samuel Goldthwaite, son and administrator to
Joseph Goldthwaite the elder; previous grant made under
false suggestion. (Nov. 1780). Revoked and administration with will granted to son Samuel Goldthwaite, executor
to his grandfather Joseph Goldthwaite the elder who died
before administering, with similar powers reserved to son
Benjamin Goldthwaite. (Nov. 1780).

Golightly, Culchett, of St. Andrew's, Berkeley Co., South
Carolina. Probate to Charles Pinckney with similar powers
reserved to Hon. Edward Fenwicke, George Austin and Land-
grave Edmund Bellinger. (Mar. 1756).

Gomme, James, of Charles Town, North America, widower.
Administration to father John Gomme. (May. 1787).

Gooch, William the younger, of Virginia. Administration to
Robert Cary, attorney for relict Eleanor Gooch in Virginia.
(Jan. 1744).

Goodrich, Danby and Thomas, of Virginia, infants. Administration to uncle Sir Abstrupus Danby. (Nov. 1703).

Gordon, Alexander, formerly of Norfolk, Virginia, but late of
Kensington, Middlesex. Limited administration with will
to Lewis Wolfe with similar powers reserved to Peter
Elmsly. (Mar. 1799).

Gordon, James, Colonel of 80th Regiment who died at New York,
bachelor. Administration to mother Elizabeth Gordon, widow.
(May 1784).

Gordon, Patrick, chaplain of H.M.S. *Lenox* who died in New
York Province. Administration to brother James Gordon.
(Jan. 1703).

Gore, Charles, of Philadelphia, Captain of 35th Regiment of
Foot under Hon. Lieutenant-General Otway. Limited admini-
stration to Thomas Brown, attorney for relict Rebecca
Gore in Philadelphia. (June 1764).

Gorham, John, of Boston, New England, Captain of an Independent
Company at Nova Scotia but who died at St. Martin in Fields,
Middlesex. Administration to Jonathan Barnard, attorney
for relict Elizabeth Gorham at Boston. (July 1752).
Goring, Lovet, of Inner Temple, London. Probate to Susan.
wife of Joshua Lambe of Roxbury, New England, administra-
trix of named executor Lovet Saunders deceased, attorney
for Elizabeth Saunders, mother and next of kin of said
Lovet Saunders, in Boston. (Apr. 1710).
Gorstich, Thomas, of New York. Administration to mother Jane
Gorstich, widow, and brother John Gorstich. (Aug. 1714).
Goswell, John, of Virginia, bachelor. Administration to
sister Elizabeth Goswell. (Sept. 1734).
Gough, Charles, of Maryland. Administration to Joshua Noguier,
guardian of son Thomas Gough. (Nov. 1700).
Goffe, Daniel, Captain of a Company in H.M. American Regiment
commanded by Colonel William Gooch. Administration to
Jonathan Barnard, attorney for relict Mary Goffe in New
England. (Aug. 1744).
Gould, James, of Exeter who died at Trenton, New Jersey.
Administration to principal creditor Elizabeth Gould,
spinster; relict Ann Gould and minor children Elizabeth
and Francis Gould cited but not appearing. (Feb. 1742).
Gold, Richard, Lieutenant of 47th Regiment of Foot who died
at Boston, widower. Administration to Charles Yarburgh,
Henry Yarburgh and John Kilvington, guardians of only
children Charles and Joyce Gold. (Dec. 1777).
Goven, John, of New York, after of H.M.S. *Launceston*, but who
died on H.M.S. *Assistance*. Administration to relict Elizabeth Goven. (Feb. 1747).
Grace, William, master of merchant ship *Owen* who died at Boston,
New England. Probate to Catherine Hunter, widow. (Sept.
1748).
Graham, Anne, of West Hall, Dunsyre, Clydesdale, Scotland,
widow. Administration to John Graham, attorney for only
child Hugh Graham in Philadelphia. (Aug. 1727).
Graeme, David, of Charles Town, South Carolina. Probate to
relict Anne Graeme. (Apr. 1778).
Graham, John, of Charles Town, South Carolina, bachelor. Pro-
ate to William Littleton. (May 1755).
Grant, Alexander, sergeant of 2nd Batallion of 42nd or Royal
Highland Regiment under Lord John Murray, who died at Havana.
Administration to Duncan Campbell, attorney for relict
Barbara Grant in New York. (Mar. 1766).
Grant, John, of New York City who died at Kensington, Middle-
sex. Probate to Sir James Grant with similar powers reser-
ved to brother Alexander Grant, Ludovick Grant and James
Trasch. (May. 1781).
Grant, Neal, of New York, Lieutenant of 77th Regiment of Foot.
Administration to relict Hellen Grant. (Aug. 1763).
Grave, John, formerly of Dublin, Ireland, but late of Anna-
polis, Maryland. Probate to brother Thomas Grave. (July
1757).
Grave alias Graves, Leonard, of Charles Town, South Carolina.
Administration with will to nephew Leonard Grave; brother
William Grave and William Burrows having died before
executing, and father Robert Grave having died in lifetime
of testator.. (Dec. 1799) Further grant March 1819.

Gray, Ellis, of Boston, Mass. Limited probate to Thomas Dolbeare. (Aug. 1782).

Gray, Harrison, of Boston, Mass., but late of Newman Street, St. Marylebone, Middlesex. Probate to son Harrison Gray with similar powers reserved to sons Lewis and John Gray. (Jan. 1795).

Gray, James, surgeon of 21st Regiment of Foot who died at Philadelphia. Probate to father John Gray. (Dec. 1771).

Gray, John, Captain of an Independent Company in Georgia and Governor of the Fort there, bachelor. Administration to Henry Davidson, attorney for brother and next of kin Robert Gray at Crich, Scotland. (Aug. 1770).

Gray, Thomas, of Boston, Mass. Limited probate to Thomas Dolbeare. (Aug. 1782).

Grayson, John, of merchant ship *Prince Frederick* of Whitehaven, Virginia, bachelor. Administration to Benjamin Grayson, attorney for mother Mary Grayson, widow, at St. Bees, Cumberland. (Sept. 1733).

Greaves, Adam, of Charles Town, South Carolina, and of H.M.S. *Rose*, bachelor. Probate to Edward Jasper, attorney for Edward Stevens in South Carolina. (Apr. 1738).

Green, Richard, of Jamaica who died at New York City. Administration to brother and next of kin William Green. (May 1794).

Green, Thomas, of Strutton Major, King and Queen Co., York River, Virginia, widower. Administration to Elizabeth Green, relict and executrix of nephew and next of kin John Green deceased. (Oct. 1729).

Greenwood, Isaac, of Boston, New England, who died in Barbados on ship *Norwich*. Administration to John Grimla, attorney for relict Anne Greenwood in Boston. (July 1700).

Greenwood, Isaac, of H.M.S. *Rose*, widower. Administration to James Crockatt, attorney for principal creditor Gideon Norton in Charles Town, South Carolina. (Nov. 1746).

Gregory, John, of H.M.S. *Southampton* who died in Virginia. Administration to relict Margaret Gregory. (Oct. 1702).

Greig, David, formerly of St. Botolph Aldgate, London, but late of New York, bachelor. Administration to John Claphin, attorney for mother Isabel Murison, widow, at Tearn, Scotland. (Oct. 1788).

Gresham, Otway, of the neighbourhood of Boston, New England. Probate to Edward Benskin, executor Frances Benskin having died. (Nov. 1717).

Gresley, Jeffery, of King William Co., Virginia. Administration to daughter Jane Grammar Gresley; relict Mary, now wife of Robert Gaines, cited but not appearing. (Apr. 1791).

Grice, Caesar, of Maryland. Administration to brother John Grice; relict having died. (Aug. 1754).

Grierson, James, of Augusta, Georgia, Colonel of Loyal Militia Regiment, who died at St. Paul, Georgia. Probate to son Thomas Grierson with similar powers reserved to Andrew Johnson and John Glen. (Feb. 1789).

Griffin, James, Lieutenant of General Shirley's Regiment who died at Oxford, Mass. Administration with will to Thomas Kast, attorney for relict Prudence Griffin and William Watson in Mass. (Sept. 1773).

Griffith, Edward, formerly of Charles Town, North America,
but late of City of Chester. Probate to William Greenwood
and William Higgins with similar powers reserved to Walter
Thomas and Charles Goodwin; relict Martha now having
married James McNeill. (Oct. 1785).

Griffiths, Andrew, surgeon of H.M.S. *Proteus* and *Guadeloupe*
who died at New York. Probate to brother Richard Griffiths.
(Feb. 1782).

Griffiths, James, of Port Royal, Carolina, who died in Palace
of St. James, Westminster, Middlesex. Probate to father
John Griffiths. (Feb. 1709).

Griffiths, John, of New York City. Administration with will
to daughter Cornelia, Baroness de Diemar, wife of Frederick
Baron de Diemar; relict Jane Griffiths and sons John and
Anthony Griffiths having died before executing. (Dec.
1799).

Grimes, Gilbert, of Stepney, Middlesex, who died at Panama or
Porto Bello in America. Probate to relict Eleanor Grimes.
(Dec. 1722).

Grismond, Charles, Ensign at Annapolis Royal in North America
who died in General Evans' Regiment in Scotland. Administration to relict Anne Grismond. (Mar. 1723).

Groombridge, Walter, of Philadelphia. Administration to John
Norton and Henry Daniel, guardians of only child Jane
Groombridge. (July 1710).

Grove, Grey, Captain of 23rd Regiment of Foot who died in
New York, bachelor. Administration to sister Mary, wife
of Corbett Hale. (Sept. 1777).

Grove, Samuel, of St. Helena, Granville Co., South Carolina.
Limited administration with will to relict Jane Grove.
(May 1777).

Grover, John, of King's College, Cambridge, who died in Georgia,
bachelor. Administration to mother Carolina, wife of
William Kindon, she having retracted a former renunciation.
(Nov. 1774).

Grover, Joseph alias Jotham, of merchant ship *Providence*,
bachelor. Administration with will to William Lancaster,
attorney for grandmother in Boston, New England. (May 1710).

Grover, William, formerly of Reading, Berkshire, but late
Chief Justice of East Florida, who died at sea. Probate
to son John Grover. (Jan. 1768).

Gudgeon, Henry, of New York City, Lieutenant in Sir William
Pepperell's Regiment, who died at Oswego. Administration
to relict Martha Gudgeon. (July 1765).

Guest, John, of Philadelphia, widower. Probate to John Geast.
(Apr. 1708).

Guillume, Peter, master of brigantine *Jane and Margaret* who
died in Virginia, bachelor. Probate to father John Guillume.
(Feb. 1702).

Gulline, William, Lieutenant of a New York Independent Company
of Foot who died at Havana, bachelor. Administration to
John Cuthbert, attorney for nephew John Gulline at Stran-
raer, Wigtownshire, Scotland. (Dec. 1763).

Gulliver, Elijah, of Milton, Suffolk Co., New England, and
H.M.S. *Vigilant* and *Superbe*, bachelor. Administration to
Henry Rainsdon, attorney for brother Samuel Gulliver in
New England. (July 1754).

Gurney, Daniel, of Christ Church, Middlesex, who died in
    North America, bachelor. Administration to Ann, wife
    of Joseph Piggot, administratrix to John Kettle deceased
    who was half brother and only next of kin. (July 1788).
Guyon, Stephen, 2nd Lieutenant of 23rd Regiment of Royal
    Welch Fusiliers who died at George Town, North America,
    bachelor. Administration to father Henry William Guyon.
    (Aug. 1784).
Gwinnett, Ann, formerly of Wolverhampton, Staffordshire, but
    late of Georgia. Administration with will to Peter Belin,
    husband and administrator of daughter Elizabeth Belin
    formerly Gwinnett. (May 1785).
Gwyn, John, of Charles Town, South Carolina, bachelor.
    Administration to creditor John Owen. (Nov. 1757).
Gyles - see Giles.

Hackett, John, who died in Maryland on merchant ship *Oxford*.
    Administration to principal creditor Thomas Watson. (Apr.
    1729).
Hackett, John, of Pennsylvania, bachelor. Probate by solemn
    affirmation to brother Thomas Hackett; no executor named
    and father John Hackett dying before administering.
    (Feb. 1731).
Haines - see Haynes.
Hall, John, of St. Marylebone, Middlesex, who died at Williams-
    burg, Virginia, bachelor. Administration to mother Ann
    Hall, widow. (Sept. 1787).
Hall, Jonathan, Lieutenant of 34th Regiment of Foot who died
    at New York, bachelor and bastard. Administration to Sir
    Thomas Clavering for the use of the King. (Feb. 1768).
Hall, Robert, of Marlborough, Prince George Co., Maryland.
    Administration with will to Thomas Sprigg, attorney for
    James Haddock and Nolden Jefferson in Maryland. (May 1720).
Hall, William, of Virginia, bachelor. Administration to
    mother Elizabeth, wife of Richard Fox. (Mar. 1713).
Hall, William, of Mount Facitus, South Carolina, bachelor.
    Administration to brother Robert Hall. (Jan. 1786).
Hallett, Elizabeth, of St. Edmund the King, London, who died
    in New York, widow. Administration to Henry Barton,
    guardian of daughter Elizabeth Hallett. "Pauper."
    (July 1723). Regranted to Elizabeth Hallett on her coming
    of age. (Sept. 1724).
Halley, Francis, of All Hallows Staining, London, who died in
    Virginia. Probate to Edmund Halley and Richard Pyke.
    (Sept. 1702).
Haman, Richard, of St. Olave, Southwark, Surrey, who died on
    merchant ship *New York* in New York. Probate to relict
    Anne Haman. (Feb. 1717).
Hambeton/Hambleton, John - see Hamilton.
Hamerton, Pinchback, of Virginia, bachelor. Probate to
    Hannah, wife of Richard Cloke. (Dec. 1729).
Hamilton, Andrew, of Philadelphia. Administration with will
    to Ferdinando John Paris, attorney for William Allen,
    James Hamilton and Andrew Hamilton in Pennsylvania. (Dec.
    1742).

Hamilton, Douglas, of Suffolk, Virginia, bachelor. Administration to brother Archibald Hamilton. (July 1783).

Hamilton, Hugh, of Pensacola, Lieutenant of H.M. Forces, bachelor. Administration to brother and next of kin Andrew Hamilton. (Apr. 1793).

Hamilton, James, of Vienna, Maryland, bachelor. Administration to sister and next of kin Margaret Howe, widow. (Feb. 1772).

Hamilton alias Hambleton alias Hambeton, John, of H.M.S. *Canterbury*, bachelor. Administration with will to Owen Gray, administrator to named executor Thomas McKenly deceased and attorney for William Gale in New York, principal creditor of said McKenly; legatee David Chancelor having died before administering. (Mar. 1750).

Hamilton, Mary, of Philadelphia, widow. Administration with will to Lady Ann Hamilton, attorney for Samuel Duffield in Philadelphia. (Dec. 1794).

Hamilton, Paul, formerly of Charleston, South Carolina, but late of Clerkenwell, Middlesex. Limited probate to Robert Williams and limited double probate to Rev. Alexander Hewat. (Jan. 1798).

Hammell, John, of New York, surgeon of 3rd Batallion of late New Jersey Volunteers. Administration to David Thomas, attorney for relict Hannah Hammell in New York. (Aug. 1797).

Hammer, Martin, of merchant ship *Pertuxan Merchant* who died in Virginia, widower. Administration to Gustavus Hammer, guardian of children Anne Catherine, Beren and Martin Hammer in Scotland or at sea. (Aug. 1704).

Hammerton, Elizabeth, of Charles Town, South Carolina. Administration with will to Nathaniel Hollier; named executors Ann de la Brasseur, Joseph Barry, Adam Beauchamp and Thomas Bolton cited but not appearing, and son Hollier Hammerton having died. (Jan. 1750).

Hammand, Thomas, of Newport, North America, widower. Administration to son Benjamin Hammand. (July 1786).

Hampton, John, of Somerset Co., Maryland. Limited probate to brother Robert Hampton. (Aug. 1722).

Hamson, Daniel, of H.M.S. *Mermaid* who died on merchant ship *Hamilton*, bachelor. Administration with will to Thomas Newby, attorney for John Newby in New England. (June 1715).

Hance, Peter - see Hans.

Handy, Charles, of Newport, Rhode Island. Probate to sons John and Thomas Handy and to Stephen Deblois with similar powers reserved to sons Levin and William Handy. (Mar. 1796).

Hanford, Elnathan, of Norwall, Connecticut, seaman of H.M.S. *Weymouth* who died in Bombay Hospital. Administration to James Perrot, attorney for relict Ann Hanford at Norwall. (Nov. 1769).

Hannam, Minty, formerly of St. John, Southwark, Surrey, but late of Dorchester Co., Maryland. Administration to cousin german Hester Read; relict Mary Holland formerly Hannam cited but not appearing. (Apr. 1791).

Hans alias Hance, Peter, of merchant ship *Providence* who died in Virginia. Probate to relict Sarah Hans with similar powers reserved to Robert Townsend. (Nov. 1708).

Hanton, William, of Ramsgate, Kent, master of merchant ship
Sarah. Limited administration to Rodrigo Pachecor to
recover debts owed to William Yeomans and Gabriell Escott
of South Carolina. (Aug. 1736). Limited administration
to relict Sarah Hanton. (Jan. 1737).

Harding, William, of Virginia, bachelor. Probate to Adriana
Dunn alias Oakley, wife of Samuel Dunn. (Nov. 1742).

Hardy, John, of West Florida, bachelor. Administration to
father Rev. Joseph Hardy. (July 1775).

Harley, John, of H.M.S. *Terrible* who died in Long Island
Hospital. Probate to Elizabeth Halfpenny, spinster.
(July 1781).

Harman, John, of Bermondsey, Surrey, who died on merchant
ship *Forward* in Virginia. Probate to relict Mary Harman.
(Dec. 1728).

Harman, Thomas, of Poplar, Stepney, Middlesex, who died in
Virginia, bachelor. Administration to principal creditor
Mary Fisher, widow. (Apr. 1701).

Harmer, George, formerly of Bristol but late of Albemarle Co.,
North America. Administration with will to John Lambert;
no executor named. (Apr. 1799).

Harries - see Harris.

Harris, Benjamin, of Newbury Port, Mass. Administration to
creditor Joseph Hooper; relict Lucy Harris having died
before administering and only child Mary, wife of said
Hooper, cited but not appearing. (Apr. 1779).

Harris, John, of St. Stephen's, Northumberland Co., Virginia.
Probate to relict Hannah, now wife of Thomas Cralle.
(Sept. 1723).

Harries, John Hill, of Priskilly, Pembrokeshire, Lieutenant
of 33rd Regiment of Foot who died at Boston, bachelor.
Administration to father John Harries. (June 1778).

Harris, Richard, of Pennsylvania, who died at St. Stephen,
Coleman Street, London. Limited probate to Theodore
Eccleston. (Mar. 1701).

Harris, Richard the younger, Lieutenant in Colonel Cane's
Regiment who died in America. Administration by decree to
James Rane, executor to father Richard Harris. (Feb. 1723).
Revoked and granted to Francis Marshall, executor to James
Rane now deceased. (Jan. 1726).

Harris, Robert, of H.M.S. *Hampshire*, bachelor. Administration
to Margaret, wife of Magnus Alexander, attorney for sister
Isabel, wife of William Tilley, in New England. (May 1700).

Harris, Robert, of H.M.S. *Essex* Prize who died in Virginia.
Administration to Susan Biddell, grandmother of children
Robert, Sarah, Mary and Elizabeth Harris. (July 1700).

Harris, Samuel, of Boston, New England, who died on merchant
ship *Martha and Hannah*. Probate of nuncupative will by
decree to brother Amos Harris. (Jan. 1721).

Harrison, George, of Philadelphia. Administration to sister
and only next of kin Rachel, wife of Samuel Jones; relict
Elizabeth Harrison *?having died*.

Harrison, Lother, of St. Margaret, Westminster, Middlesex,
who died on merchant ship *Mary* in Carolina. Administration
to relict Catherine Harrison. (Apr. 1720).

Harrison, Robert, of Augusta, Georgia. Probate to Charles
Sumerson and Thomas Nickelson; relict Mary Harrison
renouncing. (Feb. 1776).

Harrison, Samuel, Lieutenant of Artillery Train who died at
   Albany, North America. Administration to creditor James
   Taylor; mother and only next of kin Ann Robins renouncing.
   (Oct. 1759).
Hart, Andrew, of Wapping, Middlesex, who died on merchant
   ship *Amity* in Virginia. Probate to Robert Wilson.
   (Nov. 1723).
Hart, Charles, of Charles Town, South Carolina, widower.
   Administration to sister Mary, wife of Sidney Harris.
   (Dec. 1758).
Hart, John, of Cumberland Town, New Kent Co., Virginia, bache-
   lor. Administration to James Miller, attorney for brother
   and next of kin Patrick Hart in New York City. (Dec. 1779).
   Revoked and granted to James Miller as attorney for mother
   Elizabeth Smith, widow. (Dec. 1780).
Hart, John, of H.M.S. *Avenger* who died in Long Island Hospital,
   bachelor. Administration to father John Hart. (Apr. 1784).
Hart, Thomas, of New York City. Probate to relict Esther Hart.
   (Jan. 1774).
Harvey, Nicholas, Lieutenant of Captain Clarke's Independent
   Company of Foot who died at Albany, New York, bachelor.
   Administration to brother Rev. Peter Harvey; mother Jane
   Harvey renouncing. (Dec. 1750).
Harvey, Peter, of New England, bachelor. Administration by
   decree to principal creditor Joseph Davis; sister Deborah
   Oakley, widow, renouncing. (Oct. 1719).
Harvey, Stephen, of Saratoga, North America, Lieutenant of
   62nd Regiment of Foot, bachelor. Administration to brother
   Eliab Harvey. (Dec. 1782).
Harvey, Thomas, of H.M.S. *Deptford*, bachelor. Administration
   to Rebecca, wife and attorney of Abraham Allaway in Boston,
   New England. (Aug. 1707). Revoked and granted to sister
   Elizabeth, wife of Thomas Sly. (Sept. 1707).
Harwar, Thomas, of Essex Co., Virginia, widower. Limited
   administration to son Thomas Harwar. (Nov. 1704).
Haslehurst, Mary, of Philadelphia who died at sea, widow.
   Administration to mother Mary Abraham, widow. (Jan. 1736).
Haslewood, William, Lieutenant in Royal American Regiment who
   died in North America, bachelor. Administration with will
   to father Edward Haslewood; no executor named. (May 1759).
Hasted, Thomas, of Stepney, Middlesex, who died in Virginia,
   widower. Administration to John Hogg the younger, guardian
   of children Judith Hogg alias Hasted, Reynol and Thomas
   Hasted, revoking previous grant of February 1698. (Feb.
   1704). Revoked and granted to Mary Hone, widow, guardian
   of son Thomas Hasted. (Apr. 1706).
Hastings, John, master of ship *James* who died in Virginia.
   Administration with will to William Finlason, attorney
   for only sister Janette Hastings at Preston Pans, Scotland;
   executor William Brock renouncing. (Sept. 1707).
Hatch, Matthew, of St. Leonard Eastcheap, London, who died in
   Georgia, bachelor. Administration with will to Thomas
   Gorst; no executor named. (Mar. 1765).
Haviland, Margaret, of New York City. Administration to
   husband Joseph Haviland. (June 1768).
Hawes, William, of Virginia, bachelor. Administration to
   brother Henry Hawes. (May 1735).

Hawkes, John, formerly of Whitechapel, Middlesex, but late of
Norfolk, Virginia, bachelor. Administration to brother
William Hawkes. (Jan. 1790).

Hawkins, John, of Queen Anne Co., Maryland. Probate to son
Ernault Hawkins. (Nov. 1719).

Hawkins, John, of H.M.S. *Essex* and late of H.M.S. *Juno* who
died in New York Hospital. Probate to Elizabeth Yarworth.
(June 1767).

Hawkins, Mary, of Boston, New England, widow. Probate to
Randolph Hopley the younger with similar powers reserved
to Randolph Hopley the elder. (Feb. 1721).

Hawkins, Philip, formerly of South Carolina and Islington,
Middlesex, but late of St. Croix in West Indies. Probate
to brother John Hawkins with similar powers reserved to
John Lewis Jervies, George Cook and John Owen. (Feb. 1782).

Hawkins, William, of Boston, New England, surgeon. Probate to
relict Dorothy Hawkins. (Apr. 1702).

Hay, Alexander, of Charles Town, South Carolina. Probate to
Francis Mercer. (July 1776).

Hay, Charles, of H.M.S. *Tamer* who died at Boston, New England,
widower. Administration to only children Eleanor and
Anna Maria Hay. (June 1773).

Hayes, Rebecca, of Carolina, spinster. Administration to
third cousin and next of kin Richard Hayes. (Jan. 1736).

Haines, Anna Maria, formerly of Great Russell Street, Covent
Garden, Middlesex, but late of Marmion, Virginia, spinster.
Administration to brother Thomas Haines.

Haynes, Thomas, of Warwick Co., Virginia. Administration
with will to James Wilkes, attorney for Andrew Haynes in
Virginia. (Sept. 1746).

Haynes, Herbert, of Abingdon, Gloucester Co., Virginia, who
died at St. Peter Cornhill, London. Probate to Job Wilkes,
attorney for relict Sarah Haynes and father Thomas Haynes
in Virginia. (Dec. 1737).

Hazleton, William - see Heselton

Head, George, of Philadelphia who died in Charles Town, South
Carolina, bachelor. Administration to brother Thomas Head;
father Rowland Head renouncing. (Nov. 1734).

Heale, George, of Lancaster City, Rappahannock, Virginia.
Administration to Arthur Bayly, attorney for son George
Heale in Virginia, the named executor. (Mar. 1709).

Hele, Warwick, of Pennsylvania, widower. Administration to
principal creditor Michael Hammond. (Mar. 1711).

Healy, William, of H.M.S. *Boreas* and *Alcide* who died in hospital at Governor's Island, New York. Probate to Thomas
Healy. (July 1783).

Heath, Henry, of Fredericksburg, Virginia. Administration to
relict Susanna Heath. (Sept. 1772).

Heath, William, formerly of Topsham, Devon, but late of New
York City. Administration to brother and next of kin David
Heath; relict Sarah Heath renouncing. (Feb. 1789).

Heathcote, Gilbert (July 1731), Mary (July 1731), Elizabeth
(Feb. 1736), William (Feb. 1736), all of New York Province.
Administration to Samuel Baker, attorney for mother Martha
Heathcote, widow, in New York.

Heathcote, William, of New York Province, bachelor. Administration to mother Martha Heathcote, widow. (Jan. 1723).

Hedges, Thomas, of Wilmington, North Carolina, widower.
Administration to brother Joseph Hedges. (Dec. 1769).
Helcott, Matthew, of H.M.S. *Robust* who died in New York.
Administration to sister Anne, wife of Benjamin Cole.
(Jan. 1783).
Hele - see Heal.
Hemard, Peter, of Stepney, Middlesex, who died in Virginia.
Probate to relict Elizabeth Hemard. (Mar. 1719).
Henderson, Henry, of H.M.S. *Culloden* who died at Long Island
Hospital, bachelor. Administration to cousin german
William Gunn. (Apr. 1782).
Henderson, James, of New York City. Probate to relict Tessia
Henderson and daughter Margaret, wife of Joseph Haviland.
(Feb. 1760).
Henderson, James, Lieutenant of 78th Regiment of Foot who
died in New York. Administration to John Ogilvie,
attorney for relict Elizabeth Henderson in New York.
(Oct. 1770).
Henderson, James, surgeon of Royal Artillery who died at New
York, bachelor. Administration to sister Margaret, wife of
Robert Marshall. (Apr. 1781).
Henly, Henry, of Virginia who died at sea. Administration to
brother John Henly. (Mar. 1700).
Herault, John, of Charles Town, South Carolina, bachelor.
Administration to second cousin and next of kin Henry Ayme.
(Mar. 1705).
Herbert, William, of Scarborough, Yorkshire, who died in Phila-
delphia. Probate to William Herbert. (May 1778).
Heron, Margaret - see Moncrieffe.
Herring, William Edward, formerly of St. Marylebone, Middlesex,
but late of Charleston, South Carolina, widower. Admini-
stration to brother and only next of kin Sampson George
Herring. (May 1789).
Hesletine, James, of St. Mary le Bow, Durham, widower. Admini-
stration to Thomas Philpot, attorney for nephew and niece
Charles Hesletine and Catherine, wife of James Fraizer in
Maryland. (June 1765).
Heselton alias Hazleton, William, of Virginia, mate of merchant
ship *Resolution*. Administration to relict Hannah Heselton.
(Jan. 1766).
Hewetson, Thomas Wallis, Lieutenant of Marines who died at
Boston. Administration to James Fitter, attorney for brother
Boyle Hewetson at Kilkenny, Ireland. (May 1777).
Hewett, William, surgeon and Ensign of 28th Regiment of Foot
who died at Charles Town, South Carolina, bachelor. Admini-
stration with will to John Cole, attorney for brother and
next of kin Thomas Hewett in Cork, Ireland; executors
Arthur Price and Lionel Chalmers, doctor of physick,
renouncing. (Dec. 1766).
Hewgill, Henry, master of merchant ship *Lord Middleton* who
died at Savannah, Georgia. Administration with will to
sister Cordelia, wife of Daniel Kitchen; executor Sir
Thomas Coxhead renouncing. (Apr. 1798).
Hewson, Mary, of Pennsylvania, widow. Limited probate to James
Blunt with similar powers reserved to Miles Satterthwaite.
(Apr. 1796).

Hext, Edward, of Charles Town, South Carolina. Probate to
David Hext and John McCall with similar powers reserved
to Thomas Hext, John Bee the younger, Jonathan Bryan and
Philip Prisleau. (Dec. 1742).

Hicks, Jacob, of Portsmouth, Newport Co., Rhode Island,
private in Lieutenant-Colonel Hargill's Company who died
at Havana, apprentice to Robert Burrington the younger
at Portsmouth. Limited administration to Joseph Sherwood of Throckmorton Street, London, attorney for said
Burrington. (Dec. 1765).

Higgins alias Higgons, John, of H.M.S. *Dunkirk* who died in
New England, bachelor. Administration to sister and
next of kin Elizabeth, wife of Thomas Pattison. (Oct.
1711).

Higgins, Robert Harpur, Lieutenant of 52nd Regiment of Foot
who died at Boston. Administration to mother Mary, wife
of James Robinson. (Apr. 1776).

Higginson, John, of Maryland, bachelor. Administration to
brother Robert Higginson. (Jan. 1746).

Higgons, John - see Higgins.

Higgs, William, of Pennsylvania, bachelor. Administration
to brother John Higgs. (Oct. 1709).

Hildyard, William, of New Providence, America, late Lieutenant in Governor Tinkers Company. Administration to
grandmother Elizabeth Hildyard, guardian of only child
Hannah Hildyard; relict Hannah Hildyard having died.
(July 1756).

Hill, Adam, of Talbot Co., Maryland. Probate to William
Campbell with similar powers reserved to Ebenezer Mackie
and Robert Campbell. (Mar. 1768).

Hill, Allen, of Bermondsey, Surrey, who died in Virginia.
Administration to relict Mary Hill. (Dec. 1726).

Hill, Littleton, Lieutenant on H.M.S. *Scorpion* who died in
South Carolina, widower. Administration to George Hill,
uncle and guardian of only child Littleton Hill. (May
1752).

Hill, Martha, of St. Saviour, Southwark, Surrey, but late of
Virginia, spinster. Administration to brother Thomas
Hill. (Dec. 1778).

Hill, Samuel, of Charles Town, South Carolina. Probate to
James Alexander with similar powers reserved to James
Dawson. (Aug. 1787).

Hill, William, of H.M.S. *Lynn*, bachelor. Administration to
John Bradford, attorney for half brother William Abraham
at Charlestown, New England. (Jan. 1750).

Hill, Willoughby, of ship *India King* who died in Virginia.
Probate to relict Joanne Hill. (May 1703).

Hinchman, John, of Burlington, New Jersey. Administration
with will to James Bell, attorney for John Hinchman Stokes,
Joseph Atkinson alias Hatkinson and Hinchman Bispham at
Burlington. (June 1790).

Hiorns, William, of Philadelphia but late of Natchez, West
Florida. Probate to brother Francis Hiorns. (June 1781).

Hitchins, Thomas, Ensign in Colonel Venderduson's Independent
Company who died in South Carolina, bachelor. Administration to principal creditor George Daniel. (Oct. 1749).

Hobby, Charles, of Boston, New England, but late of St. James,
Westminster, Middlesex. Limited administration to Stephen
Mason of Islington, Middlesex, merchant. (June 1715).

Hobkirk, John, of New York City. Administration to relict
  Hannah Hobkirk. (Jan. 1780).
Hockenhull, Richard, of South Carolina, widower. Administration to creditor Austin Ashby; brother George Hockenhull
  and John Howe, guardian of nephew Chadwell Hockenhull,
  renouncing. (May 1733).
Hockley, Thomas, of Philadelphia. Probate to Samuel Smith
  with similar powers reserved to Jacob Duche, James Reynolds
  and William Garriques. (Dec. 1781).
Hockley, William Branson, of Philadelphia, bachelor. Admini-
  stration to nephew Richard Hockley Wilcocks. (Jan. 1796).
Hodd, Thomas, of Virginia, bachelor. Administration to Lucy
  Swinhoe, spinster, executrix of mother and next of kin
  Hannah Hodd, widow. (Nov. 1797).
Hodges, Nathaniel, of Gravesend, Kent, who died at Providence
  Island, bachelor. Administration to brother George Hodges;
  mother Mary Hodges having died. (July 1748).
Hodgskinson, Christopher, of Virginia. Administration to
  sister and next of kin Anne, wife of Richard Walley.
  (Apr. 1718).
Holding, Edward, master of merchant ship *Friends Goodwill* who
  died at Boston, New England, bachelor. Probate to Mary
  Pomfrett, widow. (Feb. 1751).
Holditch, James, of Carolina. Administration to Richard Boys,
  attorney and father of Susan Holditch in Carolina. (Mar.
  1702).
Houldsworth, Michael, of Jamaica who died in New York. Admini-
  stration to relict Mary, now wife of Thomas Nuttall. (Jan.
  1706).
Hollamby, James, of New York City. Administration with will
  to Alexander Goudge, attorney for Luke Bird and Thomas
  Goudge in New York. (Apr. 1780).
Hollowell, John, of Philadelphia. Administration to Elizabeth
  Linch, widow, attorney for relict Mary Hollowell at Phila-
  delphia. (Feb. 1779).
Holmes, James, of H.M.S. *Prince George* and *Laystoffe* who died
  in Virginia on H.M.S. *Oxford*. Administration to relict
  Mary Holmes. (Mar. 1709).
Home, Charles, of New York. Probate to William Home with
  similar powers reserved to William Jameson, James Henderson
  and James Rochead. (Feb. 1748).
Hookamer, Jacob - see Vandrez.
Hooker, William, of New York City but formerly of H.M.S.*Advice*,
  Lynn and *Suffolk* who died on H.M.S. *St. George*. Administration to William Bryant, attorney for relict Cloe Hooker
  in New York. (Feb. 1749).
Hooker, William, Captain of 31st Regiment of Foot who died at
  Pensacola, West Florida, widower. Administration to
  creditor James Gibson; others with title cited but not
  appearing. (July 1767).
Hope, Henry, of North Carolina who died in Liverpool, Lancashire, widower. Administration to brother John Hope,
  attorney for father Archibald Hope. (Nov. 1738).
Hopkins, William, of Virginia who died at St. Dunstan in West,
  London, bachelor. Administration to brother James Hopkins
  pending production of will. (Feb. 1735).

Hopton, William, of Charles Town, South Carolina. Administration with will to John Hopton, attorney for daughters Mary Christianna and Sarah Hopton, for Nathaniel Russell and Samuel Legare, and for relict Sarah Hopton in South Carolina. (Aug. 1788).

Hornbe, Robert, of ship *Benjamin* who died in Virginia. Probate to relict Elizabeth Hornbe. (Aug. 1704).

Horrocks, Rev. James, of Bruton parish, Williamsburg, Virginia, but late of St. Olave, Hart Street, London, who died at Oporto, Portugal. Administration to relict Frances Horrocks. (May 1772).

Horsmanden, Daniel, of New York City. Probate to Miles Sherbrooke with similar powers reserved to Thomas Hayes. (Apr. 1786).

Hoskins, Richard, of Pennsylvania but late of St. Stephen, Coleman Street, London. Limited probate to Theodore Eccleston with similar powers reserved to Philip Collins and John Groves. (Mar. 1701).

Houghton, John, of Charles Town, South Carolina. Probate to surviving executor John Owen. (Apr. 1751).

Houldsworth - see Holdsworth.

Howard, Michael, of Talbot Co., Maryland. Probate to brother Francis Howard with similar powers reserved to Samuel and Herbert Hyde and to Adam and Michael William Howard. (May 1738). Administration of estate unadministered by Francis Howard now deceased to Christopher Plunkett, son of Ann Plunkett, widow; said Francis Howard dying intestate, Samuel Hyde renouncing, and Herbert Hyde, Adam and Michael William Howard, Daniel Delany and Walter Carmichael all having died. (Aug. 1757).

Howell, William, of Boston, New England, widower. Administration to son Joseph Howell.

Howson, Thomas, of Maryland. Probate to mother Mary Howson. (June 1718).

Hoyle, Samuel, of St. Catherine Creechurch, London, who died at Rappahannock, Virginia, bachelor. Administration to mother Anne Atkinson, widow. (Apr. 1708).

Hubbard, Nathaniel, of Newhaven, Connecticut, surgeon's mate of H.M. Regiment of Foot who died at Havana, bachelor. Administration to Phineas Lyman, attorney for brother Leverett Hubbard at Newhaven. (Dec. 1763).

Hudson, Abednego, of New Bern, North Carolina. Administration to Thomas Blount, attorney for relict Ann Hill at New Bern. (July 1787).

Hudson, John, of ship *Paget* and of Boston, New England. Probate to Jane, wife of William Jenkinson. (July 1702).

Huger, Daniel, of Berkeley Co., South Carolina. Limited administration with will to Thomas Corbett, attorney for Francis Lejan the elder and Francis Lejan the younger in South Carolina. (Jan. 1756).

Hughes, David, of Bristol, late of the ship *Lackey*, who died in Pennsylvania. Administration to brother and next of kin John Hughes. (June 1772).

Hughs, John, of Fort Albany, Hudsons Bay, bachelor. Probate to brother and next of kin William Hughs. (Nov. 1726).

Hughes, Richard, of Georgia, bachelor. Administration to great aunt Jemima Elliott, widow, guardian of nephew and next of kin Philip Hughes. (Mar 1763) Revoked and granted to cousin and next of kin Richard Hughes, previous grant having been obtained under false pretences. (May 1765).

Hughes, Robert, of Stepney, Middlesex, who died on H.M.S. *Tartar* in Virginia. Probate to relict Mary Hughes. (May 1727).

Hughes, William, of Boston, New England, bachelor. Administration to John Carling, attorney for brother John Hughes in Boston. (Mar. 1731).

Huisman, Abraham, of New York City. Limited probate to Joseph Mico of London, merchant. (Dec. 1748).

Huling, John, of H.M.S. *Triton's* prize, bachelor. Administration to Charles Lodwick, attorney for brother Alexander Huling in New York. (Nov. 1711).

Humble, William, of New York City. Probate to Mary Spark, spinster. (June 1778).

Hummerston, Thomas, formerly of St. Margaret Lothbury, London, but late of North America, bachelor. Administration to brothers and sister James and William Dunn Hummerston and Elizabeth, wife of William Hibbert. (June 1783).

Humphries, Richard, formerly of Cork, Ireland, after of St. John, Southwark, Surrey, but late of New Orleans. Probate to John Burrell and William Hance. (Jan. 1797).

Humphries, Thomas, of Christ Church, Surrey, who died in Maryland. Probate to relict Jane Humphries; no executor named. (Nov. 1722).

Hunt, Charles, formerly of Queen Street, St. Marylebone, Middlesex, but late of Williamsburg, North America. Probate to surviving executor Richard Adams. (Dec. 1794).

Hunt, John and Nicholas, of Virginia, bachelors. Administration to sisters and next of kin Mary Hunt and Willielma, wife of Francis Rawlings. (May 1702).

Hunt, John, of Virginia, widower. Administration to principal creditor William Moore; the children cited but not appearing. (Sept. 1718).

Hunt, John, of Taunton, Somerset, who died at Charles Town, South Carolina, widower. Administration to creditor Betty Wansbrough, widow; only child John Hunt renouncing by his uncle and guardian William Hunt. (Apr. 1760).

Hunt, John, of Newport, Rhode Island, who died on H.M.S. *Valiant*. Administration by his solemn declaration to Joseph Sherwood, attorney for relict Carolina Hunt in Rhode Island. (Sept. 1763).

Hunter, John, of Norfolk, Virginia, who died in New York City. Probate to Thomas McCulloch with similar powers reserved to James Parker. (Apr. 1783).

Hunter, John, formerly of Little England, Virginia, but late of Bath. Probate to Archibald Hamilton and Osgood Hamilton; Benjamin Colborne renouncing. (Apr. 1791).

Hunter, William, formerly of Bristol but late of Philadelphia. Administration with will to Robert Lewis, attorney for relict Susanna Hunter at Philadelphia. (Dec. 1796).

Hussey, John, Lieutenant-Colonel of 47th Regiment of Foot under Lieutenant-General Peregrine Lascelles who died in North America, bachelor. Administration to brother Richard Hussey; mother Elizabeth Hussey, widow, renouncing. (Dec. 1760).

Hutchin, Frederick, of Deptford, Kent, who died in Virginia
on merchant ship *Forward*. Administration to principal
creditor John Lutwyche; relict Anne Hutchin renouncing.
(July 1727).

Hutchins, Charles, of Maryland. Administration to relict
Dorothy Hutchins. (Oct. 1701).

Hutchins, John, quartermaster of 17th Regiment of Dragoons
who died at New York, bachelor. Administration to brother
Joseph Hutchins. (July 1777).

Hutchings, Noy Willey, of Charles Town, South Carolina,
bachelor. Administration to mother and only next of kin
Sarah Hutchings, widow. (Apr. 1792).

Hutchings, Richard, of Charles Town, South Carolina. Probate
to nephew William Hutchings. (Feb. 1791).

Hutton, Charles, of Ploxen, Virginia, bachelor. Administration to nephew and next of kin John Hutton; mother Jane
Hutton, widow, renouncing. (Sept. 1722).

Hutton, Robert, of H.M.S. *Southampton* who died in Virginia,
bachelor. Administration to principal creditor Christiana
Thompson. (June 1703).

Hyde, Catherine, of St. Giles in Fields, Middlesex, spinster.
Administration to Henry, Earl of Clarendon, father and
attorney of Edward, Viscount Cornbury, in New York.
(June 1708).

Imer, Rev. Abraham, of Congrees, South Carolina. Administration to James McKenzie now husband and attorney of relict
Ann in South Carolina. (Jan. 1775).

Ingersoll, Jared, of Newhaven, Connecticut. Administration
with will to Dennis de Berds, attorney for Jared Ingersoll at Philadelphia. (Feb. 1783).

Inglis, Thomas, formerly of Charles Town, South Carolina,
but late of Jamaica, bachelor. Administration to sister
Sarah Inglis; mother Mary Inglis, widow, renouncing.
(Aug. 1788).

Ingoldsby, Richard, Captain who died in New York. Administration to son George Ingoldsby, attorney for relict
Mary Ingoldsby in New York. (July 1719).

Ingraham, George, of New England but late of H.M.S. *Newcastle*
and *Grafton*. Probate to Robert Smith. (June 1764).

Ingram, Thomas, of Birmingham, Warwickshire, who died in
Maryland. Administration to principal creditor Thomas
James; relict Ann Ingram renouncing. (July 1717).

Inman, Mary, of Chesterfield, Derbyshire, who died in South
Carolina, spinster. Probate to Thomas Pike. (Nov. 1769.).

Inman, Robert, of Colonel Burr's Marines of H.M.S. *Windsor*
who died at Boston, New England. Administration to relict
Elizabeth Inman pending production of will. (Aug. 1712).

Issabell, Robert, of Philadelphia, bachelor. Administration
to mother Ann, wife of William Cock. (Oct. 1781).

Izard, Mary, of Carolina. Probate to husband Ralph Izard.
(July 1700).

Izard, Ralph, of Berkeley Co., South Carolina. Administration
with will to Ralph Izard, attorney for Daniel Blake, Henry
Middleton and Benjamin Smith in South Carolina. (May 1763).

Jackman, Joseph John, of Surry Co., Virginia, who died at
Deal, Kent. Probate to relict Mary Jackman. (May 1714).
Jackson, Arthur, of Bristol who died at Quary Creek, Potomack
River, Stafford Co., Virginia, bachelor. Administration
to father Arthur Jackson. (July 1712). Revoked and
administration with will granted to sisters Elizabeth,
wife of James Kelson, and Rachel, wife of Joseph End;
named executors being dead. (Nov. 1713).
Jackson, Edward, of Boston, New England. Administration with
will to Nathaniel Paice, attorney for surviving executors
Daniel Marsh, Samuel Sewall and Thomas Cushing at Boston;
relict Dorothy Jackson having died before executing.
(May 1763).
Jackson, Harry, of Philadelphia, Lieutenant in H.M. Forces,
bachelor. Administration to David Thomas, attorney for
sister and only next of kin Sarah, wife of Edward Miles,
at Liverpool, Lancs Co., North America. (Aug. 1797).
Jackson, John, of Boston, Mass., Ensign of 64th Regiment,
bachelor. Administration to Charles Lincoln, attorney
for brother and next of kin Richard Jackson in Dublin,
Ireland. (May 1783).
Jago, John, negro of merchant ship *Humphrey* who died in
Virginia, bachelor. Probate to John Coldham, father and
guardian of John Coldham; no executor named. (Dec. 1739).
James, Elisha, of Bristol who died in Virginia. Administra-
tion to relict Hester James. (Nov. 1706).
James, Thomas, of Charles Town, South Carolina, bachelor.
Administration to father John James. (July 1759).
Jarvis, Edward, of Rhode Island, bachelor. Administration
to sister and next of kin Elizabeth, wife of Edward Sharp
by decree. (Jan. 1722).
Jauncey, James, formerly of New York City but late of St.
Marylebone, Middlesex. Probate to son William Jauncey
with similar powers reserved to son Thomas John Jauncey
and daughter Mary Jauncey. (July 1790).
Jay, Peter, formerly of Rye, Westchester Co. but who died at
Poughkeepsie, Dutchess Co., New York. Administration with
will to James Daltera, attorney for sons Sir James Jay,
John and Frederick Jay, and for Egbert Benson in North
America. (May 1785).
Jeane, John, Collector of Brunswick, North Carolina, widower.
Administration to principal creditor David Deacon; sister
and only next of kin Jenney, wife of Richard Score, renoun-
cing. (May 1752).
Jeckell, John, of New York, widower. Administration to
brothers William and Samuel Jeckell and sister Esther,
wife of Robert Almoney. (May 1783).
Jeffrey, Joseph, carpenter of H.M.S. *Apollo* who died at New
York. Probate to Edward Trythall. (Feb. 1779).
Jefferies, John, of H.M.S. *Scorpion* who died in North Caro-
lina, bachelor. Administration to mother Catherine
Jefferies, widow. (Jan. 1777).
Jeffreys, Peter, of merchant ship *Prosperous Ann* who died in
Maryland, bachelor. Probate to brother Robert Jeffreys.
(Jan. 1733).
Jefferys, William, of merchant ship *Mary and Francis* who
died in Virginia, bachelor. Probate to John Jefferys.
(Jan. 1715).

Jekyll, John, of Boston, New England. Administration to
Thomas Sandford, attorney for relict Margaret Jekyll at
Boston. (June 1748). Revoked on death of Thomas Sandford
and Margaret Jekyll and granted to son Rev. John Jekyll.
(Nov. 1769).

Jenney, John, of St. Mary at Hill, London, who died in
Virginia, bachelor. Administration to Edmund Strudwick,
executor to brother Samuel Jenney deceased; nieces and
next of kin Jane Wyldbore and Mary ?Formoson renouncing.
Grant of August 1676 revoked. (July 1734).

Jennifer, Daniel de St. Thomas, of Patuxen River, Maryland,
who died at St. Botolph Bishopsgate, London. Administration to creditor Jonathan Forward; relict Elizabeth and
daughters Mary and Elizabeth Jennifer cited but not
appearing. (Apr. 1730).

Jennings, Samuel, of Wingan, South Carolina, widower. Administration to son Samuel Jennings. (Dec. 1745).

Jenys, Thomas, of Charles Town, South Carolina. Probate to
Stephen Bedon with similar powers reserved to Elizabeth
Gibbes, Branfill Evance and Paul Jenys. (Oct. 1750).

Jephson, Christopher, Ensign of William Shirley's Regiment
of Foot who died in New England, bachelor. Administration to mother Elizabeth Jephson, widow. (Sept. 1750).

Jerningham, Henry, of St. Mary's Co., Maryland. Limited
administration with will to daughter Frances Henrietta
Jerningham. (May 1775).

Jesson, Robert, of Pennsylvania, widower. Probate to Rebecca
wife of Solomon Goade. (June 1740).

Johns, John, of St. Botolph Bishopsgate, London, who died in
Carolina. Probate to relict Frances Johns. (Jan. 1700).

Johnson, Abraham, of St. Dunstan in East, London, who died
in Maryland. Administration to relict Mary Johnson.
(Aug. 1701).

Johnson, Andrew, of merchant ship *Sussex* who died in Virginia,
bachelor. Probate to sister Martha Tilbury alias Splidt,
wife of Thomas Tilbury. ((Apr. 1708).

Johnson, Robert, Governor of South Carolina. Limited administration with will to son Robert Johnson. (Aug. 1735).

Johnson, William, Captain of H.M.S. *Lizard*, bachelor.
Administration to Fairfax Overton, attorney for father
Sir Nathaniel Johnson in Carolina. (Oct. 1701). Revoked
on death of Overton and granted to son Robert Johnson as
attorney. (Jan. 1709).

Johnson, Sir William, of Johnson Hall, Tryon Co., New York.
Administration with will to Samuel Baker, attorney for
son Sir John Johnson, Daniel Claus, Guy Johnson, Robert
Adams, Dr. John Dease and Joseph Chew in America. (Feb.
1776).

Johnston, Francis, Lieutenant of 38th Regiment of Foot who
died at Philadelphia, bachelor. Administration to cousin
german Thomas Noble; sister Grace Johnston renouncing.
(Dec. 1778).

Johnston, Gabriel, of Edenhouse, North Carolina, and Governor
who died in 1753. Limited administration with will to
Alexander Anderson, attorney for Samuel Johnston now in
Carolina. (Aug. 1791). Revoked and granted to Alexander
McDougall, attorney for Hannah Bruce, formerly Ferrier,
wife of Robert Bruce, and Elizabeth Ferrier, both at Edin-

burgh, daughters and executrices of Rev. Robert Ferrier
who was sole executor to Elizabeth Ferrier, sister of
Gabriel Johnston; Samuel Johnston, relict Frances Johnston and Henry Johnston having died. (Mar. 1795).

Johnston, Lewis, formerly of Edinburgh but late of Georgia.
Probate to daughters Elizabeth, Rachel and Ann Johnston
with similar powers reserved to William Johnston, John
Wood and James Hume. (Apr. 1798).

Johnston, Robert, formerly of Virginia but late of St. Olave
Hart Street, London. Probate to James Russell. (Apr.
1766).

Jolland, Charles, of H.M.S. *Grafton* and *Raisonable* who died
at Rhode Island Hospital, bachelor. Administration to
father Robert Jolland. (Jan. 1780).

Jones, Allen, of Bourbon, Virginia. Administration with will
to William Murdock, attorney for William Goosley at York,
Virginia. (Oct. 1792).

Jones, George, late of Philadelphia who died in Worcester.
Limited administration with will to Elizabeth Clay.
(Feb. 1752).

Jones, Hugh, of Calvert Co., Maryland. Administration with
will to Barbara Jones, attorney for Thomas Cockshutt and
John Bigger in Maryland. (June 1704).

Jones, John, of Pennsylvania. Probate to Joanne Jones, the
relict. (Dec. 1723).

Jones, John, of H.M.S. *Mermaid* who died at South Carolina,
bachelor. Administration to father John Jones. (May
1754).

Jones, John, formerly of St. Bride, London, but late of New
York, bachelor. Administration to brother and only next
of kin Robert Jones. (May 1790).

Jones, Lewis, of St. Helena, South Carolina. Probate to
brother John Jones with similar powers reserved to Gabriel
Manigault and Charles Purry. (Oct. 1748).

Jones, Mary Ann, of Boston, Mass., widow. Probate to son
Edward Jones and James Hughes. (Nov. 1791).

Jones, Robert, of Henrico, King William Co., Virginia, bachelor. Administration to brother and next of kin Richard
Jones. (Aug. 1771).

Jones, Simon, of Maryland who died at sea, bachelor. Administration to mother Margaret, wife of Anthony Royston.
(July 1776).

Jones, Thomas, of Virginia, bachelor. Administration to
father Richard Jones. (Nov. 1724).

Jones, Thomas, formerly Judge of Supreme Court of New York
but late of Hoddesdon, Broxbourne, Hertfordshire. Probate
to relict Ann Jones. (Aug. 1792).

Jones, William, of Rotherhithe, Surrey, who died in Virginia.
Probate to Thomas May. (Dec. 1718).

Jones, William, of Philadelphia, bachelor. Administration
to sister Mary Jones. (May 1735).

Jones, William, purser of H.M.S. *Coventry* who died in New
York. Probate to relict Rachael Jones. (July 1765).

Jones, William (*calendared as Evan*), formerly of Charles Town,
South Carolina but late of St. Martin in Fields, Middlesex. Probate to sister Margaret Jones with similar powers
reserved to Richard Downes and Theodore Gaillard. (May
1774).

Jordan, Jane, of Virginia, widow. Administration to niece and only next of kin Susanna Jane Purdue, (formerly Browne) wife of William Purdue. (Oct. 1792).

Jose, John, master of *John Adventure* who died in Boston, New England. Limited administration to John Ive, attorney for ship's owners. (Nov. 1706).

Jouet, John Troup, of Elizabeth Town, New Jersey, Ensign on half pay of 3rd Batallion of New Jersey Volunteers, bachelor. Administration to creditor Thomas Courtney; father Rev. Cavalier Jouet renouncing. (July 1794).

Juckes, Edward, of South Carolina. Probate to Dorothy Juckes. (Nov. 1715).

Julin, Carls, of ship *Charles Town Packet*, bachelor. Probate to Johannes Scheelhase with similar powers reserved to his wife Sarah Scheelhase. (Sept. 1760).

Kearny, Philip, of Perth Amboy, New Jersey. Limited administration with will to John Abraham Denormandie, attorney for Isabella Kearny and Andrew Eliot in North America. (Mar. 1783).

Kearny alias Burley and afterwards Ravaud, Susannah, of Perth Amboy, Middlesex Co., New Jersey. Administration to Anthony Merle, attorney for husband Philip Kearny in Perth Amboy. (Mar. 1746).

Kearsley, Margaret, of Philadelphia, widow. Limited administration with will to Phineas Bond. (Aug. 1779).

Keech, Thomas, surgeon of merchant ship *Goodwill* who died in Maryland. Probate to George Fisher. (Nov. 1717).

Keeling, Charles, of New York City who died in Bay of Honduras. Administration to brother Anthony Keeling; relict Catherine Keeling cited but not appearing. (July 1787).

Keen, Arthur - see Kyne.

Keith, James, formerly of Charles Town, South Carolina, but late of Blairshinnock, Banffshire, Scotland. Limited probate to William Irvine, George Gerrard and Robert Telder. (Nov. 1788).

Kelly, Edmond, of Baltimore, Maryland, widower. Administration to only child Frances Kelly. (Nov. 1794).

Kelly, James, of merchant ship *Friendship* who died at Rhode Island. Probate to Jane Nance, spinster. (May 1778).

Kemp, George, formerly of East Florida but late of Nassau, doctor of physick, bachelor. Administration to Thomas Finlayson, attorney for cousin german and only next of kin Agnes Muir alias Ferguson at Haddington, Scotland. (July 1789).

Kennan, William, of Richmond Co., Virginia, bachelor. Administration to Robert Wallace Johnson alias Johnston, doctor in physick, attorney for sister and next of kin Janet, wife of John Wallace, at Dumfries, Scotland. (Feb. 1765).

Kerr, Thomas - see Carr.

Kettell, John, of H.M.S. *Merlin*, bachelor. Administration to John Coles, attorney for brother Jonathan Kettell at Charles Town, New England. (May 1757).

Keylock, Anthony, of New England, bachelor. Administration
to cousin and next of kin Frances Smith, widow. (Oct. 1711).
Kibble, Stephen, of New York City. Probate to surviving
executor William Butler with similar powers reserved to
James Dole and Benjamin James. (Jan. 1782).
Kidgell, Nicholas, of Stepney, Middlesex, who died at Charles
Town, America. Probate to Sarah Kidgell; no executor
named. (July 1727).
Kilpin, William, of Virginia, bachelor. Administration to
brother and next of kin James Kilpin. (Aug. 1716).
Kincaid, George, formerly of Christ Church, Georgia, but late
of Exeter, Devon. Probate to relict Marion Kincaid and
brother Patrick Kincaid with similar powers reserved to
Basil Cowper and Samuel Douglass. (Oct. 1791).
King, Anne, of South Carolina, widow. Administration to sister
Joanne, wife of William Cripps. (Mar. 1740).
King, Daniel, of Annapolis Royal, Arundell Co., Maryland,
who died at sea on merchant ship *Content*. Administration
to relict Anne King. (Nov. 1725).
King, Eusebius, of Bristol, Prince George Co., Virginia.
Administration with will to Isham Randolph, attorney for
William Randolph of Henrico Co., Virginia. (Sept. 1711).
Revoked on death of William Randolph and administration
granted to Richard Oakly. (Jan. 1713).
King, James, of Glasgow, Scotland, having property in Virginia.
Limited probate to father James King and mother Elizabeth
King. (Nov. 1788).
King, John Curle, of Virginia, formerly of H.M.S. *Port Royal*
and *Orford* but who died at St. Martin in Fields, Middlesex.
Probate to William Boyd with similar powers reserved to
James Casey. (Nov. 1763).
King, Nathaniel, of Boston, New England, who died on H.M.S.
York. Administration with will to Thomas Newman, attorney
for relict Mary King in Boston. (Nov. 1747).
King, Samuel, of Bristol who died at Gliucester, Virginia,
bachelor. Administration to brother John King. (Feb. 1745).
King, Seth, Captain of 1st Connecticut Regiment of Foot who
died at Havana, bachelor. Administration to Phineas Lyman,
attorney for father Josiah King at Suffield, Connecticut.
(Nov. 1764).
King, William, of merchant ship *Cambridge* who died in or near
Maryland, bachelor. Administration to principal creditor
William Gray. (Dec. 1732).
King, William, formerly of Ipswich, Suffolk, but late of Phila-
delphia, bachelor. Administration to father Stephen King.
(Oct. 1795).
Kinnersley, William, of Philadelphia, bachelor. Administra-
tion to nephew William Kinnersley; brother and sister and
next of kin Richard Kinnersley and Hannah, wife of William
Fencott renouncing. (Apr. 1714).
Kinnicutt, Edward, of Providence, Rhode Island, who died at
St. Bartholomew by Exchange, London. Administration to
creditor William Stead; relict Mary Kinnicutt and children
Lydia, Elizabeth and Sarah Kinnicutt cited but not appearing.
(Oct. 1754).
Kirk, Thomas, of St. James, Duke's Place, Middlesex, who died
in Virginia. Limited administration to Barbara Kirk pending
production of will. (May 1741).

Kirkland, Moses, formerly of South Carolina but late of St.
Andrew, Jamaica. Probate to relict Catherine Kirkland
with similar powers reserved to Thomas Edgehill and John
Bruce. (July 1789).
Kitts, William, of York River, Gloucester Co., Virginia,
bachelor. Administration to sister and next of kin
Elizabeth Kitts. (Sept. 1710).
Knapp, Jonathan, of Killingley, Connecticut, soldier of H.M.
Regiment of Foot in Connecticut who died at Havana.
Administration to Phineas Lyman, attorney for relict
Sarah Knapp at Killingley. (Dec. 1763).
Knapton, Albin, of Carolina. Administration to James Brent,
guardian of daughter Margaret Knapton. (Mar. 1708).
Knight, John, of Abington, Montgomery Co., Pennsylvania.
Administration with will to Abel Evans, attorney for Isaac
Knight and Jonathan Tyson at Abington, executors of Isaac
Knight deceased, who was named executor to testator.
(Apr. 1793).
Knight, Richard, of Norfolk, Virginia. Administration to
brother and next of kin Benjamin Knight; relict having
died before administering. (May 1771).
Knight, William, of Williamsburgh, Virginia. Probate to
brother Robert Knight. (Jan. 1771).
Knighton, John, of Maryland, bachelor. Administration to
mother Mary, wife of Ellis Farnworth. (Sept, 1720).
Knipe, William, of Portsmouth, New England, and late of H.M.S.
Centurion and *America*. Probate to Robert Ratsey. (Nov.
1750).
Knolles, John, surgeon's mate of West Florida Hospital.
Probate to William Street. (Sept. 1767).
Knolton, Christian David, formerly of New York City but late
of New Providence Island. Administration to Jarvis
Roebuck, guardian of only child Catherine Knolton. (July
1787). Revoked and granted to Roebuck as attorney for
Catherine Knolton now come of age; relict Jennet Arabella
Knolton having died before administering. (Nov. 1788).
Nott, Edward, Vice-Governor of Virginia. Probate to Susan
Leighton. (Nov. 1706).
Knott, Jeremiah, of Charles Town, South Carolina. Administra-
tion to David Lucas, administrator to Sarah Knott deceased,
only sister and next of kin; relict Isabella Knott having
also died. (Feb. 1765).
Knott, Jeremiah, of Charles Town, South Carolina, bachelor.
Administration to nephew and next of kin Luke Knott. (Feb.
1773).
Knowles, Robert, of H.M. Artillery Train who died in Pennsyl-
vania, bachelor. Administration to father John Knowles.
(Apr. 1761).
Nox, Thomas, of H.M.S. *Hornet* who died at Brunswick, North
Carolina. Administration with will to Thomas Howard,
attorney for Michael Cashio Howard in Douai, Flanders,
and Patrick Howard at Angiers, France. (Mar. 1768).
Kyne alias Keen, Arthur, of H.M.S. *Gosport*, bachelor. Admini-
stration to Houghan Tober, husband and attorney of sister
Rachel Tober, in New England. (June 1705). Declared null
May 1709.

Lacy, Patrick, of H.M.S. *Essex* Prize who died in Virginia, bachelor. Probate to Thomas Conaway. (Aug. 1700).

Ladstone, William, of Shadwell, Middlesex, who died on merchant ship *Joseph and Thomas* in Virginia. Administration to relict Mary Ladstone. (Aug. 1709).

Laffette, Mary, of Port Royal, South Carolina. Administration to daughter Jane, wife of Charles Blundy; husband Peter Laffette having died before administering. (Mar. 1752).

Lake, Charles, Rector of St. James' parish, Ann Arundell Co., Maryland, clerk. Administration with will to Messenger Monsey, doctor of physick, attorney for William Keene and Rev. Samuel Keene in Maryland. (Apr. 1765).

Lamb, Stephen, of H.M.S. *Tartar* who died in Long Island Hospital, bachelor. Administration to father William Lamb. (Mar. 1778).

Lambert, Jonathan, of Boston, New England. Administration to John Charnock of Whitechapel, Middlesex, mariner, attorney for relict Elizabeth Lambert in Boston. (July 1711).

Lambert, Vincent, of Maryland who died a prisoner in France. Probate to father Edward Lambert. (July 1703).

Lambert, William, of Boston, New England. Administration with will to Thomas Lane, attorney for nephew William Lambert in Boston. (Mar. 1750).

Landen, Henry, of Maryland, bachelor. Administration to sister Hannah, wife of Thomas Linthall. (Jan. 1737).

Landifield, William, master of transport ship *Ranger* who died at Boston, bachelor. Administration to brother and only next of kin Thomas Landifield. (Mar. 1776).

Lane, John, of North Carolina, bachelor. Administration to sister Elizabeth, wife of Rev. Rodney Croxall; mother Bridget Lane, widow, renouncing. (Aug. 1748).

Lane, Martha, of Blandford, Dorset, who died in North Carolina, spinster. Probate to Thomas Fitzherbert. (Dec. 1756).

Lang, Benjamin, of Portsmouth, New England, who died on H.M.S. *Hind*. Administration to Thomas Adams, attorney for relict Elizabeth Lang in Portsmouth. (Mar. 1750).

Langhorne, William, of Maryland, bachelor. Administration to sister and next of kin Elizabeth, wife of John Hall. (May 1716).

Lanman, William, of Boston, New England. Probate to son William Lanman. (Sept. 1726).

Larmount, John, of Boston, New England, bachelor. Administration to principal creditor Edward Blackstock; brother and next of kin Adam Larmount renouncing. (June 1720).

Larner, of St. Martin in Fields, Middlesex, Lieutenant of Major-General Richard O'Farrell's 22nd Regiment of Foot, who died at Albany, North America. Administration pending production of will to Ann Lynes, wife of Thomas Lynes, daughter of William and Mary Ashburn of Kersley near Coventry, Warwickshire. (Aug. 1758).

Lavington, Stephen, formerly of Arundell Street, St. Clement Danes, Middlesex, but late of South Carolina. Limited administration with will to Edward Codrington, attorney for John Lightfoot and Samuel Redhead at Antigua. (Dec. 1759).

Law, John, of H.M.S. *Pembroke*, bachelor. Administration with will to Joseph Argent, attorney for Elizabeth Partridge at Boston, New England. (May 1750).

Lawrence, Richard, of H.M.S. *Squirrell* who died overseas.
  Administration with will to Peter Warre, attorney for relict
  Mary Lawrence at Boston, New England. (Jan. 1742).
Lorence, William, of transport ship *Firm* who died at Charles
  Town, South Carolina, bachelor. Administration to uncle
  and next of kin Thomas Lorence. (Oct. 1783).
Lawson, Robert, of Maryland. Administration to relict Margaret
  Lawson. (Oct. 1714). Revoked on death of Margaret Lawson
  and granted to Robert White, guardian of daughter Margaret
  Lawson. (Dec. 1715).
Laxon, Thomas, of H.M.S. *Jason*, who died at Long Island Hospi-
  tal, bachelor. Administration to Matthew Laxon; other
  son John Laxon having died before administering. (Apr.
  1784).
Lay, Benjamin, of Abington, Pennsylvania. Administration with
  will by his solemn affirmation to Samuel Cook; wife Sarah
  Lay having died in testator's lifetime. (July 1760).
Lea - see Lee.
Leach, John, of H.M.S. *Nassau* who died in New England, bachelor.
  Administration by decree to Mary Lightfoot, wife and
  attorney for principal creditor Matthew Lightfoot now at
  sea on H.M.S. *Sheerness*. (Nov. 1722).
Lechmere, Anthony, of Charles Town, South Carolina, bachelor.
  Administration to principal creditor John Lane; brother
  Nicholas Lechmere renouncing. (Aug. 1783).
Le Cocq, Peter, of Liverpool, Lancashire, but late of Boston,
  Mass. Probate to relict Elizabeth Le Cocq. (Mar. 1799).
Ledain, George, of H.M.S. *Rippon's* Prize and H.M.S. *Cornwall*,
  bachelor. Administration to Benjamin Hallowell the younger,
  attorney for mother Mary Ledain, widow, at Boston, New
  England. (Feb. 1750).
Ledger, John, of Williamsburg, Virginia. Probate to James
  Minzies. (Apr. 1779).
Ledwidge, John, of H.M.S. *Southampton* who died in Virginia.
  Administration to relict Sarah Ledwidge. (June 1703).
Ley, Aden, of York Town, Virginia, Captain of Colonel Warge's
  Regiment of Foot who died at Goree. Administration to
  relict Mary Ley. (May 1712).
Lee, Alice, of Mount Pleasant, Burlington Co., New Jersey.
  Administration to husband John Lee. (Mar. 1785).
Lee, Charles, formerly of Westminster, Middlesex, but late of
  Berkeley Co., Virginia, Major-General in the service of the
  United States of America. Administration with will to Sir
  Robert Kerries and Charles Kerries, attornies for Alexander
  White in Frederick Co., Virginia; other executor Charles
  Mym Thurston cited but not appearing. (June 1785).
Lee, Isaac, of Rappahannock River who died at Stepney, Middle-
  sex. Limited administration with will to William Dawkins
  alias Dawkings. (Nov. 1727).
Lee, James, of Hackensack, Bergen Co., New Jersey, widower.
  Administration to Christopher Benson, attorney for children
  William and John Lee, Tabitha wife of John Oats, Catherine
  wife of John Smith, Justina Ridgeway, widow, Elizabeth wife
  of James Van Gelder, and Mary wife of Christopher Benson,
  in America. (Mar. 1763).
Lea, Sarah, (formerly Brown), wife of William Lea of Philadelphia. Administration to son William Lea; husband having
  died before administering. (Oct. 1749).

Lee, William, of Dartmouth, Devon, master of merchant ship
Prosperous who died in North Carolina, bachelor. Admini-
stration to mother Elizabeth Lee, widow. (June 1761).
Lee, William, of Philadelphia, bachelor. Administration to
sister Ann Lee. (Apr. 1778).
Leeth, Thomas, of merchant ship *Anne and Mary* who died in
Virginia. Probate to Jane Holmes alias Usher, wife of
John Holmes. (May 1711).
Leman, Hickford, of Piscatua, Maryland, bachelor. Probate
to Daniel Cooper. (Aug. 1732).
Le Neve, Michael, of Maryland, bachelor. Administration to
father Edward Le Neve. (Sept. 1707).
Lenthall, Phillip, of Philadelphia. Probate to son John
Lenthall. (Jan. 1724).
L'Escott, Frances, of Charles Town, South Carolina, widow.
Administration with will to George Chardin, attorney for
Zachariah Villepontoux and Isaac Mazyck in South Carolina.
(Sept. 1753).
Levett, Elizabeth, of Maryland, widow. Probate to James
Haddock and Margaret Clarke alias Buchanan, now wife of
George Buchanan. (Dec. 1730).
Levett, Francis, of St. Augustine, East Florida. Probate to
relict Juliana Levett. (Oct. 1786).
Lewis, Daniel, of Charles Town Hospital, South Carolina,
bachelor. Administration to mother Martha Lewis, widow.
(Aug. 1784).
Lewis, John, marine of Colonel Jeffery's Regiment, of H.M.S.
Launceston and after of H.M.S. *Vigilant* and *Mermaid* who
died in Hampton Hospital, Virginia, bachelor. Administra-
tion to father John Lewis.
Lewis, John, of Charles Town, South Carolina, who died in St.
Thomas Hospital, Southwark, Surrey. Probate to John
Taylor and Thomas Hardwick with similar powers reserved
to relict Sarah Lewis. (July 1753).
Lewis, John, of Bluefields, North America, bachelor. Admini-
stration to aunt Elizabeth Gourley. (July 1794).
Ley - see Lee.
Leyburn, George, formerly of Maryland and late of Liverpool,
Lancashire, master of merchant ship *Benedict*. Limited
administration pending production of will to brother Peter
Leyburn. (Dec. 1782).
Liddell, Archibald, master of merchant ship *Elliott* who died
in Charles Town, South Carolina. Probate to Archibald
Elliott with similar powers reserved to Abraham Cridland
alias Creedlan. (June 1748).
Lidgett, Charles, of Boston, New England, who died at St.
Bride, London. Limited administration with will to relict
Mary Lidgett. (Mar. 1701).
Lillingstone, Mary Ann, of Maryland. Administration by decree
to Robert Myre the younger, attorney for husband Carpender
Lillingstone in Maryland. (Dec. 1721).
Lillystone, John, of Holborn, Middlesex, and Philadelphia,
who died on ship *Rowser*, bachelor. Administration to
mother Hannah Lillystone. (June 1751).
Linch - see Lynch.
Lindesay, John, of New York. Administration to relict Penelope
Lindesay. (Apr. 1753).
Linn - see Lynn.

Linton, Ann, formerly of Rotherhithe, Surrey, but late of
    Philadelphia. Administration to Thomas Gilbert, surviving
    executor of the husband John Linton deceased; only next
    of kin sister Mary, wife of William Nichols, and niece
    Maria Butcher, spinster, a minor, cited but not appearing.
    (Nov. 1785).
Linzee, John, formerly Captain the Royal Navy but late of
    Milton, Mass. Administration with will to William Burgess,
    attorney for Thomas Amory at Boston. (Apr. 1799).
Lithgow, William, of Wilmington, North Carolina. Probate to
    Sir Peter Thompson with similar powers reserved to Job
    Pearson. (July 1754).
Littler, William, Captain of 3rd Batallion of Royal Americans
    who died at Boston, New England, bachelor. Administration
    to mother Dorothy Littler, widow. (Feb. 1765).
Livingston alias Ash, Anne, of Charles Town, South Carolina.
    Administration by decree to husband William Livingston.
    (Aug. 1721).
Livingstone, Henry, Ensign in British American forces who
    died at New York, bachelor. Administration to Charles
    Cooke, attorney for father John Livingstone in New York
    City. (Apr. 1786).
Livingston, John, of New London, Connecticut, who died at
    St. James, Westminster, Middlesex. Probate to James
    Douglass with similar powers reserved to Elizabeth Living-
    ston. (May 1720).
Livingstone, William, of Bodlorme, Linlithgow Co., Scotland,
    but formerly Lieutenant on half pay of Independent Company
    of Foot in South Carolina. Administration to Alexander
    Small, attorney for sister and next of kin Grisel, wife
    of William Nimmo at Bodlorme; relict Helen Livingstone
    having died. (June 1770).
Lloyd, Henry, formerly of Boston, Mass., but late of Bryanston
    Street, St. Marylebone, Middlesex. Probate to Katharine
    Lloyd with similar powers reserved to nephew Henry Smith.
    (Apr. 1796).
Lloyd, John, of Sarphley, St. James, Goose Creek, South Caro-
    lina. Administration with will to John Nickleson, admini-
    strator to son John Lloyd deceased, attorney for daughter
    Sarah Lloyd,a minor; relict Sarah Lloyd and executors
    Ralph Izard and Benjamin Wareing having died without
    executing. (June 1746).
Lloyd, John, of Goose Creek, Berkeley Co., South Carolina,
    minor. Administration to John Nickleson, guardian of
    sister Sarah Lloyd. (June 1746).
Lloyd, Sarah - see Waring.
Lock, John, of merchant ship *Rappahanock*, bachelor. Admini-
    stration to sister Alexandra Gun. (Sept. 1725).
Locker, James, of Liverpool, Lancashire, who died in Virginia,
    bachelor. Administration to sister and next of kin Hannah
    Locker. (June 1722).
Loge, Abraham, private in Rhode Island Regiment of Foot who
    died at Havana. Administration by his solemn declaration
    to Joseph Sherwood, attorney for relict Hannah Loge at
    Rhode Island. (Dec. 1765).
Lodge, Edward, of Stepney, Middlesex, who died in Maryland.
    Administration to principal creditor Samson Burrows.
    (Mar. 1700).

Lofthouse, Alvara, of St. Katherine by Tower, London, master
of merchant ship *Judith* who died at St. Augustine, East
Florida. Probate to sister Mary, wife of William Thomas,
with similar powers reserved to Peter Simon. (May 1778).

Logan, George, of Princess Anne Co., Virginia, who died in
Glasgow. Probate to relict Isabella Logan. (Aug. 1781).

Logan, Margaret, of South Carolina. Administration to husband
William Logan. (May 1791).

Logan, William, of Philadelphia. Limited administration with
will to David Barclay, attorney for son George Logan,
doctor in physic, in New York; executors cited but not
appearing. (June 1780).

Loge - see Lodge.

Lomas, John, of Annapolis, Maryland, but late of Glasgow.
Administration with will to John Mill, attorney for James
Johnson in Virginia. (Nov. 1757).

Long, Richard, of merchant ship *Hope* who died in South Carolina. Administration to principal creditor Jeremy Mackneer
at sea on H.M.S. *Grafton*. (Jan. 1719).

Longland, John, commander of sloop *Eastmain* who died at Albany
Road, bachelor. Administration to niece Lucy Sweet;
previous grant of February 1758 to pretended next of kin
cousin german Elizabeth Thomas, widow, and of December 1757
to pretended creditor Mary Hallam, widow, now revoked as
being made on false pretences. (June 1758).

Longley, Robert Benjamin, of Boston, Mass., master of merchant
ship *Salus*. Administration with will to creditor Francis
Henry Christin; father Robert Longley renouncing. (Dec.
1792).

Lorence, William - see Lawrence.

Lormier, Lewis, of South Carolina. Administration to principal
creditor James Lardant; relict Jane Lormier and brother
and sisters and only next of kin David Lormier, Ann Gueront
and Ann Rachel Michel cited but not appearing. (May 1749).

Loughton, Sarah, of Charles Town, Carolina, who died in Barbados. Administration to husband Edward Loughton. (Mar.
1701).

Lovell, William King, 2nd Lieutenant of Royal Regiment of
Artillery who died on Long Island, New York, bachelor.
Probate to sister Alisha Skingle Lovell. (Oct. 1776).

Lovett, Thomas, of Belfast, Ireland, or of Virginia, who died
at sea on H.M.S. *Falkland*. Administration to principal
creditor William Browne. (July 1709).

Lowe, Henry, of St. Mary's Co., Maryland. Probate to daughters
Elizabeth, wife of Henry Darnall, and Dorothy, wife of
Francis Hall; sons Henry and Bennet Lowe having died.
(Sept. 1731).

Lowe, Thomas, of New York City, bachelor. Administration to
sister Margaret, wife of Richard Linaker. (Apr. 1782).

Lowndes, Roger, Lieutenant of H.M.S. *Happy* who died in South
Carolina, bachelor. Administration to brother Robert
Lowndes. (Oct. 1735).

Lucas, Charles, of merchant ship *Hopewell* who died in Maryland.
Probate to Edward Poulter. (June 1722).

Lucas, William, of H.M.S. *Warwick* who died in Virginia on
H.M.S. *Sea Horse*, bachelor. Administration to Benjamin
Bristowe. (June 1738).

Ludlam alias Carter, Anne, of South Carolina, widow. Administration to son Thomas Carter. (Aug. 1729).
Ludwell, Philip, of St. Martin in Fields, Middlesex, having
property in Virginia. Limited probate to daughter Hannah
Philippa Ludwell with similar powers reserved to daughters
Frances and Lucy Ludwell. (May 1767).
Luscombe, Thomas, of Boston, New England. Administration to
mother Sarah Luscombe, widow. (Apr. 1700).
Lycett, William, Lieutenant of Marines who died at New York,
bachelor. Administration to Frances Layton, spinster,
executrix of creditrix Frances Russell now deceased;
brother and only next of kin John Lycett renouncing.
(Feb. 1778).
Lyde, Byfield, of Boston, Mass., but late of Halifax, Nova
Scotia, widower. Administration to son Edward Lyde.
(Mar. 1777).
Lymburner, Matthew, formerly of St. Andrew, New Brunswick,
but late of Penobscot, Mass. Administration to Robert
Shedden, attorney for relict Margaret Lymburner at St.
Andrew. (Mar. 1789).
Linch, John, of New York City. Administration to relict
Elizabeth Linch. (Mar. 1778).
Lyne, Joseph, of Blackfriars, London, who died in Virginia on
H.M.S. *Shoreham*. Administration to relict Abishag Lyne.
(May 1701).
Linn, William, of Charles Town, South Carolina, bachelor.
Administration to Fergus Baillie, attorney for sisters and
next of kin in Scotland Janet, wife of Anthony Ellis,
Jeane Aitkine, widow, and Agnes, wife of William Campbell.
(Feb. 1735).
Lyon, George, formerly of Cape Fear, North America, Colonel
of Royal North Carolina Regiment, bachelor. Administra-
tion to Walsingham Collins, attorney for nephews and next
of kin John Dunlop and Colin Campbell at Port Glasgow,
Scotland. (Aug. 1790).
Lyon, Nathan, soldier in H.M. Regiment of Foot of Connecticut
who died at Havana. Administration to Phineas Lyman,
attorney for father Ephraim Lyon in Connecticut. (Dec.
1763).
Lyon, Seth, soldier in H.M. Regiment of Foot of Connecticut
who died at Havana. Administration to Phineas Lyman,
attorney for father Jonathan Lyon in Connecticut. (Dec.
1763).

Macaulay, Daniel, chief mate of merchant ship *Georgia* who
died in America. Administration to brother George Macaulay.
(Dec. 1770).
McBryde, Thomas, of Charles Town, South Carolina, bachelor.
Administration to father Edward McBryde. (Sept. 1795).
McClentock, Alexander, of Charles Town, New England, who died
on H.M.S. *Otter*, bachelor. Administration to William
Lance, attorney for father William McClentock in Charles
Town. (Jan. 1753).
McCloud, John, of New York, sergeant of 42nd Regiment of Foot.
Administration to John Small, attorney for relict Isabella,
now wife of Peter Barclay, in New York. (Mar. 1765).

McCrackan, John, of Old Glenlure, Galloway, Scotland, who
died in New Haven, New England. Probate to James McDouall
with similar powers reserved to father Andrew McCrackan.
(Feb. 1769).

Macdonald, Alexander, late of Kingsburgh, Isle of Skye,
Captain of late Regiment of North Carolina Volunteers.
Administration to Andrew Lawrie, attorney for relict
Annabella Macdonald at Mugstole, Isle of Skye. (May 1798).

McDonald, Donald, formerly Major and after Lieutenant-Colonel
on half pay of American Provincials at Chatham but late
of Edinburgh. Probate to relict Jane McDonald. (May 1789).

McDonald, Evan, of Charles Town, South Carolina, widower.
Administration to only child Katherine Cramond, widow.
(Mar. 1764).

Macdonald, James, of Anson Co., North Carolina. Administration to relict Isabella Macdonald. (Oct. 1784).

McDonaugh, John, formerly of New Orleans, Louisiana, but late
of Judd Place, Somer Town, St. Pancras, Middlesex. Probate
to John Tate and Martin French with similar powers reserved
to James Canick, John Joyce and John Turnbull. (Dec. 1797).

Mackenzie, Duncan, of New York, bachelor. Probate to Alexander Mackenzie. (Apr. 1736).

McEvers, Charles I., of New York, who died on merchant ship
Mary, bachelor. Administration to brother James McEvers;
mother Elizabeth Baynard renouncing. (Dec. 1794).

McFadyen, Daniel, formerly of Glasgow but late of New York
City. Limited administration with will to Thomas Maude,
attorney for relict Elizabeth McFadyen in New York. (June
1781).

McGregor, William, private of 1st Batallion of 42nd or Royal
Highland Regiment who died at Havana. Administration to
Duncan Campbell, attorney for relict Mary McGregor in New
York. (Mar. 1766).

McGuiry, Laughlin, of New York who died on merchant ship
Monmouth, bachelor. Probate to Thomas Parker. (June 1750).

McIntosh, Alexander, of Charles Town, South Carolina, bachelor.
Administration to brother William McIntosh; father John
McIntosh renouncing. (Apr. 1772).

Mackintosh, Charles, of New York, but late of St. Martin in
Fields, Middlesex, who died at sea. Administration to
principal creditor Alexander Mackintosh; relict and children cited but not appearing. (June 1749). Declared null
by Act of Court and administration with will granted to
John Fell, husband and attorney of relict, now Susanna
Fell in New York. (June 1750).

Macintosh, Gregor, of New York, sergeant of 42nd Regiment of
Foot who died at Havana. Administration to Samuel Willis,
attorney for relict Catherine Macintosh at New York.
(June 1765).

Mackintosh, James, formerly of Mobile, West Florida, but late
of Chicksaw Nation in North America. Administration with
will to Charles Graham, attorney for brother John Mackintosh;
sole executor Daniel Ward cited but not appearing. (Apr.
1787).

Mackintosh, Lachlan, of Charleston, South Carolina. Limited
probate to Simon Mackintosh. (Oct. 1789).

Mackintosh, Robert, of New York City who died on Tortola,
bachelor. Administration to brother Alexander Mackintosh.
(Apr. 1782).

McIsaac, Malcolm, of New York, bachelor. Administration to father Archibald McIsaac. (Mar. 1781).

Mackay, Robert, Lieutenant on half pay of 88th Regiment of Foot who died in Virginia, bachelor. Administration to John Crocker, attorney for mother and next of kin Jean Mackay at Rothesay, Isle of Bute, Scotland. (Sept. 1772).

McKenzie, Alexander, private of 2nd Batallion of 42nd Royal Highland Regiment who died at Havana. Administration to Duncan Campbell, attorney for relict Margaret McKenzie in New York. (Mar. 1766).

Mackenzie, Duncan, of New York, bachelor. Probate to Alexander Mackenzie. (Apr. 1736).

McKenzie, John, formerly of St. George, Middlesex, who died in Pensacola. Probate to Nicholas Sanders. (Feb. 1782).

Mackenzie, Robert, corporal of 77th Regiment who died at Amboy. Probate to Donald Mackenzie; no executor named. (May 1764).

Mackey, William, of transport ship *Tweed* who died at Savannah, bachelor. Administration to William Thornton, attorney for father Robert Mackey at Woodhaven, Scotland. (May 1781).

McKenley, Thomas, of H.M.S. *Cornwall*, bachelor. Administration to Owen Gray, attorney for principal creditor William Gale in New York. (Mar. 1750).

McKinley, Duncan, of Wapping, Middlesex, and merchant ship *Royal Prince*, who died at Southwark, Surrey. Administration to Isabell, wife of William Betts, in Boston, New England, administratrix to principal creditrix Margaret Rogers now deceased. (Apr. 1725).

Mackinen, Robert, of 35th Regiment who died at Pensacola, West Florida, bachelor. Administration to creditor Hunt Fitzgerald; uncle and only next of kin Robert Makinen cited but not appearing. (Feb. 1767).

McLatchie, Charles, of East Florida. Administration to John McLatchie, uncle and guardian of children James and Elizabeth McLatchie. (June 1796).

Macleod, Mary, of Fayette Ville, North Carolina, spinster. Administration to Hector Mackay, attorney for brother and next of kin Norman Macleod. (Aug. 1793).

McMullin, John, of Calf Pasture, Virginia, cook of H.M.S. *Charlestown*. Administration to relict Jane McMullin. (Feb. 1783).

McNab, Archibald, Lieutenant of 42nd Regiment who died at New York, bachelor. Administration to Henry Davidson, attorney for sisters Catherine, wife of Robert McAlpin, and Ann, wife of Even Cameron, in Scotland. (June 1767).

McNeil, Thomas, formerly of South Carolina but late of New Providence. Administration to Lewis Wolfe, attorney for relict Margaret, now wife of Robert Lightfoot, at New Providence. (Mar. 1790).

McNicol, Colin, soldier of 77th Regiment who died at Amboy, New Jersey. Limited administration pending production of will to cousin german and next of kin Archibald McNicol. (May 1764).

Macombe, James, of Cloak Lane, London, who died at New York. Administration to relict Margaret Macombe. (Feb. 1797).

McPhearson, Colin, Quartermaster of 42nd Regiment who died at New York, bachelor. Administration to John Small, attorney for mother Ann McPhearson, widow, at New York. (Mar. 1765).

McPherson, Mary, formerly of Tryon Co., New York, but late
of River Raisin, Quebec. Administration to James Phyn,
attorney for son James McPherson at River Raisin. (July
1792).

Mace, Sandford, Ensign of General Oglethorpe's Regiment of
Foot who died in Georgia, bachelor. Administration to
brother James Mace. (Mar. 1745).
Maddox, Jonathan, of H.M.S. *Lizard* who died in New York
Hospital, widower. Administration to Elizabeth, wife of
William Richards, aunt and guardian of children Martha,
Elizabeth and William Maddox. (Mar. 1779).
Mahier, Richard, of New England who died at Rotherhithe,
Surrey. Limited administration with will to John Lloyd.
(Apr. & July 1721).
Maiden, William, of Philadelphia, bachelor. Administration
to William Bruce, attorney for father John Maiden at
Dundee, Scotland. (Apr. 1756).
Mainwaring, William, Captain of H.M.S. *Arundell* who died at
Virginia, bachelor. Administration to father Gilbert
Mainwaring. (May 1764).
Maitland, Hon. Richard, of New York City, Deputy Adjutant-
General of H.M. Forces. Administration with will to
James Syme, attorney for Rev. John Ogilvie, William McAdam,
William Bruce and Thomas Montcrieffe in New York City;
brother Hon. Alexander Maitland, Major-General of H.M.
Forces, renouncing. (July 1773).
Malcolm, Farquhar, formerly of Georgia but late of Bow Street,
St. Margaret, Westminster. Probate to Neill Malcolm.
(May 1791).
Malcolm, John, of Norfolk, North America, bachelor. Admini-
stration to Mark Noble Daniell, attorney for mother Jane
alias Jean Malcolm at Madderly, Scotland. (Dec. 1793).
Mallortie, David, of Port Royal, South Carolina, commander
of merchant ship *Susannah*, bachelor. Probate to father
James Mallortie. (Oct. 1736).
Mallory, Florisabella alias Flourisbelly, of King William Co.,
Virginia, spinster. Probate to William Mallory and Thomas
Avora. (Sept. 1769).
Mallory, William, of Virginia. Administration with will to
son William Mallory; relict Mary Mallory having died
without executing. (Sept. 1769).
Manby, Aaron, of Kingston, Jamaica, who died at Savannah,
Georgia. Limited probate to Joseph Lane the younger with
similar powers reserved to Edward Manby and Joseph Lane
the elder. (Apr. 1780).
Manigault, Gabriel, of South Carolina. Probate to grandson
Joseph Manigault with similar powers reserved to Bacott
Samuel Proleau the younger, Peter Bonnetheare and Gabriel
Manigault. (Oct. 1784).
Man, Edward, of New York, bachelor. Administration to sister
Martha Man. (Mar. 1707).
Mann, William, formerly of Jamaica but late of Pensacola,
West Florida. Limited administration with will to sister
Elizabeth, wife of John Walker. (Dec. 1781).

Marbin, Thomas, of Stepney, Middlesex, who died in Maryland,
master of ship *Sarah and Hannah*. Probate to relict Sarah
Marbin. (Feb. 1713).
Marquois, William, First Lieutenant of Royal Artillery who
died at South Carolina, bachelor. Administration to
father Thomas Marquois. (Mar. 1783).
Marr, Andrew, of Charles Town, South Carolina. Limited
probate to James Carsan with similar powers reserved to
relict Ann Marr, George Haig and John Fisher. (Sept. 1786).
Limited double probate to John Fisher since deceased.
(Jan. 1789).
Marsden, William, sergeant of 64th Regiment who died at
Spiking Devil, North America, bachelor. Administration
to daughter Betty, wife of Benjamin Bottomley. (Feb. 1785).
Marsh, Joseph, of H.M.S. *Romney* who died in Boston, New
England, bachelor. Probate to Thomas Marston. (Dec. 1770).
Marsh, Joseph, of New Hampshire but late of Fredericksburgh
Province, Quebec. Administration to James Phyn, attorney
for relict Susannah Marsh at Fredericksburgh. (Nov. 1790).
Marsh, Thomas, of Queen Anne Co., Maryland. Administration
with will to Joseph Reed, attorney for Ezekiel Forman at
Philadelphia; other surviving executors James Frisby,
John Thompson and Samuel Thompson renouncing. (Apr. 1784).
Marshall, George, of merchant ship *Bayly* who died in Virginia,
bachelor. Probate to Anne, wife of Edward Coggin, with
similar powers reserved to said Edward Coggin. "Pauper."
(June 1720).
Marshall, Henry, of Boston, New England, bachelor. Admini-
stration to cousin and next of kin Richard Marshall.
(Jan 1733). Revoked and granted by decree to aunt Sarah
Percival, widow. (Nov. 1733).
Marshall, James, of St. Philip's, Charles Town, South Carolina.
Administration to John Ritchie, attorney for brother and
next of kin John Marshall at Aberdeen, Scotland. (June
1767).
Marshall, John, of merchant ship *Resolution* who died in Mary-
land. Probate to relict Sarah Marshall. (Dec. 1717).
Marshall, John, formerly of Islington, Middlesex, but late
of Virginia, bachelor. Administration to sister Frances
Peers Smith, wife of Owen Smith; mother Ann Marshall,
widow, having died. (May 1793).
Martin, John, Captain of Royal North Carolina Regiment.
Administration with will to Hector Mackay, attorney for
Angus Martin, Donald Martin and Malcolm McLeod in Scotland.
(Jan. 1793).
Martin, Michael, of Boston, New England. Probate to relict
Sarah Martin. (Mar. 1701).
Martin, Richard, of Bristol who died in Virginia. Probate to
Nathaniel Wraxall, Lyonel Lyde and Andrew Pope. (June 1721).
Martyn, Richard, of Portsmouth, New Hampshire, who died on
H.M.S. *Princess Amelia* at Lisbon, bachelor. Administration
to William Slayton, attorney for mother Jane Martyn at
Portsmouth. (Apr. 1737).
Martyn, Samuel, of Charles Town, South Carolina. Administra-
tion to relict Elizabeth Martyn. (Oct. 1734).
Martindale, Jonathan, of H.M.S. *Europe* who died at Long Island
Hospital, bachelor. Administration to mother Mary, wife
of John Grave. (July 1782).

Martineau, Matthew, of Philadelphia. Administration to
Honorius Combauld, attorney for relict Sarah Martineau at
Philadelphia. (Mar. 1799).

Mason, Arthur, of New England, bachelor. Administration to
brother and next of kin Nicholas Mason. (Feb. 1718).

Mason, Hugh and Hester, of Water Towne, New England. Administration to Benjamin Franklin, attorney for sons John and
Joseph Mason in New England. (May 1702).

Mason, John Baptist, of ship *South River Merchant*, bachelor.
Administration to principal creditor John Roberts. (Feb.
1710).

Mason, Peter, of Bristol who died in Virginia, bachelor.
Administration to sister Matilda, wife of William Collins;
mother Matilda Mason having died. (Jan. 1751).

Mason, Thomas, of Cecil Co., Maryland, who died in Philadelphia,
bachelor. Probate to Andrew Duche, husband of sister Mary
in Philadelphia; named executor John Copson renouncing.
(June 1732).

Master, Robert, bachelor of physick of Savannah, Georgia,
physician to British Army at Santo Domingo, bachelor.
Administration to father Rev. Robert Master. (Apr. 1798).

Masurer, Philip, of Stepney, Middlesex, who died in New York
on merchant ship *Elizabeth* of London. Administration to
relict Elianor Masurer. (July 1702).

Mather, Richard, Captain of 1st Batallion of Royal Americans
who died at Pitburgh, America, bachelor. Probate to
brother Thomas Mather; no executor named. (Apr. 1763).

Matthews, Isaac, of St. John, Southwark, Surrey, master of
merchant ship *Joseph and Elizabeth* who died in New York,
widower. Administration to principal creditor Robert Wood;
only child Sarah Matthews renouncing. (Apr. 1741).

Matthews, John, of H.M.S. *Launceston* and *Mermaid*. Administration to Joseph Basherwile, attorney for relict Sarah
Matthews in Boston, by solemn affirmation; administration
of April 1747 to principal creditor Israel Harlow the
younger revoked by Act of Court. (Sept. 1749).

Matthews, Lowther, Lieutenant of 62nd Regiment who died at
Rhode Island, bachelor. Administration to brother John
Matthews. (Sept. 1781).

Matthews, Mary, formerly of Bishop Waltham, Hampshire, but
late of South Carolina, spinster. Administration to James
Guillitt alias Guillet, surviving executor to brother and
only next of kin Charles Matthews deceased. (Mar. 1799).

Mathews, Stephen, of South Carolina, widower. Administration
to son Stephen Mathews. (Mar. 1740).

Matthews, Thomas, of Boston, New England, who died on H.M.S.
Eltham. Probate to Richard Crafts. (Dec. 1746).

Mattison, Oliver, of H.M.S. *Lyme*. Administration to John
Coles, attorney for relict Mary Mattison in Boston, New
England. (July 1750).

Mauduit, William, of Maryland. Administration to creditor
Jasper Mauduit; relict Mercy Mauduit and children Jasper,
Elizabeth Lamy, Deborah Jackson and Anne Ruth Mauduit cited
but not appearing, and other child William Isaac John
Mauduit renouncing by his guardian Thomas Wright. (Nov.
1750).

Mauduit, William, of Bladenburgh, Maryland. Administration
to son William Mauduit; relict Mary Mauduit having died
before administering. (Sept. 1786).

Mauroumet, John, midshipman of private warship *Boyne* and
late Lieutenant in New York Provincials who died at Havana.
Administration with will to James McKenzie, now husband
of relict Ann, in South Carolina; executors Thomas
Grollier and John Mairac having died before administering.
(Jan. 1775).

Maxfield, Jeremiah, of Bristol, Rhode Island, and Providence
Plantations, New England, who died on H.M.S. *Lyon*,
bachelor. Administration to Thomas Lane, attorney for
father Joseph Maxfield in Bristol. (June 1753).

May, Thomas, of ship *Hopeful Jacob* who died in Virginia.
Administration to relict Martha May. (Jan. 1700).

May, William, of H.M.S. *Rose* who died in South Carolina.
Administration to George Ryall, guardian of son William
May; relict Mary May having died before administering.
(Aug. 1739).

Maybank, David and Susan of Christ Church, Berkeley Co.,
South Carolina. Administration with wills to Samuel Wragg,
attorney for Susan Bond alias Maybank, wife of James Bond,
and Thomas Barton in South Carolina. (Feb. 1725).

Maynard, Henry, of Dublin, Ireland, who died in Virginia.
Probate to relict Henrietta Maynard. (Oct. 1727).

Maynard, William, Lieutenant of 2nd Regiment of Foot Guards
who died in North Carolina. Administration with will to
brother Henry Maynard. (June 1781).

Mease, Edward, of Pensacola, West Florida, bachelor. Administration to cousin german and next of kin Michael Driver
Mease. (Mar. 1781).

Medhurst, Thomas, of Virginia. Administration to relict Anne
Medhurst. (Sept. 1713).

Medlicott, Edmund, of Charles Town, South Carolina, bachelor.
Administration to sister Mary, wife of John Andrews.
(May 1717).

Mendes, Isaac, of Pensacola, West Florida. Probate to
William Barrow with similar powers reserved to William
Aird, Arthur Neil and Alexander Solomons. (July 1769).

Mercer, James, Captain of General Webb's Regiment of Foot
who died at Albany, North America, bachelor. Probate to
uncle Robert Fenton. (Feb. 1759).

Mercer, James Francis, Lieutenant-Colonel of Sir William
Pepperell's late Regiment who died at Oswego, North America,
bachelor. Administration to Andrew Douglas, attorney for
brother William Mercer at Perth, Scotland. (July 1760).

Mercer, Richard, of Charles Town, South Carolina. Probate
to relict Grace Mercer with similar powers reserved to
John McCall the younger. (Apr. 1788).

Merchant, William, of Boston, New England, who died in Barbados. Administration to creditor James Johnson; relict
and child or children and others interested cited but not
appearing. (Apr. 1756).

Mercier, Thomas, Lieutenant of General Lascelles' Regiment of
Foot who died at Louisburgh, bachelor. Administration to
father Philip Mercier. (July 1759).

Merefield, Edward, of German Town, Pennsylvania. Probate
to Vernon Merefield (in will called Merryfield), son;
with similar powers rserved to Benjamin Condy. (July 1768).
Merrick, Dennis, of the Hokills, Pennsylvania. Administra-
tion to principal creditor Richard Chope. (Nov. 1702).
Mayrick, Walter, of merchant ship *Providence* who died in
Virginia, bachelor. Administration to principal creditor
Dennis Fox. (Oct. 1703).
Metcalfe, John, of King and Queen Co., Virginia, who died at
sea, bachelor. Probate to Thomas Metcalfe with similar
powers reserved to Samuel Metcalfe, John Craven and Daniel
Ker. (Mar. 1762).
Metcalfe, Richard, of Lewis, Pennsylvania, widower. Admini-
stration to daughter Elizabeth Metcalfe. (July 1763).
Metcalfe, Simon, formerly of Prattsburgh, Charlotte Co., New
York, but late of Albany, New York. Administration with
will to Alexander Ellice, attorney for relict Catherine
Metcalfe. (Feb. 1797).
Mew, Noel, of Providence Plantation, New England, and Newport,
Rhode Island. Administration with will to Thomas Zachary,
attorney for relict Mary Mew in Newport. (Apr. 1700).
Meyrick - see Merrick.
Middleton, Arthur, of St. James, Goose Creek, South Carolina.
Administration with will to William Middleton, attorney
for Sarah Middleton, widow, in South Carolina; other
executor Henry Herwood having died. (Aug. 1740).
Middleton, James, of Philadelphia, Lieutenant of H.M.S.
Launceston. Administration by his solemn declaration to
David Barclay, attorney for relict Mary Middleton in Phila-
delphia. (Aug. 1746).
Middleton, Thomas, of Charles Town, South Carolina. Administra-
tion with will to John Shoolbred, attorney for daughter
Mary alias Polly, wife of James Shoolbred, at Charles Town;
brother Henry Middleton renouncing and Ralph Izard, John
Deas, Robert Gibbes, and relict Elizabeth Middleton cited
but not appearing. (Mar. 1799). Further grants August
1803, July 1806 and September 1820.
Midford, John, John, of St. Dunstan in East, London, merchant,
Limited administration to Brian Philpott to recover debts
in Virginia and Maryland. (Mar. 1735). Further grant in
June 1742.
Midford, William, of Inner Temple, London, who died in Charles
Town, South Carolina, bachelor. Administration to sister
Frances Burton, widow. (Aug. 1746).
Milam - see Mylam.
Miller, Henry, of H.M.S. *Fame* who died in Long Island Hospital.
Administration with will to Samuel Davis and Jacob Aaron,
attornies for Jane Donaldson of Plymouth, Hampshire *(sic)*.
July 1783).
Mills, Andrew, of New York, purser of H.M.S. *Greyhound*. Probate
to relict Eleanor Mills. (Feb. 1750).
Mills, George, of merchant ship *Betty*, bachelor, who died in
Virginia. Administration to principal creditrix Jane
Sutherland. (Dec. 1712).
Mills, John, of Alexandria, Virginia, widower. Administration
to nephew and next of kin John James Harrop. (Jan. 1786).

Mills, William Henry, formerly of South Carolina, after of
Nassau, but late of City of Chester. Limited probate to
John Simpson with similar powers reserved to Thomas Moss,
William Moss and James Hepburn. (Aug. 1790).

Milne, James, Lieutenant and surgeon of 2nd Batallion of
Royal Americans and surgeon of hospital at Fort Pitt,
bachelor. Administration to brother and next of kin
Robert Milne. (Jan. 1765).

Milner, William, of H.M.S. *Enterprise*, Lieutenant of Colonel
Churchill's Regiment of Marines, who died at Boston, New
England, bachelor. Administration to mother Anne Milner,
widow. (Nov. 1713).

Milward, Robert, of Yanoak near Swinnards Bay, James River,
Virginia, bachelor. Administration to principal creditor
Marmaduke Carver the younger by decree; sisters and next
of kin Mary, wife of John Dudley, and Anne, wife of
William Gilbert, renouncing. (July 1718).

Minnick, Christian, of Bristol, Bucks Co., Pennsylvania.
Probate to Joseph Plant with similar powers reserved to
son John Minnick, Seymour Hart and William McIlwaine.
(July 1786).

Minott, Theophilus, of Boston and H.M.S. *Gloucester* and
Windsor, bachelor. Administration to William Walford,
attorney for sister Mechetabel Cooper, widow, in Boston,
New England. (Nov. 1705).

Mitchell, Benjamin, of Niagara, North America, bachelor.
Administration to father William Mitchell. (Dec. 1761).

Mitchell, James, quarter gunner of H.M.S. *Renown* who died in
Rhode Island Hospital, bachelor. Administration to mother
Elizabeth Mitchell, widow, at Montrose, Scotland. (Apr.
1781).

Mitchell, Joseph, of merchant ships *Oxford* and *Essex Loan* who
died in Virginia. Administration to relict Rebecca
Mitchell. (Nov. 1710).

Molloy, John, of merchant ship *Offer* who died in Virginia,
bachelor. Administration by decree to father Daniel Molloy.
(Feb. 1722).

Moncrieff, Isabella, of Pembroke who died at St. Augustine,
East Florida, widow. Probate to daughter Christiana
(formerly Scott) wife of Jacob Vanbraam. (Oct. 1779).

Moncrieffe, formerly Heron, Margaret, of New York. Administration to Charles Gould, attorney for husband Thomas
Moncrieffe in New York. (Dec. 1764).

Moncrieffe, Thomas, of New York, Major in H.M. Service,
widower. Administration to Thomas Vaughan, attorney for
son Edward Cornwallis Moncrieffe at Dungannon, Ireland.
(July 1792).

Moncrief, William, Captain of Queen's Rangers who died at New
York, bachelor. Administration to father James Moncrief.
(Feb. 1790).

Money, John, Lieutenant of 63rd Regiment who died in North
Carolina, bachelor. Administration to father Rev. Thomas
Money. (May 1781). Revoked on death of father and granted
to mother Margaret Money, widow. (Oct. 1793).

Monck, Edward, of South Carolina, bachelor. Administration to
mother Joan Monck, widow. (July 1713).

Monk, John, of Charles Town, South Carolina. Limited probate
to William Monk and James Horsnell. (Oct. 1789).

80

Montgomerie, John, Governor of New York, widower. Administra-
tion to Robert Dalrymple, attorney for principal creditor
Sir John Anstruther in Scotland; sister and next of kin
Elizabeth, wife of Patrick Ogilvy, renouncing. (Mar. 1732).
Montgomery, Samuel the elder, of Savannah, Georgia, widower.
Administration to John Simpson and Crawford Davison,
attornies for only children Samuel, William and Jane
Montgomery, and Mary, wife of John Wilson, at Savannah.
(June 1797).
Moody, Ann, of York Co., Virginia. Administration to husband
Mathew Moody. (Feb. 1760).
Moore, Alexander, of Boston, Mass., who died at sea. Probate
to John Lane. (Feb. 1794).
Moore, Elizabeth - see Quigly.
Moor, Ferguson, of Philadelphia, seaman of H.M.S. *Argonaut*.
Administration to William Coningham, attorney for relict
Jane Moor at Philadelphia. (Oct. 1798).
Moore, Sir Henry, Governor of New York. Probate to relict
Dame Catharine Maria Moore. (June 1770).
Moore, Mary, of New York. Administration to husband William
Moore. (Apr. 1784).
Morley, David, of Brompton, North Carolina, bachelor. Admini-
stration to brother Philip Morley. (Jan. 1752).
Morrant, John, of H.M.S. *Perseus* who died in Long Island
Hospital, bachelor. Administration to Jane Dalton, spin-
ster, attorney for mother Mary Morrant, widow, at Harts-
bourne, Northamptonshire. (Jan. 1780).
Morrey, Anne, of Philadelphia. Administration to husband
Richard Morrey by his solemn affirmation. (Mar. 1749).
Morrey, Richard, of Philadelphia. Administration with will
to John Strettell, attorney for surviving executor John
Bazelee at Philadelphia; relict Sarah Morrey having died
before executing. (Nov. 1756).
Morrey, Sarah, of Philadelphia, widow. Administration to
John Sprettell, attorney for son Stephen Williams at Phila-
delphia. (Nov. 1756).
Morris, John, of St. George, Hanover Square, Middlesex,
Controller of Customs at Charles Town, South Carolina, who
died at Kingston, Jamaica. Probate to relict Elizabeth
Morris. (Mar. 1778).
Morris, John, Lieutenant-Colonel of H.M. Corps of New Jersey
Volunteers. Administration to John Turner and William
Goodall, attornies for relict Sarah Morris at Montreal.
(Jan. 1797).
Morris, Rachael - see Weems.
Morris, Thomas, of East Florida. Administration with will to
William Murdock and Horatio Clagett, administrators to
daughter Rachel, relict of William Weems, and attornies
for said William Weems at Arundell Co., Maryland; execu-
tors James Penman, Robert Payne, Peter Gimel and John
Martin having died. (June 1797).
Morris, William of Anne Arundell Co., Maryland, bachelor.
Administration to sister and only next of kin Rachel, wife
of William Weems. (Apr. 1793). Revoked on death of said
Rachel Weems and granted to William Murdock and Horatio
Clagett, her administrators, attornies for husband William
Weems at Anne Arundell Co. (June 1797).

Morrisey, John, of H.M.S. *Greyhound* who died at New York, bachelor. Administration to brother Thomas Morrisey. (Apr. 1752).

Morison, Malcolm, formerly of Fredericksburgh, Dutchess Co., North America, and late of Annapolis, Nova Scotia, but who died at Quebec. Administration to son Archibald Morison; relict Mary Morison cited but not appearing. (Jan. 1790).

Morse, Henry, of Williamsburg, Virginia. Probate to Thomas Woodall with similar powers reserved to Benjamin Waller and Robert Prentis. (Dec. 1775).

Mortier, Abraham, of New York City. Probate to brother David Mortier with similar powers reserved to relict Martha Mortier and Goldsbrow Banyar. (Jan. 1785).

Moreton, Anthony, Lieutenant of General Oglethorpe's Regiment of Foot who died in Frederica, Georgia, bachelor. Probate to Niel alias Neal Holland with similar powers reserved to Thomas Bosom. (July 1749).

Morton, John, of Carolina. Probate to relict Anne, now wife of Thomas Wills; executor Robert Cuthbert having died and his mother Elinor Cuthbert renouncing. (Mar. 1706).

Morton, Joseph the elder, of Carolina, widower. Probate to daughter in law Anne, now wife of Thomas Wills. (Mar. 1706).

Mott, Edmund, of New York, bachelor. Administration to principal creditor Joseph Bentham; sisters Bridget and Elizabeth Mott renouncing. (Feb. 1705).

Motteux, Benjamin, of South Carolina, bachelor. Probate to brother John Anthony Motteux. (Dec. 1725).

Moultrie, Cecilia, of St. Augustine, East Florida, widow. Administration to son James Moultrie. (Mar. 1781).

Mowate, Alexander, of H.M.S. *Chatham* who died in Philadelphia on merchant ship *Tyger*, bachelor. Administration to father Roger Mowate. (Mar. 1717).

Muller, Albert, of Bristol who died in South Carolina, bachelor. Administration with will to nephew Walter Lougher, guardian of Lyon (?Lyder) Muller. (Jan. 1729). Revoked and granted to Walter Lougher as administrator to Lyder Muller. (Jan. 1738).

Munday, Joseph, of Deptford, Kent, who died in Virginia on merchant ship *Nicholson*. Administration to relict Susan Munday. (Apr. 1702).

Munday, Richard, of Stepney, Middlesex, master of merchant ship *Europa* who died in Virginia, bachelor. Probate to Samuel Bonham. (Aug. 1738).

Munro, Malcom, sergeant in Captain John McNeill's Company of 1st Batallion of Highland Regiment who died at Long Island, New York, bachelor. Administration to cousin german and only next of kin Hugh Ross. (May 1766).

Murdoch alias Murdock, Robert, of Trenton, North America. Probate to Rev. Hugh Dixon and James Riddle. (July 1759).

Murray, Rev. Alexander, of Philadelphia. Limited probate to Rev. John Chalmers and Roderick McLeod. (Dec. 1795).

Murray, Captain Charles, who died in America. Administration to principal creditor Theophilus Rabiniere. (June 1700).

Murray, John, Captain-Lieutenant of 55th Regiment of Foot who died in North America, bachelor. Administration to Henry Davidson, attorney for brothers Duncan and Evan Murray in Edinburgh. (May 1759).

Murray, John, formerly of Rutland, Mass., after of Cowbridge,
    Glamorgan, but late of New Brunswick. Probate to relict
    Deborah Murray and children Deborah and Thomas Murray.
    (Oct. 1795).
Muschamp, George, of Potoxen, Maryland, bachelor. Administra-
    tion to sister and next of kin Elizabeth Muschamp. (Aug.
    1713).
Myatt, Joseph, of Albany Fort, America, widower. Probate to
    Thomas Bird and Richard Staunton. (Nov. 1730).
Myers, Arthur, of Bristol who died in Boston, Mass., bachelor.
    Administration to cousins german and next of kin Jane,
    wife of Bashan Carter, John Robinson and William Robinson.
    (Jan. 1787).
Milam, John, of Bristol who died in Virginia. Administra-
    tion to Dorothy, wife of Edward Dyer, aunt and guardian
    of children John and Elizabeth Milam. (Dec. 1701).

Nanfan, John, Vice-Governor of New York. Administration to
    Middleton Chamberlain, attorney for relict Elizabeth
    Nanfan in Barbados. (Feb. 1708).
Neilson, Richard, of Brigadier Guise's Regiment of Foot who
    died in Carolina, bachelor. Probate to William Chancellor.
    (Feb. 1743).
Nelson, Paschall, formerly of Boston, New England, but late
    of St. Margaret, Westminster, Middlesex. Probate to
    nephew John Temple with similar powers reserved to nephew
    John Nelson. (Sept. 1760).
Neve, Timothy, of Ludlow, Shropshire, who died at Manopolis
    Town, Maryland, bachelor. Administration to Thomas Hughes,
    attorney for father William Neve in Ludlow. (Nov. 1746).
Nevin, James, of New Hampshire. Probate to Thomas Lane with
    similar powers reserved to James Cummins, Theodore Atkin-
    son and relict Isabella Nevin. (June 1769).
New, Thomas, of Bristol who died in Pennsylvania. Limited
    administration with will to relict Elizabeth, now wife of
    Joseph Reynolds. (Jan. 1732).
Newall, John, of Bath Town, North Carolina, bachelor. Admini-
    stration to brother James Newall; father James Newall
    renouncing. (Nov. 1772).
Newberry, Roger, of Windsor, New England, Captain in the
    American Regiment who died in West Indies. Administration
    with will to Christopher Kilby, attorney for relict Eliza-
    beth Newberry and Roger Wolcott. (Aug. 1744).
Newcomen, Samuel, of Charles Town, South Carolina, bachelor.
    Administration to mother Hannah Newcomen, widow. (Dec.
    1792).
Newdigate, Nathaniel, of Warwick, Rhode Island, widower.
    Administration to Thomas Sandford, attorney for daughter
    Sarah Mumford, widow. (Jan. 1750). Revoked on death of
    Thomas Sandford and granted to William Stead as attorney
    for Sarah Mumford at Newport. (Sept. 1756).
Newell, John, of Holborn, Middlesex, who died in New York.
    Administration to relict Catherine Newell. (May 1729).

Newman, John, of New England who died on H.M.S. *Spence*, bachelor. Administration to brother Thomas Newman. (Feb. 1739).

Newman, John, of New York, bachelor. Administration to brother Thomas Newman; father John Newman renouncing. (Dec. 1744).

Newman, Robert, of New York, seaman of H.M.S. *Pandora*. Probate to relict Mary Newman. (Oct. 1783).

Newman, Roger, of Baltimore Co., Maryland. Administration with will to sister Susan, wife of Caleb Coatsworth, attorney for Charles Greenberry in Maryland. (Dec. 1704).

Newton, Ambrose, of Pitsburgh, America, bachelor. Administration to brother and next of kin Isaac Newton. (July 1772).

Newton, Edward, of Maryland, bachelor. Administration to father James Newton. (Nov. 1725).

Newton, William, formerly of New York City but late of Dacre Street, St. Margaret, Westminster, Middlesex. Probate to relict Mary Newton with similar powers reserved to Dennis Carleton. (Mar. 1790).

Nicholas, William, of H.M.S. *Winchelsea* who died in Virginia, bachelor. Probate to Thomas Page. (Oct. 1734).

Nicoll, Andrew, Captain-Lieutenant of Captain Hubert Marshall's Company who died in New York City. Probate to Rev. James Orem with similar powers reserved to Richard Nicholls and George Burnet. (Feb. 1749).

Nicoll, John, late Controller of Customs at Rhode Island who died at Long Island. Administration to relict Penelope Nicoll. (Aug. 1782).

Nicholl, William, of Charles Town, North America, bachelor. Administration to brother Robert Nicholl; mother Mary Heane, widow, having died before administering. (Nov. 1787).

Nicholls, John, of Philadelphia who died at sea on merchant ship *Dorothy*. Probate to Charles Willing. (Mar. 1751).

Nicholls, Richard, of New York City. Administration with will to Francis Donaldson, attorney for surviving executor Richard Harrison in New York City. (Oct. 1783).

Nichols, Stephen, of Newport, Rhode Island and H.M.S. *Vigilant* who died at Louisburg, bachelor. Administration with will to Benjamin Wickham, attorney for Samuel Pool at Newport; no executor named. (July 1751).

Nicholls, William, of Kent Co., Pennsylvania. Probate to William Nicholls. (Mar. 1700).

Nicholson, Hon. Francis, Governor of South Carolina, who died at St. George, Hanover Square, Middlesex. Probate to Kingsmyll Eyre. (Mar. 1728).

Nicholson, Henry, Lieutenant of General Amherst's Regiment of Foot who died at Louisburgh, bachelor. Administration with will to Sampson Barber, attorney for Richard Burton in Germany. (Oct. 1758).

Nicholson, Joseph, formerly of Charles Town, South Carolina but late of Hackney, Middlesex. Administration with will to son Samuel Nicholson; executors Robert Raper, Richard Downes and Aaron Loocock cited but not appearing and William Greenwood renouncing. (June 1783).

Nicholson, William, of Anne Arundell Co., Maryland, merchant.
Limited administration with will to William Hunt with
similar powers reserved to Elianor Foster, Anne and Elizabeth Nicholson. (Feb. & July 1720).

Nicoll - see Nicholl.

Nisbit, Elizabeth - see Wallace.

Noble, Nevill, of New York. Administration to creditors
Richard Clay and Hilton Wray; relict Samuel *(sic)* Noble
and children Charles and Mark Noble cited but not appearing. (July 1787).

Nockold, Samuel, of New York, widower. Administration by
decree to brother and next of kin Robert Nockold. (June
1719).

Noke, William, of Annapolis Royal, Maryland. Administration
to sister Elizabeth, wife of Joseph Sandell; relict Ann
Noke having died before administering and mother Elizabeth,
wife of John Stone, renouncing. (Feb. 1783).

Norris, Andrew, of Boston, New England, but formerly of merchant ship *Friendship* and H.M.S. *Bideford*, widower.
Administration to brother Richard Norris. ((June 1753).

Norris, Isaac, of Philadelphia, widower. Administration to
daughters Mary and Sarah Norris by their solemn declaration.
(Aug. 1767).

North, Stephen, of Boston, New England, who died at St. Botolph
Aldgate, London. Probate to Francis North. (Jan. 1723).

Norton, James, of H.M.S. *Ardent* who died in New York Hospital,
bachelor. Administration to father John Norton. (Jan.
1780).

Norton, Samuel, formerly of Yarmouth, Norfolk, but late of
New York City. Probate to relict Martha Norton. (Dec.
1791). Further grant February 1815.

Nourse, formerly Fouace, Sarah, of Philadelphia. Administration to son Joseph Nourse; husband James Nourse having
died before administering. (June 1785).

Nott - see Knott.

Nowell, Thomas, of St. Dunstan in West, London. Administration
with will to Martha, wife of John Marshall, in New England;
named executor Alexander Nisbett renouncing. (May 1713).

Nox - see Knox.

Nugent, Walter, Lieutenant of 2nd Batallion of Marines who
died at Long Island. Administration to relict Rebecca
Nugent. (Jan. 1777).

Odeway, Isaac, of Christ Church, Middlesex, who died in Maryland, widower. Administration to only child Elizabeth,
wife of William Herrick. (Feb. 1779).

Ogden, David, formerly of Rathbone Place, Middlesex, after of
Newark, New Jersey, and late of Flushing, New York. Probate
to son Nicholas Ogden with similar powers reserved to
Aaron Burr, Richard Varrick, Peter Kemble and Richard
Stockton. (Oct. 1799).

Ogden, Thomas, master of ship *Thomas and Elizabeth* who died
in Virginia. Probate to relict Alice Ogden. (Aug. 1704).

Ogilvie, Henry, of Dundee, Scotland, who died at Pensacola.
Administration to relict Hannah, now wife of David Scott.
(Feb. 1785).

Ogilvie, Rev. John, of New York City. Administration with will to Frederick Philipse, attorney for surviving executor Margaret Ogilvie, widow, in New York. (May 1786).

Ogilvie, Patrick, of Boston, New England, widower. Administration to John Lloyd, guardian of only child Margaret Ogilvie. (Nov. 1718).

Ogilvie, William, Captain of Independent Company who died in New York, bachelor. Administration to Joseph Mico, attorney for brother Rev. John Ogilvie in Montreal. (Aug. 1763).

Ogle, Samuel, Lieutenant-Governor of Maryland. Probate to Benjamin Tasker and Colonel Benjamin Tasker. (Sept. 1755).

Ollier, Jane and Ponz, of Charles Town, South Carolina. Administration to Thomas Elliot, attorney for mother Mary Satur, widow, in South Carolina. (Nov. 1737).

O'Neill, John, Lieutenant of Prince of Wales American Regiment. Administration to David Thomas, attorney for relict Margaret O'Neill in Philadelphia. (May 1792).

Opie, Thomas, of Bristol, mariner, who died in Virginia. Probate of will requesting tombstone to be sent Virginia to sister Susan Opie. (July 1703).

Orange, William, formerly of Norfolk, Virginia, but late of Liverpool, Lancashire. Probate to John Sparling, William Bolden, Richard Kent and William Charles Lake. (June 1789).

Oreck, William, of ship *Arseller* who died in Virginia, bachelor. Administration to Catherine, wife and attorney of principal creditor Simon Symondson at sea on ship *Speedwell*. (Dec. 1706).

Ormandey, John, of ship *Anne and Mary (and of Maryland)* who died overseas, bachelor. Probate to Arthur Holme. (Aug. 1700).

Ormsby, Eubule, Lieutenant of 35th Regiment who died at West Florida. Probate to sister Mary Ormsby. (June 1768).

Oswin, Thomas, of merchant ship *Essex* who died at York River, Virginia. Probate to father Christopher Oswin. "Pauper." (Dec. 1721).

Overing, Henry John, of Newport, Rhode Island, and Providence Plantations. Administration to Henry Overing, attorney for relict Mary Overing at Newport. (Aug. 1784).

Owen, Joseph, of St. Botolph Bishopsgate, London, who died in Virginia. Administration to brother Benjamin Owen. (Oct. 1709).

Owen, Thomas, of Granvill Co., South Carolina. Probate to brother Jeremiah Owen with similar powers reserved to Joseph Wragg and William Yeomans. (July 1738).

Owen, William, of Bath, North Carolina, bachelor. Administration to uncle and principal creditor Thomas Walker; sister and next of kin Elizabeth Owen renouncing. (Jan. 1735).

Oyles, Phillip, of Maryland, bachelor. Probate by solemn declaration to brother Thomas Oyles. (Nov. 1710).

Packharness alias Peckharness, John, of New York City. Probate to Richard Peckharness with similar powers reserved to brother and sister Richard and Deborah Peckharness. (Nov. 1796).

Page, John, of Gloucester Co., Virginia, who died at Bethnal
Green, Stepney, Middlesex, merchant. Probate to son John
Page. (Jan. 1719).

Paine - see Payne.

Palmer, Anthony, Lieutenant of Lieutenant-General Dalzel's
Regiment in Leeward Islands who died in Philadelphia.
Probate to Robert Lowe with similar powers reserved to
relict Elizabeth Palmer. (May 1749). Revoked and granted
to said Elizabeth Palmer. (July 1750).

Palmer, Eliakim, of St. Peter le Poor, London, having estate
at Boston, New England. Limited probate to Beeston Long,
Henry Norris and William Palmer. (May 1749).

Palmer, Thomas, of Virginia. Probate to Nicholas Palmer with
similar powers reserved to relict Mary Palmer. (Nov.
1768).

Parham, Joseph - see Parrum.

Park, Elizabeth, widow, formerly Elizabeth Chambers, widow,
formerly Elizabeth Watson, spinster, of Bury St. Edmunds,
Suffolk, who died in Savannah, Georgia. Administration to
sister Sarah Elliott, widow. (July 1770).

Parke, Graves, of Virginia, master of merchant ship *Gooch*.
Probate to Edward Randolph with similar powers reserved to
John Randolph. (Aug. 1731).

Parke, Thomas, of H.M.S. *Peach* who died at New York, bachelor.
Administration to sisters Grace Parke and Mary, wife of
John Sowerby. (Nov. 1780).

Parker, Benjamin, of Boston, New England, bachelor. Limited
administration to John Hiller of Bread Street, London,
attorney *pendente lite* for Robert Robinson. (Dec. 1772).

Parker, John, of Virginia. Administration with will to John
Purvis, attorney for William Colsen in Virginia. (Aug. 1701).

Parker, John, of Morton, Thornbury, Gloucestershire, who died
in Pennsylvania, bachelor. Administration with will to
cousin german and next of kin Isaac Reach; executors in
trust William Gregory and Thomas Allway and brother William
Parker having died. (Apr. 1750).

Parker, John, formerly of Enfield, Middlesex, but late of
Annapolis, Maryland, widower. Administration to son and
next of kin George Parker. (May 1799).

Parker, Joseph, of Charles Town, South Carolina, bachelor.
Administration to brother George Parker of Lambs Conduit
Street, St. George the Martyr; mother Katharine Parker
renouncing. (July 1785).

Parker, Josiah, of Charles Town, North America, Lieutenant on
half pay of late Regiment of New Jersey Volunteers.
Administration to David Thomas, attorney for relict Levina
Parker at Charles Town. (Nov. 1796).

Parkin alias Perkins, John, seaman of H.M.S. *Eagle* who died
at New York, bachelor. Probate to brother Henry Parkin.
(Apr. 1777).

Parkin, Thomas, of New York City. Limited administration
with will to nephew Thomas Parkin. (May 1795).

Parnel, James, of Pennsylvania. Probate to Ambrose Stevenson.
(Oct. 1725).

Parnell, Moses, of Southampton, Long Island, New York, widower.
Administration to son Moses Parnell. (July 1756).

Parr, Henry, of Boston, New England, bachelor. Administration to father Richard Parr. (Aug. 1753).

Parrum alias Parham, Joseph, of Stepney, Middlesex, who died in Boston, New England. Administration to Jane Parrum. (Aug. 1701).

Parsons, Edward Lambert, of James Town, Virginia, who died passenger on merchant ship *Warwick*, master Charles Lasker, bachelor. Administration to cousin german and only next of kin John Lambert, administrator to brother and only next of kin John Temple who died before administering. (May 1778).

Parsons, John Temple, of Chester Town, Maryland, bachelor. Administration to cousin german and only next of kin John Lambert. (May 1778).

Paston, John, of Old Stratford, Warwickshire, who died in America. Probate to mother Elizabeth Paston. (June 1711).

Paston, Robert, Captain of H.M.S. *Feversham*. Administration with will to Benjamin Edmonds, attorney for Adolph Philips in New York; sentence of July 1712 appointing Thomas Sandford as attorney now revoked. (Jan. 1713).

Pastree, George, of Boston, New England, who died on armed vessel *Boston Packet*, bachelor. Administration by his solemn affirmation to Anthony Hodgson, attorney for grandmother Margaret Pastree in Boston. (Aug. 1751).

Pateshall, Robert, of Boston, Mass., Captain of 40th Regiment of Foot, bachelor. Administration to Dennys de Berdt, attorney for brother and only next of kin Richard Pateshall at Boston. (Aug. 1763).

Patten alias Potten, John, Lieutenant of 48th Regiment of Foot who died at Havana. Administration to John Pritchard, attorney for relict Mary Patten at Trinity parish, New York. (Jan. 1765).

Patterson, John, of Farmington, Connecticut, Captain of 1st Connecticut Regiment of Foot who died at Havana. Administration with will to Phineas Lyman, attorney for relict Ruth Patterson in Connecticut. (Jan. 1765).

Paterson, Robert, Lieutenant of 17th Regiment of Light Dragoons who died at Charles Town, South Carolina. Probate to John Wilson with similar powers reserved to brother William Paterson. (July 1781).

Pattison, George, of merchant ship *Betty* who died in Virginia, bachelor. Probate to mother Jane Pattison, widow. (Jan. 1722).

Pattison, John, of South Carolina who died on H.M.S. *Windsor*. Probate to daughter Isabella, wife of George West. (Feb. 1742).

Patton, formerly Petifer, Mary, of Savannah, Georgia. Administration to John Patton, attorney for husband John Patton in Savannah. (Jan. 1775).

Paxton, Charles, formerly of Boston, New England, but late of St. James, Westminster, Middlesex. Probate to William Burch and Thomas Palmer. (Feb. 1788).

Paxton, Wentworth, of Boston, New England, but formerly of Rotherhithe, Surrey. Administration to son Charles Paxton; relict Faith Paxton having died. (Feb. 1751).

Payne, Edmund, of Stepney, Middlesex, who died in Maryland. Probate to Catherine Payne. (July 1708).

Pain, James, of H.M.S. *Tartar* who died in Long Island Hospital. Probate to Jane Cotterell, spinster. (Aug. 1778).

Paine, William, of ship *Charles* who died in Virginia. Probate to relict Susan Paine. (Nov. 1710).

Paynter, Lovell, of merchant ship *Loyal Judith* who died at Philadelphia, bachelor. Administration to creditor John Lemon; great uncle and next of kin John Paynter renouncing. (Aug. 1741).

Peachy, Mary, of Virginia. Probate to Thomas Walker with similar powers reserved to Susan Walker. (Jan. 1717).

Peake, Christopher, of Deptford, Kent, who died in Virginia on merchant ship *Mary*. Administration to relict Anne Peake. (Dec. 1726).

Peak, Samuel, of Boston, New England, master of H.M.S. *Lowestoft*. Administration to Samuel Partridge, attorney for relict Elizabeth, now wife of Edward Marshall, at Boston. (Feb. 1753).

Pearman, Ann, of Annapolis, Maryland, spinster. Administration to Zachariah Hood, attorney for uncle and next of kin Thomas Hyde at Annapolis. (Jan. 1785).

Pearson, John, of Mount Airy, Richmond Co., Virginia, widower. Administration to son John Pearson. (July 1766).

Pearson, Joseph, of Shadwell, Middlesex, master of merchant ship *Providence* who died in Maryland. Administration to relict Elianor Pearson. (Jan. 1726).

Pearson, Richard, of H.M.S. *Shoreham* who died in New York, bachelor. Administration to principal creditor Samuel Wood. (Sept. 1730).

Peckharness - see Packharness.

Pecknell, Elizabeth, of New York City. Probate to William Orcher Huddleston and daughter Rebecca, wife of said William. (Nov. 1786).

Peele, Robert, of Maryland, bachelor. Administration to brother John Peele. (Jan. 1734).

Peele, Samuel, of Maryland, bachelor. Administration to brother John Peele. (Aug. 1733).

Peers, Joseph, of H.M.S. *Princesse* who died at Long Island Hospital. Probate to Henry Gillis. (Aug. 1783).

Peet, Joseph, formerly of St. Mary's, Nottingham, but late of Philadelphia, widower. Administration to sister and next of kin Abigail, wife of James Newton. (Feb. & Mar. 1797).

Pelham, Penelope, of Boston, New England, spinster. Administration to William Pelham, attorney for half brother and next of kin Peter Pelham at Greenville Co., Virginia. (Feb. 1790).

Pelham, William, of Boston, New England, bachelor. Administration to William Pelham, attorney for brother Peter Pelham at Greenville Co., Virginia. (Feb. 1790).

Penman, James, formerly of Charles Town, South Carolina, but late of St. Paul, Covent Garden, Middlesex. Probate to William Drummond and Thomas Young with similar powers reserved to Sir William Forbes and Spencer Man. (Nov. 1789). Double probate January 1794.

Penn, John, of Philadelphia. Probate to relict Anne Penn with similar powers reserved to John Fishbourne Mifflin. (Jan. 1796).

Penn, Richard, of St. Marylebone, Middlesex, having estate in America. Limited probate to relict Hannah Penn. (Mar. 1771).

Penny, John, of H.M.S. *Roebuck* who died in Philadelphia, bachelor. Administration to mother Elizabeth, wife of Peter Sawrey. (Feb. 1779).

Pepperell, Andrew, formerly of Portsmouth, New Hampshire, but late of St. Marylebone, Middlesex. Probate to Sir William Pepperell with similar powers reserved to George Atkinson. (July 1783).

Pepperell, Sir William, late of Kittory, York Co., Mass. Probate to grandson William Pepperell, formerly William Pepperell Sparhawk, with similar powers reserved to relict Dame Mary Pepperell and grandson Nathaniel Sparhawk. (Nov. 1768).

Perira, Emanuel, of New York and transport ship *Juliana*. Probate to Emanuel Bandira. (Apr. 1780).

Perkins, Catherine, of Charles Town, South Carolina. Administration to William Perkins, attorney for husband Samuel Perkins in Charles Town. (July 1746).

Perkins, John - see Parkin.

Perkins, Nathaniel, carpenter of H.M.S. *Ardent* who died in New York Hospital. Probate to John Taplin. (Nov. 1779).

Perroneau, Alexander, of Charles Town, South Carolina. Limited administration with will to Robert Wells and Aaron Loocock. (Sept. 1781).

Perroneau, Ann - see Petrie.

Perroneau, Henry, of Charles Town, South Carolina. Limited administration with will to James Crockatt of London, merchant, attorney for Benjamin D'Harriette and Henry, Alexander and Arthur Perroneau in South Carolina. (Aug.1755).

Perroneau, Henry, formerly of Charles Town, South Carolina, then of Stepney, Middlesex, after of St. Pancras, Middlesex, but late of Ramsgate, Kent. Probate to nephew Robert Cooper, Robert William Powell and Benjamin Savage with similar powers reserved to Dr. Alexander Garden, John Hopton, John Savage, Hon. Rawlin Lowndes, Isaac Motte and Edward Penman. (Nov. 1786).

Peters, John, of York Co., Virginia, bachelor. Administration to William Evans, attorney for mother Mary, wife of John Evans, in York Co. (Oct. 1759).

Peters, John, of Vermont, New York, Colonel of Queen's Rangers who died in Canada. Administration to relict Ann Peters. (May 1790).

Peterson alias Petterson, Gilbert, who died in Virginia on merchant ship *Prince Royal*, bachelor. Probate to James Carrack. (Jan. 1724).

Petifer, Mary - see Patton.

Petrie, formerly Perroneau, Ann, of Charles Town, South Carolina. Administration to Robert Williams, attorney for husband Edmund Petrie at Charles Town. (June 1787).

Petterson, Gilbert - see Peterson.

Pheasant, Rachel - see Bartlett.

Philipps, Erasmus John, Captain of 35th Regiment of Foot who died at New York. Administration with will to daughter Ann Fenwick, widow, administratrix of mother Ann Philipps. (Sept. 1780).

Philips, Frederick, formerly of New York but late of Chester. Administration to son Frederick Philips; relict Elizabeth Philips renouncing. (Oct. 1785). Further grant February 1822.

Phillipps, Giles, formerly of Ipswich, Suffolk, but late of
Pensacola, West Florida. Probate to relict Elizabeth
Phillipps. (Jan. 1766).

Phillips, Gillam, of Boston, Mass. Administration with will
to Samuel Prince, administrator with will of wife Mary
Phillips who died without executing. (Aug. 1782).

Phillips, Henry, of Boston, New England, who died at Rochelle,
France. Administration to mother Hannah Phillips, widow.
(July 1729).

Philips, John, of Pennsylvania, widower. Administration to
James Philips, son and executor to nephew and only next
of kin William Philips who died before executing. (June
1775).

Phillips, John, of H.M.S. *Sultana* who died in Virginia.
Administration to brother Thomas Phillips; relict Elizabeth Phillips cited but not appearing. (July 1779).

Phillips, Mary, of Boston, Mass., widow. Limited administration with will to Samuel Prince, attorney for Benjamin
Faneuil and George Bethune. (Aug. 1782).

Philips, Nasel, of merchant ship *Brunswick* who died in Boston,
New England. Probate to William Thompson with similar
powers reserved to his wife Joanna Thompson. (Feb. 1739).

Phillips, Thomas, of Maryland, clerk, bachelor. Administration to sister Elizabeth, wife of Lewis Lloyd. (Sept.
1739).

Philips, Thomas, of Boston, New England, Captain in Colonel
Gooch's American Regiment, who died in Jamaica, widower.
Administration to Robert Farmar, attorney for only children,
spinsters; all others with interest cited but not appearing.
(Dec. 1747).

Philipps, William, of Boston, New England. Probate to John
Lovelock. (Dec. 1727).

Phillips, William, of Stepney, Middlesex, who died in Virginia
on merchant ship *Alexander*, bachelor. Administration to
principal creditor Dugall Ferguson. (Aug. 1728).

Phillips, William, Major-General of H.M. Forces who died in
New York City. Administration with will to legatee in
trust William Collier; no executor named and Elizabeth
Macaulay, formerly Browne, now wife of Rev. Angus Macaulay
renouncing. (Apr. 1783). Revoked on death of William
Collier and granted to Thomas Forsyth; Elizabeth Macaulay
renouncing. (Nov. 1797).

Phipps alias Sergeant, Lady Mary, of Boston, New England.
Administration with will to John Metcalfe, attorney for
Spencer Phipps alias Bennett. (Jan. 1707).

Piggott, Rev. George, chaplain of Colonel John Wynyard's
Regiment of Marines who died at Jamaica. Administration
to son Rev. George Piggott, attorney for relict Sarah
Piggott in New England. (June 1743).

Pyke, John, of Philadelphia, bachelor. Administration to
mother Margaret Pyke, widow. (Apr. 1704).

Pike, John, clerk of H.M.S. *Resolution*, *Iris* and *Jersey* but
late of New York City. Probate to Jane, wife of Thomas
Griffin, formerly Jane North. (Apr. 1793).

Pinckney, Charles, of Charles Town, South Carolina. Probate
to son Charles Cotesworth Pinckney with similar powers
reserved to relict Elizabeth Pinckney and son Thomas
Pinckney. (Mar. 1769).

Pine, Robert Edge, of Philadelphia. Probate to relict Mary
Pine. (Dec. 1789).

Pine, Stephen, formerly of Ulster, New York, but late of
King's Co., North America, widower. Administration to
Samuel Waddington, substitute attorney for only child
Alpheus Pine in King's Co. (May 1789).

Pinhorne, John, of Halifax, Nova Scotia, Lieutenant of 45th
Regiment of Foot under Hugh Warburton, bachelor. Administration to Joseph Mico, attorney for sister and next of
kin Mary Pinhorne in New York. (Mar. 1765).

Pinhorne, Mary, of New York City, widow. Administration to
George Streetfield, attorney for son John Pinhorne in New
York. (May 1740).

Pitcher, James, of New York City. Probate to sister Grace
Pitcher with similar powers reserved to William Porter,
and Cornelius Clopper. (May 1783). Further grant March
1800).

Pitkin, James, Lieutenant of 1st Connecticut Regiment of Foot
who died at Havana, bachelor. Administration with will to
Phineas Lyman, attorney for brother Daniel Pitkin at Hartford, Connecticut. (Jan. 1765).

Pitman, Henry, of Limehouse, Stepney, Middlesex, who died in
Carolina. Administration to relict Elizabeth Pitman.
(May 1701).

Plaisted - see Playsted.

Planck, John, of Serjeants Inn, Fleet Street, London, who died
in Wilmington, North America, bachelor. Administration to
creditor Peter Planck; sisters Mary and Sarah Planck
renouncing. (Dec. 1795).

Platts, Christopher, of King and Queen Co., Maryland, who died
at St. Andrew, Holborn, Middlesex, clerk. Administration
to sister Christiana Topham alias Platts, widow. (Nov.
1700).

Plaxton, George, of Barbados who died at Salem, New England.
Administration to brother William Plaxton. (Apr. 1736).

Playsted, Edward, of H.M.S. *Shoreham* who died in Virginia,
bachelor. Administration to father James Playsted. (May
1701).

Plaisted, Francis, of Boston, New England, who died at sea.
Administration to principal creditor Judith Butler, widow;
relict Hester, now wife of James Gooch the younger, and
children cited but not appearing. (Jan. 1733).

Plesto, Edward, of Maryland, bachelor. Probate to niece and
next of kin Mary, wife of Charles Boardman, administratrix
to sister Catherine Eates alias Yeats; executors Thomas
Smith and William Thomas renouncing. (Aug. 1727).
Revoked and granted to William Yeates, son of Catherine
Eates alias Yeates; Mary Boardman, Thomas Smith and William
Thomas having died. (Dec. 1735).

Plowden, Catherine of Carolina and Florence of Havre de Grace,
France, spinsters. Administration to sister Anne Queladur
alias Plowden, wife of Yves Queladur. (Feb. 1718).

Plowden, Frances, of Carolina, widow. Administration to
daughter Anne, wife of Yves Queladur. (Apr. 1717).

Plummer, Benjamin, of Portsmouth, New Hampshire. Probate to
Thomas Plummer with similar powers reserved to Theodore
Atkinson. (Mar. 1741).

Pogson, Rev. George, of Charles Town, North America, bachelor and bastard. Administration to Rev. Thomas Preston for the benefit of the King. (Oct. 1798). Further grant November 1816.

Poiteuin alias Poitevin alias Potovin, Sebastian, of Dartmouth, Devon, master of the *Pelican* of Dartmouth, who died in or near New England, bachelor. Administration to brother and next of kin Raymond Poiteuin. (Jan. 1716).

Poizer, Thomas, soldier of 22nd Regiment of Foot who died in Captain Campbell the elder's Company at Mobile, West Florida, bachelor. Probate to Elizabeth, wife of William Chipman. (June 1767).

Pomeroy, Robert, seaman of H.M.S. *Vigilant* and *Vindictive* who died at Philadelphia. Probate to relict Ann, now wife of Robert Hunter. (Mar. 1790).

Poole, Richard, formerly of East Florida but late of Roseau, Dominica. Administration to Robert Payne, attorney for relict Hannah Poole at Roseau. (Sept. 1790).

Poole, Thomas, physician to Lord Howe's fleet who died at Long Island, bachelor. Administration to brother Edward Poole. (Sept. 1778).

Pope, Alexander, of Jamaica who died at Philadelphia, bachelor. Administration to brother Thomas Pope. (Mar. 1787).

Pope, Francis, formerly of Bristol but late of Rhode Island. Probate by his solemn declaration to John Harford with similar powers reserved to Thomas Powell. (July 1788).

Pope, Mary, of Newport, Rhode Island, spinster. Administration to James Davenant, attorney for father Francis Pope at Newport. (Aug. 1749).

Porter, Frederick, of Boston, New England, Captain of 3rd Batallion of Royal American Regiment. Administration with will to William Hodshon, attorney for Metatiah Brown, James Bowdoin and relict Mahettable Porter in Boston. (Feb. 1762).

Porter, Thomas, of New York. Probate to George Streatfield, attorney for John Fred in New York. (July 1724).

Porteus, Edward, of Gloucester Co., Virginia. Limited administration with will to Geoffrey Jeffreys, attorney for relict Margaret Porteus in Virginia. (Oct. 1700).

Potovin, Sebastian - see Poiteuin.

Potten, John - see Patten.

Pottinger, James, Lieutenant of Major Rogers' Company of Rangers who died at Ticonderoga, bachelor. Administration to mother Agnes Pottinger. (Feb. 1764).

Potts, Joseph, of Philadelphia, Lieutenant on half pay of Royal Navy. Administration with will to Oliver Toulmin, attorney for relict Miriam Potts in Philadelphia. (Sept. 1773).

Potts, Joseph, of Maryland. Probate to brother Selby Potts. (Apr. 1777).

Powell, Hugh, of Bridgnorth, Shropshire who died in Philadelphia, bachelor. Administration to sister Jane Powell. (Dec. 1771).

Powell, James, of Doore, Herefordshire, who died in Maryland, bachelor. Administration to brother and next of kin William Powell. (Apr. 1747). Revoked on death of William Powell and granted to Edward Westmore, attorney for brother Hugh Powell at Doore. (Feb. 1755).

Powell, John, formerly of Boston, New England, but late of
   Ludlow, Shropshire. Probate to Grant Allan and daughter
   Jane Powell. (June 1799).
Power, Lucy, of King William Co., Virginia, widower. Admini-
   stration to son Jack Power. (Sept. 1769).
Pratt, Caleb, of H.M.S. *York*, bachelor. Administration to
   Daniel Ballard, attorney for father Caleb Pratt in Boston,
   New England. (Jan. 1748).
Pratt, Josiah, of Boston, New England, bachelor. Administra-
   tion to brother and next of kin James Pratt. (July 1767).
Pratt, Samuel, of Boston, New England, bachelor. Administra-
   tion to brother and next of kin James Pratt. (July 1767).
Prentis, Alice, of New England, widow. Administration to
   Joseph Marion, attorney for son John Prentis in New England.
   (May 1701).
Prentis, John, of New London, Connecticut, after of St. Martin
   in Fields, Middlesex, and late commander of H.M.S. *Defence*.
   Limited probate to William Bowdoin. (Aug. 1746).
Pryce, Charles, of Savannah, Georgia. Probate to father
   Charles Pryce with similar powers reserved to William
   Stephens and James Habersham. (July 1780).
Price, Edward, of Somerset Co., Maryland, bachelor. Admini-
   stration to brother William Price. (Nov. 1714).
Price, Francis, of Maryland, bachelor. Administration to
   cousin and next of kin Richard Price. (Feb. 1714).
Price, John, of H.M.S. *Mermaid* who died in South Carolina,
   bachelor. Probate to Mary Rea. (July 1753).
Prior, James, of Newport, Rhode Island, who died on H.M.S.
   Hussar. Administration to William Maude, attorney for
   relict Lydia Prior at Newport. (June 1769).
Prichard, John, of Bell Town, Maryland. Probate to Anthony
   Donne. (Jan. 1742).
Proberts, John, of Philadelphia and merchant ship *Alexander*
   who died in St. Thomas's Hospital, Southwark, Surrey.
   Administration to William Playter, attorney for relict
   Grace Proberts in Philadelphia. (Nov. 1742).
Prout, Robert, of Bristol, after of Charles Town, South Caro-
   lina, but late of Halifax, Nova Scotia. Probate to brother
   William Prout. (Aug. 1783).
Pryce - see Price.
Purdy, Gilbert, of Ulster Co., New York, widower. Administra-
   tion to James Phyn, attorney for son David Purdy at Bay of
   Quinty, Quebec. (Dec. 1790).
Putnam, John, soldier of H.M. Regiment of Foot of Connecticut
   who died at Havana. Administration to Phineas Lyman,
   attorney for father Henry Putnam in Mass. (Dec. 1763).
Pyke - see Pike.

Quarles, Aaron, of King William Co., Virginia. Probate to
   John Quarles the younger with similar powers reserved to
   Joseph Fox and Bartholomew Dandridge. (Dec. 1771).
Quigly, formerly Moore, Elizabeth, of Virginia. Administra-
   tion to husband James Quigly. (Dec. 1789).

Rabey, Peter, of merchant ship *Rainbow* who died in Virginia,
bachelor. Administration to principal creditor Paul
Boucher. (Mar. 1705).

Rably, William, of Philadelphia who died at sea. Administration to principal creditor Richard Deeble; brother and
sister John and Mary Rably renouncing. (Feb. 1731).

Raboteau, Charles the younger, of Philadelphia. Administration to Joseph Reed, attorney for relict Mary Raboteau in
Philadelphia. (Mar. 1784).

Rae, James, of Maryland. Probate to John Glissell. (Mar.
1703).

Ragg, Andrew, of New York. Administration with will to
grandmother and next of kin Anne Ragg, guardian of daughter
Anna Ragg; executor James Gilchrist having died. (Sept.
1783).

Rainbow, Richard, of H.M.S. *Burford* who died on H.M.S. *Nonsuch*. Administration to aunt on mother's side Susan, wife
of James Scott of merchant ship *Richard and Sarah*, in New
England. (Feb. 1713).

Ramsay, Charles, of H.M.S. *Harwich* who died in America,
bachelor. Administration with will to Henry Mills, attorney for brother John Ramsay in New York. (Feb. 1761).

Ramsay, James, Captain of Independent Company of Fusiliers
who died in New York. Administration to Elenor Ramsay,
attorney for relict Catharine Ramsay in New York. (Apr.
1745).

Randall, Robert, of Virginia, bachelor. Administration to
Robert Crosby, attorney for brother and next of kin George
Randall overseas. (Nov. 1726).

Randolph, Edward, of Acquamat, Virginia. Administration with
will to Sarah, wife of John Howard, guardian of minor
daughter Sarah Randolph. (Nov. 1703).

Randolph, Hon. Peter, of Chatsworth, Henrico Co., Virginia,
Surveyor-General of Customs for Middle Western District
of America. Administration with will to William Robertson
Lidderdale, attorney for Archibald Cary, Richard Randolph
and John Wayles, and for Seth Ward now in Virginia.
(Oct. 1768).

Ranolds - see Reynolds.

Raper, Robert, of Charles Town, South Carolina. Limited
administration with will to William Raper. (Oct. 1789).

Ratcliff, James, of 62nd Regiment of Foot who died at Boston.
Administration to uncle and next of kin Robert Ratcliff.
(Apr. 1781).

Ravaud, Ferdinand, of New York. Administration to Sampson
Broughton, husband and attorney of relict Mary Broughton
alias Ravaud, and for only child Susan Ravaud in New York.
(Sept. 1708). Revoked on death of Sampson Broughton and
granted to Mark Anthony Ravaud as attorney. (May 1714).

Ravaud, Susan - see Kearny.

Rawlins, Joseph, formerly of St. Christopher's but late of
Baltimore, Maryland. Probate to surviving executor
William Manning with similar powers reserved to John
Hutchinson Nallwin and Edward Fleming Akers. (Apr. 1797).

Reade, Alexander, of Middlesex Co., Virginia. Limited probate
to surviving executor George Thornburgh. (July 1767).

Reid, Andrew, of Charles Town, South Carolina. Administration
with will to John Tunno, attorney for Robert Johnson, John
Wagner at Charles Town. (June 1784).

Reade, Hayden, 1st Lieutenant of Marines on half pay who died
at New York, bachelor. Administration to mother Mary
Reade, widow. (Dec. 1796).

Read, James, of Beaufort, South Carolina. Administration to
relict Elizabeth, now wife of John Hammond. (July 1791).

Redwood, Abraham, formerly of Newport, Rhode Island, but late
of Mendon, Mass. Probate to son Abraham Redwood with
similar powers reserved to Joseph Clarke. (Feb. 1789).

Reece, Thomas, of Philadelphia. Administration to relict
Sarah Reece. (Mar. 1777).

Reeks, Nicholas, of merchant ship *William and Sarah* who died
in Maryland. Probate to Samuel Spurrier. (Oct. 1734).

Reeve, James, of Bristol who died on passage to Pennsylvania.
Administration to father Charles Reeve; relict Jane Reeve
having gone to Pennsylvania. (Aug. 1714).

Reeves, Charlotte, of Charles Town, South Carolina. Probate
to James Murray and James Freshfield with similar powers
reserved to sister Ann Elliott, spinster. (Dec. 1789).

Reid - see Read.

Remington, Jonathan, of New England who died on H.M.S. *Pearle*.
Administration to Jeremiah Fones, attorney for relict
Larana Remington in New England. (Oct. 1751).

Remnant, John, of H.M.S. *Pearl* who died in Virginia, bachelor.
Probate to John Macky. (Feb. 1743).

Remnant, John, formerly of St. Giles in Fields, Middlesex,
but late of Alexandria, North America, bachelor. Administration to brother and next of kin Richard Remnant.
(July 1793).

Remsen, Peter, of New York City. Probate to son and surviving
executor Simeon Remsen. (July 1792).

Renton, Joseph, of merchant ship *Rose* who died in Virginia,
bachelor. Probate to Cuthbert Birkley. (July 1742).

Ranolds, Samuel, of H.M.S. *Fox* who died in South Carolina,
bachelor. Probate to Richard Miller. (Aug. 1732).

Ricard, Francis, of Jersey but late of 29th Regiment of Foot
who died in New England, bachelor. Administration to
Noah Le Cras, attorney for father Edward Ricard in Jersey.
(Mar. 1773).

Rice, David, of Annapolis in America. Probate to relict Anne
Rice. (Sept. 1724).

Richards, John, of Teston, Kent, who died in Virginia, widower.
Administration to creditor John Thunder. (Mar. 1745).
Revoked on death of John Thunder and granted to his executor
John Watkins. (Oct. 1765).

Richards, William, of St. Martin in Fields, Middlesex, who died
on merchant ship *Easter* in Carolina. Probate to relict
Elizabeth Richards. (June 1722).

Richardson, Richard, who died in Pennsylvania. Administration
to principal creditor John Marsden. (June 1700).

Richardson, William, of Maryland who died at Rotherhithe,
Surrey. Probate to Thomas Plumsted by his solemn affirmation. (Mar. 1732).

Richardson, William, of Kensington, Middlesex, then of Cross
Oak, Wiltshire, who died at Pensacola. Administration with
will to sister and next of kin Mary, wife of Rev. William
Robinson; executors Thomas Athawes having died and Samuel
Commeline renouncing. (Feb. 1769). Revoked on death of
Mary Robinson and granted to her son Rev. Matthew Robinson.
(Nov. 1794). Further grant July 1828.

Riddell, Susanna, of Williamsburg, Virginia, widow. Probate
to Charles Philips with similar powers reserved to
Jaquelin Ambler and Robert Andrews. (July 1790).

Riensset alias Hays, Mary, wife of John Riensset of Bath Town,
North Carolina, who died in Cork, Ireland. Administration
to son John Riensset; husband John Riensset having died.
(May 1744).

Ryley, John, of H.M.S. *Winchelsea* and *Chester* who died in
Boston, New England. Probate to Bryan Northen with similar
powers reserved to Hugh Dyer. (May 1713).

Ryley, William, of New England, bachelor. Administration to
brother and next of kin Ambrose Ryley. (June 1715).

Rimes - see Rymes.

Rimus, formerly Barrett, Ann, late of Virginia, widow.
Administration to brother Gerard Barrett. (Feb. 1755).

Ripley, John, formerly of Tower of London who died at Fort
Augustus, East Florida. Probate to mother Judith Ripley.
(Sept. 1773).

Ritchie, Peter, of Philadelphia who died at Havana, Cuba,
bachelor. Administration to Juliana, wife and attorney
of brother and next of kin William Ritchie in Philadelphia.
(Mar. 1765).

Rivett, Daniel, of Georgia. Probate to relict Barbe Rivett.
(May 1739).

Roades, William, of Maryland, bachelor. Administration to
brother Thomas Roades. (Jan. 1727).

Roberts, Humphrey, of Portsmouth, Virginia. Administration
with will to William Roberts, attorney for son Edward
Roberts at Portsmouth. (Apr. 1793).

Roberts, Sophia, of Pennsylvania, spinster. Administration
to sister Rebecca Roberts; mother Anne Roberts having
died before administering. (Nov. 1731).

Robertson, formerly Chichester, Ellen, of Virginia. Administration to husband Andrew Robertson. (Nov. 1763).

Robertson, Moses, of St. Michael, Northumberland Co., Virginia.
Administration to Newton Keene, attorney for minor children
John Willoughby, Moses and Frances Robertson in Virginia;
relict Susannah Robertson having died before administering.
(Apr. 1752).

Robertson, Paul Douglas, Lieutenant of Marines of Plymouth
Division who died at Rhode Island, bachelor. Administration to father Rev. William Robertson. (Mar. 1779).

Robey, Thomas the younger, of Derby who died at Philadelphia.
Probate to Francis Green. (Apr. 1764).

Robins, Daniel, of New Shoreham, Newport Co., Rhode Island,
private in Captain Giles Russell's Company of Rhode Island
Regiment of Foot, who died at Havana, bachelor, apprentice
to Abel Franklin of New Shoreham, yeoman. Limited administration by his solemn affirmation to Joseph Sherwood of
Throgmorton Street, London, attorney for said Abel Franklin.
(Dec. 1765).

Robins, John, of merchant ship *Britannia* who died in Virginia,
bachelor. Administration to principal creditor William
Jackson. (Feb. 1720).

Robins, Thomas, of East Linington, Warwickshire, who died in
Maryland. Administration to relict Jane Robins. (Oct.
1704).

Robinson, Joseph, master of merchant ship *Fortitude* who
died at New York, bachelor. Administration to father
Henry Robinson. (Apr. 1778).

Robinson, Joseph, quartermaster of 23rd Regiment who died at
South Carolina. Administration to son Phanas Robinson;
relict Hannah Robinson having died before administering.
(Aug. 1784).

Robinson, Richard, of New England, bachelor. Administration
to sister Catherine Robinson. (Feb. 1732).

Robinson, Thomas, formerly of Sussex Co. on Delaware but
late of Nova Scotia. Administration with will to Charles
Cooke, attorney for Peter and Burton Robinson and son
Thomas Robinson on Delaware. (Aug. 1788).

Robinson, William, of Limehouse, Stepney, Middlesex, who
died in South Carolina on merchant ship *Susanna*. Administration to relict Grace Robinson. (July 1730).

Robson, Isaac, of merchant ship *Britannia* who died in Virginia.
Probate to relict Mary Robson. (Sept. 1710).

Roche, Patrick, of Limerick, Ireland, who died at Sypruss
in South Carolina. Administration to relict Bridget Roche.
(Apr. 1726).

Roddam, Lucy, of New York. Administration to husband Robert
Roddam. (Nov. 1751).

Rogers, Anthony, of New York. Administration to Thomas Parry,
guardian of daughter Catherine Rogers; relict Catherine
Rogers renouncing. (June 1704).

Rodgers, James, of South Carolina. Probate to John Beswicke
with similar powers reserved to John Savage and Robert
Raper. (June 1763). Double probate to surviving executor
Robert Raper. (Sept. 1764).

Rogers, John, of H.M.S. *Tartar* who died on hospital ship
Jersey in New York. Probate to brother Thomas Rogers.
(Dec. 1778).

Rogers, Margaret, of Wapping, Middlesex, widow. Administration to daughter Isabella, wife of William Betts, in
Boston, New England. (Apr. 1725).

Rogers, Thomas, formerly Captain then Lieutenant-Colonel of
Georgia Militia but late of Rouen, France. Limited probate
to Walsingham Collins. (July 1790).

Rolles, Francis, of Maryland. Probate to Ernault Hawkins.
(Dec. 1724).

Romman, William, of Wood Brough, Wiltshire, who died in Philadelphia, bachelor. Probate to Richard Romman. (Mar. 1722).

Rootes, Thomas Reade, of Virginia who died at St. Faith,
London. Double probate to John Smith. (Mar. 1767).

Ropes, Jonathan, of Salem, Essex Co., New England, who died
on H.M.S. *Rumney Castle*, bachelor. Administration to
Bryan and Joanna Woolwik, attornies for father William
Ropes at Salem. (May 1715).

Rose, Hugh, of Schenectady, Albany Co., New York, Lieutenant
of Independent Company. Administration to Augustine
Oldham, attorney for relict Anna Rose at Schenectady.
(Sept. 1764).

Rose, Thomas, of South Kingstown, King's Co., Rhode Island,
Lieutenant of Captain Fry's Company of Rhode Island
Regiment of Foot, who died at Havana, bachelor. Administration by his solemn declaration to Joseph Sherwood,
attorney for his father John Rose at South Kingstown. (Dec.
1765).

Ross, Elizabeth, of Virginia, widow. Probate to Anthony
Hawkins. (Nov. 1768).

Ross, John, of Wapping, Middlesex, but late of New England.
Probate to John Thompson. (Oct. 1770).

Ross, Robert, of New York. Administration to Henry Waddington, attorney for relict Deborah Ross in New York.
(Jan. 1792).

Ross, William, of St. Martin in Fields, Middlesex, who died
on H.M.S. *Betty* in Virginia, bachelor. Administration
to mother Alexandra Ross. (Jan. 1718).

Route, Robert, of St. Dunstan in West, London, who died in
South Carolina. Administration to son Robert Route;
relict Mary Route renouncing. (Apr. 1725).

Rowbotham, Joseph, of H.M.S. *Southampton*, formerly on St.
Bartholomew the Great, London, but who died in Virginia.
Administration to relict Mary Rowbotham. (June 1703).

Rowland, John, of New England who died on passage from
France to London, mariner. Administration with will to
Francis Cane, attorney for mother Abigail Cane in New
England; named executor Joseph Dearing renouncing and
Mary Dearing having died in testator's lifetime. (July
1714).

Royall, Joseph, of Boston, New England, who died on H.M.S.
Boyne. Administration to cousin Mary Faucett (Sept.
1710). Revoked and granted to relict Mary Royall. (Jan.
1713).

Rudd, Charles, of Piscatua, Maryland, bachelor. Administration to mother Ann Rudd, widow. (Sept. 1752).

Ruggles, Timothy, formerly of Mass. but late of Wilmot, Nova
Scotia. Administration with will to John Turner, attorney for sons Timothy and John Ruggles at Wilmot. (July
1796).

Rumbold, Thomas, of All Hallows on Wall, London, who died in
Boston, New England. Administration to relict Elizabeth
Rumbold. (May 1727).

Rumley, Johan, of transport ship *Nancy* who died in New York.
Probate to Ezre alias Ellicksander Norman. (Apr. 1778).

Rundle, Daniel, of Philadelphia. Limited administration
with will to Robert Barclay, attorney for nephew Richard
Rundle in Philadelphia. (Sept. 1795).

Russell, Elizabeth, of Marblehead, Mass., widow. Probate to
son Russell Trevet with similar powers reserved to Daniel
Waldo and William Gray. (Jan. 1772). Further grant
September 1803).

Russell, Henry, of H.M.S. *Alborough* who died in South Carolina, bachelor. Administration with will to John Pick,
attorney for William Randall in South Carolina. (Aug.
1734).

Russell, John, of Brunswick Cape Fear, North Carolina,
commander of H.M.S. *Scorpion*. Probate to relict Alice
Russell. (July 1753).

Russell, William, formerly of Savannah, Georgia, but late of
Whitechapel, Middlesex. Probate to relict Jane Russell
with similar powers reserved to Francis Harris, Henry
Yonge, John Smith, Noble Wimberly Jones and Joseph Clay.
(Mar. 1769).

Ryder, William, Lieutenant of 9th Regiment of Foot who died
in Florida, bachelor. Administration to sister and next
of kin Mary Browne, widow. (Sept. 1768).

Ryland, George, formerly of St. Clement Danes, Middlesex, but
who died in New York, bachelor. Administration to sister
and only next of kin Elizabeth, wife of James White.
(Jan. 1792). Further grant to same, testator described
as having died at Philadelphia. (Jan. 1793).

Ryley - see Riley.

Rimes, Edward, of Captain Wemm's Company who died in New
York. Probate to relict Elizabeth Rimes. (Feb. 1704).

Rymes, Samuel, master of ship *Barbadoes Merchant* of Portsmouth, New England, who died at Kingsale, Ireland.
Administration to relict Mary Rymes. (Mar. 1709).

Sabine, William, Captain of 1st Batallion of Marines who died
at Boston, New England. Probate to sister Sarah Sabine.
(Mar. 1776).

St. Clair, Sir John, Deputy Quartermaster-General in America,
Lieutenant-Colonel of 28th Regiment of Foot, late of
Elizabeth Town, New Jersey. Administration with will to
Richard Moland alias Morland, attorney for relict Eliza-
beth, now wife of Dudley Templer, and for Andrew Eliot
in America. (Sept. 1769).

Sale, Nathaniel, of London who died in Charles Town, Carolina,
merchant and bachelor. Probate to Mary Johnson, widow.
(June 1711).

Salisbury, Nicholas, of Boston, New England. Administration
with will to Thomas Lane, attorney for relict Martha
Salisbury in Boston. (Nov. 1749).

Sallitt, William, of Charles Town, South Carolina, bachelor.
Administration to father James Sallitt. (Nov. 1784).

Salmon, Michael, of H.M.S. *Chatham* who died at New York.
Administration to Patrick Hart, attorney for relict
Anotice Salmon in Kilkenny, Ireland. (Mar. 1777).

Saltonstall, Mary, of Haverhill, Essex Co., Mass. Administration to Eliakin Palmer, attorney for husband Richard
Saltonstall in Mass. (Apr. 1748). Revoked on death of
Eliakin Palmer and granted to Benjamin Pemberton as attorney. (Aug. 1749). Revoked on death of Richard Saltonstall and granted to brother Thomas Jekyll. (Nov. 1769).

Salvador, Joseph, formerly of Jermyn Street, Westminster,
Middlesex, but late of Charles Town, South Carolina.
Limited probate to daughters Abigail, Elizabeth and
Susanna Salvador. (Nov. 1788).

Sampson, Henry, Captain of 31st Regiment of Foot who died in
Florida. Probate to brother Thomas Sampson. (Dec. 1772).

Sanders - see Saunders.

Sandford, John, of Virginia. Administration to William
Sanford, guardian of son John Sandford. (June -704).

Sandford, Samuel, of Accomack Co., Virginia, who died at St.
Mary at Hill, London. Probate to Catherine Sandford.
(Apr. 1710).

Sanger, Richard, of Philadelphia, bachelor. Administration
to sister Deborah, wife of Jonathan Cohner. (May 1737).

Sash, Richard, of H.M.S. *Elephant* who died on H.M.S. *Suffolk*.
Administration to Mary, wife and attorney of principal
creditor John Stott in New England. (Dec. 1711).

Satchwell, William, formerly of Bermuda but late of Philadelphia, bachelor. Administration to cousin german once
removed and only next of kin Margaret Redhead, spinster.
(Nov. 1786).

Saunders, Israel, of H.M. Regiment of Foot of Connecticut
who died at Havana, bachelor. Administration to Phineas
Lyman, attorney for father Peter Saunders. (Dec. 1763).

Sanders, John, of St. James, Goose Creek, South Carolina,
bachelor. Administration to James Crockatt, attorney for
uncle and next of kin Joshua Sanders in South Carolina.
(Mar. 1747).

Saunders, Jonathan, clerk, Minister or Rector of Lenhaven,
Princess Anne Co., Virginia. Administration to Jonathan
Matthews, attorney for relict Mary, now wife of Maximilian
Boush in Virginia. (Dec. 1702).

Sanders, Lovett, of Boston, New England, bachelor. Administration to Susan, wife of Joshua Lamb of Roxbury, New
England, attorney for mother Elizabeth Sanders in Boston,
widow. (Apr. 1710).

Saunders, Thomas, of St. Saviour, Southwark, Surrey, who died
in Virginia. Administration to relict Mary Saunders.
(Feb. 1723).

Saunders, Thomas, of Newport, Rhode Island, soldier of Captain
John Whiting's Company of Rhode Island Regiment of Provincials. Limited administration with will to Jared
Ingersoll, attorney for John Whiting in Newport. (Apr.
1765).

Saunders, William, of Philadelphia, bachelor. Administration
to Moses Delafont, attorney for mother Elizabeth, wife of
William Purjean, at St. Omer, France. (Aug. 1792).

Savage, Perez, of Salem, New England, who died at Haskenesse
in Barbary, Africa. Administration with will to nephew
by a sister Thomas Thatcher; no executor named. (May 1702).

Saxon, George, of Annapolis, Maryland, widower. Administration to daughter and next of kin Elizabeth Saxon. (July
1781).

Scandrett, James, of South Carolina, bachelor. Administration to sister and next of kin Elizabeth, wife of John Fell.
(Aug. 1770).

Scarth, Isaac, of St. Botolph Aldgate, Middlesex, who died in
Virginia. Administration to father and next of kin
Jonathan Scarth; relict Ann Scarth having died. (July
1728).

Schuyler, John Cortlandt, of Bethlehem, Albany Co., North
America, Lieutenant on half pay of H.M. marine forces.
Administration with will to brother William Schuyler;
mother Barbara Schuyler, widow, having died in testator's
lifetime. (Aug. 1797).

Scott, Andrew, of transport ship *Father's Goodwill* who died
at Newport, Rhode Island, bachelor. Administration to
father Andrew Scott. (Apr. 1779).

Scott, John, of Mattox, Westmoreland Co., Virginia. Administration with will to Elizabeth Scott, wife and attorney
of Gustavus Scott now abroad. (Dec. 1702). Probate to
brother Gustavus Scott with similar rights reserved to
son John Scott and other executors. (Aug. 1703).

Scott, John, of Charles Town, South Carolina. Administration
with will to John Shoolbred, attorney for relict Sarah
Scott, nephew Bartlee Smyth and for Thomas Winstanley in
South Carolina. (Aug. 1791).

Scott, Mary, of Virginia, spinster. Administration with will
to Ann, wife of Robert Anderson. (July 1781).

Scott, Walter, formerly of Maryland but late of St. Benet
Gracechurch, London. Probate to James Armour and John
Stewart. (Mar. 1752).

Scott, William, of Stepney, Middlesex, master of merchant
ship *Eagle* who died in New England. Administration to
relict Elizabeth Scott. (Apr. 1724).

Scott, William, of Charles Town, New England. Probate to
Philip Hall. (May 1754).

Scrivener, John, of Williamsburgh, Virginia, bachelor.
Administration to brother Francis Scrivener. (Sept. 1752).

Seaborne, Bartholomew, of H.M.S. *Mermaid* and *Suffolk* who
died in New York. Administration to relict Mary Seaborne.
(Mar. 1706).

Seamen, Benjamin, of Staten Island, New York. Probate to
Richard Seamen and son William Seamen. (Oct. 1786).

Seaman, George, of Charles Town, South Carolina. Probate to
John Deas with similar powers reserved to James Lennox,
David Deas and William Lennox. (July 1769).

Seapit, David, of Boston, New England, seaman of H.M.S.
Rippon. Probate to relict Sarah Seapit. (Aug. 1783).

Searles, William, carpenter's mate of H.M.S. *Niger* who died
in New York Hospital, bachelor. Limited administration
to mother Elizabeth Searles pending production of will.
(Mar. 1779).

Sears, Isaac, of New York City. Administration to creditor
Emanuel Elam by his solemn declaration; relict and son
Isaac Sears cited but not appearing. (Nov. 1787).

Sedgewicke, Isaac, of Virginia who died at St. Katherine
Creechurch, London. Administration to brother Thomas
Sedgewicke. (Mar. 1711).

Sergeant, Lady Mary - see Phipps.

Sewell, Adam, of H.M.S. *Phoenix* who died in Carolina, bachelor.
Probate to George Powers. (July 1741).

Shank, Matthew, Major in King's service who died in New York,
widower. Administration to brother and next of kin Moses
Shank. (July 1711).

Sharp, Elizabeth, of Tetbury, Gloucestershire, who died in
Maryland, widow. Administration to son John Sharp.
(Feb. 1781).

Sharp, John, of Lichfield, Staffordshire, who died at Hudson's
Bay. Administration to relict Isabella Sharp. (Feb.1712).

Sharp, Thomas, of Philadelphia, bachelor. Probate to John
Thomas. (Apr. 1740).

Sharp, William the elder, Lieutenant of 9th Regiment of Foot
who died in East Florida. Administration to relict
Dorothea, wife of John Hawkins. (July 1764).

Sharwin - see Sherwin.

Shaw, Lachlan, Lieutenant of Independent Company who died in South Carolina. Administration with will to George Urquhart, attorney for son Lachlan Shaw in Scotland; relict Mary Shaw, James Parsons and Francis Kinloch cited but not appearing. (Feb. 1765).

Shaw, Richard, of Virginia. Probate to Mosis Lacy. (June 1700).

Shaw, Samuel, of Virginia. Administration to father John Shaw. (Oct. 1700).

Shaw, William, of Port Royal, South Carolina, bachelor. Administration to nephew Alexander Shaw, executor of will of father John Shaw who died before administering. (May 1774).

Shearer, William, master of merchant ship *Friendship* who died in Boston, New England. Probate to John Freeman. (Dec. 1763).

Shemans, Benjamin, of Stepney, Middlesex, who died on H.M.S. *Dolphin* in Carolina, bachelor. Probate to Mary Jordan, widow. (Aug. 1723).

Shepherd, Joseph, formerly deputy chaplain of Colonel Morice's Regiment of Foot and late deputy chaplain of 21st Regiment of Foot who died in Florida. Probate to Archibald Grant. (July 1769).

Sherley - see Shirley.

Sherlock, James, of Virginia. Administration to relict Hannah Sherlock. (Jan. 1710).

Sherwin, George, Captain of 67th Regiment of Foot who died at Boston, bachelor. Administration with will to brother John Sherwin; no executor named. (Mar. 1777).

Sharwin alias Sherwin, Richard, of New York City. Administration to John McTaggart, attorney for relict Ann Sherwin at New York. (Nov. 1783).

Shields, Bryan, of H.M.S. *Blond* and *Rose* who died in Long Island Hospital. Probate to Mary Gamblin, widow. (Mar. 1781).

Shipman, Joseph, of H.M.S. *Duke*, bachelor. Administration to William Bryant, attorney for father David Shipman in New Jersey. (Feb. 1749).

Shipton, Thomas, of King and Queen Co., Virginia, widower. Administration to niece Deborah Weaver, spinster; sister and next of kin Deborah Weaver, widow, renouncing. (July 1766).

Shirley, William, of Eaton, Buckinghamshire, who died in Virginia on ship *James*. Administration to relict Catherine Shirley. (Feb. 1708).

Sherley, William, of Virginia, bachelor. Probate to Edward Bathurst. (July 1750).

Shirley, William, Secretary to General Edward Braddock who died in America, bachelor. Administration to father William Shirley. (Jan. 1757).

Shirley, William, of Boston, Mass., Lieutenant-General in H.M. service, widower. Administration to daughter Elizabeth Hutchinson, widow. (July 1788).

Short, James, of Virginia. Probate to Mungo Baikie and Joseph Clarke. (Feb. 1774).

Shower, Nathaniel, of Boston, New England, late purser of
H.M.S. *Blandford*, widower. Probate to daughter Elizabeth
Shower; sole executor Sir Joseph Hankey renouncing.
(Nov. 1761).

Shrimpton, Samuel, of Boston, New England. Administration
with will to Elizabeth Roberts, widow, mother and attorney
of executrix Elizabeth Shrimpton in Boston. (June 1700).

Shrubsole, William, of South Carolina, late Lieutenant of
Independent Company in South Carolina. Probate to relict
Elizabeth Shrubsole. (Mar. 1759).

Sibbet, Robert, of St. Luke, Middlesex, and merchant ships
Points and *John*, who died in Maryland, bachelor. Probate
to Catherine Stringfellow, apinster. (Mar. 1737).

Silvester, John, quartermaster-sergeant of 49th Regiment at
New York who died in Martinico, widower. Administration
to brother William Silvester. (Mar. 1763).

Simpson, Alexander, of Norfolk, Virginia, late master of
H.M.S. *Swallow*. Administration with will to John Gathorne,
attorney for relict Ann, now wife of William George, in
Norfolk. (June 1771).

Simpson, Henry, of All Hallows on Wall, London, who died on
H.M.S. *Eagle* in Virginia. Administration to relict Frances
Simpson. (Jan. 1704).

Simson, John, of Shadwell, Middlesex, who died on merchant
ship *Henry* in Virginia, bachelor. Administration to Susan,
wife of Luke Hall, attorney for principal creditor Edward
Bell. (Feb. 1727).

Simpson, John, of Savannah, North America, who died in Edinburgh, Scotland. Administration to relict Jean Simpson.
(Dec. 1788).

Simpson, John, of Sunbury, Georgia, bachelor. Administration
to sister Elizabeth, wife of Robert Hume. (Feb. 1791).

Simpson, Jonathan, formerly of Boston, Mass., but late of
Bristol. Limited probate to Richard Lechmere. (Oct.1795).

Simpson, Patrick, of Johns Island, South Carolina. Probate
to John Simpson with similar powers reserved to John
Thomas, Thomas Black, Adam Tunno, James Witters, James
Legare and Thomas Hanscome. (Mar. 1792).

Simson, Thomas, of New York who died at Port Royal, Jamaica.
Administration to relict Anne Simson. (Mar. 1729).
Revoked and limited probate granted to same. (Feb. 1730).

Sinclear alias Sinclair, Henry, of merchant ship *Wentworth*
who died at Boston, widower. Administration to creditor
William Shaw; father Magnus Sinclair renouncing. (Feb.
1777).

Sisson, William, of Newport, Rhode Island, and of Lieutenant-
Colonel Hargill's Company of Rhode Island Regiment of Foot,
who died at Havana, bachelor. Administration by his solemn
declaration to Joseph Sherwood, attorney for mother
Deliverance Sisson at Portsmouth, Rhode Island. (Dec.
1765).

Skene, Ann, of Annapolis Royal, Nova Scotia, who died in
Boston, New England, widow. Administration to nephew and
next of kin John Hamilton. (Apr. 1773).

Skinner. Cortlandt, formerly of New Jersey but late of Bristol.
Probate to relict Elizabeth Skinner. (Apr. 1799).

Skynner, Henry, barrack master of Artillery Train at St.
    Augustine, East Florida. Probate to Ann Samuel. (Nov.
    1781).
Skinner, Richard, late of River Mississippi near Mansack,
    West Florida, bachelor. Administration with will to
    brother Robert Skinner; no executor named. (Sept. 1775).
Skinner, Thomas, of London who died in Maryland. Probate to
    brother John Skinner. (Dec. 1706).
Skottowe, Thomas, formerly of Charles Town, South Carolina,
    but late of Kings Langley, Hertfordshire. Probate to
    brother Nicholas Skottowe with similar powers reserved to
    Edmund Bellinger the younger. (Dec. 1788). Further
    grant February 1801).
Skull, William, formerly of Bath, Somerset, but late of
    Baltimore, North America, widower. Administration to
    Mary Skull, relict and administratrix of only child
    Robert Skull deceased. (Nov. 1788).
Slater, Mary, of New York. Administration with will to
    Charles Lodwick, attorney for Mary Leaver in New York.
    (Mar. 1705).
Slatter, William, of Norfolk, Virginia, who died at Kingston,
    Jamaica, bachelor. Administration to brother Rev. Thomas
    Slatter; mother Elizabeth Slatter, widow, renouncing.
    (May 1760).
Sleigh, Joseph, of Boston, Mass. Administration to Jonathan
    Bracebridge, attorney for relict Anne Sleigh in Boston.
    June 1740).
Sliter, Robert, of Portobello, America. Probate to James
    Alworth with similar powers reserved to Mary Ruffin and
    Abigail.Sliter. (1716).
Slone, James, of Boston, New England. Probate to John Hayes
    and James Adams. (Aug. 1737).
Slorach, James, of Deptford, Kent, but late of New York.
    Administration with will to mother Esther alias Hester,
    wife of Samuel Pollard; executor John Marlar renouncing.
    (May 1782).
Slough, William, of Carolina. Probate to relict Mary Slough.
    (May 1703).
Slough, William, of Bristol who died in Virginia, bachelor.
    Administration to next of kin Mary Slough, spinster.
    (Dec. 1708).
Smaile, John, of H.M.S. *Greyhound* who died in New York.
    Probate to Alexander Bibb. (Jan. 1725).
Small, Daniel, of Charles Town, South Carolina, widower.
    Administration to aunt Sarah Cadman, widow, guardian of
    only children Isaac and Sarah Small. (Feb. 1772).
Smart, John, of St. Saviour, Southwark, Surrey, who died in
    Maryland. Probate to relict Anne Smart. (June 1720).
Smith, Alexander, formerly of Friday Street, London, but
    late of New York City, bachelor. Administration to William
    Smith and William Allan, attornies for father James Smith
    at Auldearn, Nairn, Scotland. (Feb. 1799).
Smith, Benjamin, of Charles Town, South Carolina. Limited
    administration with will to John Simpson, attorney for
    Isaac Mosse at Charles Town. (June 1791). Revoked on
    death of Isaac Mott *(sic)* and granted to John Simpson as
    attorney for daughter Mary, wife of John Gibbes, in South
    Carolina. (June 1797).

Smith, Brooke, formerly of Birmingham, Warwickshire, but late
of Philadelphia. Probate to William Russell and brother
Joseph Smith. (Mar. 1788).

Smith, Christopher, of New York who died at Portmalion,
Minorca. Administration to Christopher Smith, guardian
of children Christopher and Margaret Smith; relict Joane
Smith having died before administering. (Mar. 1731).

Smith, Daniel, soldier of 42nd Regiment of Foot of Captain
McNeal's Company who died at Elizabeth Town near New York,
bachelor. Administration to Hannah Smith, widow, mother
of nephew and only next of kin John Smith. (Apr. 1766).

Smith, Edmond, of Hopkintown, King's Co., Rhode Island, and
of Captain Giles Russell's Company of Rhode Island Regiment
of Foot who died at Havana, bachelor. Administration by
his solemn declaration to Joseph Sherwood, attorney for
mother Elizabeth Smith, widow, in America. (Dec. 1765).

Smith, Edward, smith of H.M. Artillery at New York, bachelor.
Probate to James Hannam. (July 1758).

Smith, Elizabeth, of New York. Administration to husband
Joshua Hett Smith. (Mar. 1785).

Smith, Elizabeth, of Wethersfield, Connecticut, widow.
Limited probate to brother John Scott. (Mar. 1786).

Smith, George, of Virginia who died at St. George Martyr,
Middlesex. Probate to Richard and Sarah Taylor. (Jan.
1729).

Smith, George, of transport ship *Hercules* who died at New
York, bachelor. Probate to Behrond Ehlers with similar
powers reserved to George Fisher. (Apr. 1763).

Smith, Henry, of Pennsylvania, bachelor. Administration to
principal creditor John Adams. (May 1703).

Smith, James, of Burlington, New Jersey. Probate to Sir
Thomas Mackworth. (Feb. 1733 & Apr. 1736).

Smith, James, of Hackney, Middlesex, but late of Virginia,
bachelor. Administration to daughter Frances Helen Smith,
administratrix with will to father Rev. James Smith who
died before administering. (May 1785).

Smyth, James, of Beaufort, Carolina, widower. Administration
to only child James Smyth. (Jan. 1791).

Smith, James, of New York, Lieutenant of late 79th Regiment.
Administration to David Thomas, attorney for relict Mary
Smith in New York City. (Sept. 1797).

Smith, Jane, (formerly Lilley), of Jamaica who died in Philadelphia. Administration to husband Joseph Smith. (June
1750).

Smith, John, of Maryland. Administration to relict Mary Smith.
(Aug. 1727).

Smith, John, of Hartford, Connecticut. Probate to David
Williams with similar powers reserved to relict Anne Smith.
(Jan. 1732).

Smith, John the younger, Lieutenant of 1st Connecticut Regiment
of Foot who died at Havana, bachelor. Administration to
Phineas Lyman, attorney for father John Smith at Volluntown,
Wyndham Co., Connecticut. (Nov. 1764).

Smith, John, formerly Customs Officer at Philadelphia but late
of Musselburgh, Scotland. Administration with will to
William Cooke, attorney for daughter Margaret Smith at
Musselburgh. (Mar. 1789).

Smith, Joseph, soldier of 28th Regiment who died at Crown
Point, America. Administration to relict Hannah Smith.
(Dec. 1763).

Smith, Joseph, of New York City. Administration with will to
Keene Stables, attorney for relict Dorothy Smith and
daughter Elizabeth Smith in New York City; executors
William Frederick Rhinelander and Robert Carter renouncing.
(Sept. 1795).

Smith, Nicholas, of Stepney, Middlesex, who died in Virginia.
Administration to relict Elizabeth Smith. (Nov. 1710).

Smyth, Peter, late of Brentford Butts, Middlesex, chaplain
of H.M.S. *Tilbury* who died in America, widower. Probate
to Rev. William Chilcott. (Dec. 1757).

Smith, Robert, of Kent Island, Maryland. Administration to
brother and next of kin William Smith. (Oct. 1707).

Smith, Robert, Lieutenant-Captain of Royal Artillery Train
under Lieutenant-General Braddock, who died in America,
bachelor. Administration to mother Mary Smith. (Sept.
1756).

Smith, Robert, of Savannah, Georgia, but late of Jamaica.
Probate to Benjamin Eyre with similar powers reserved to
brother Thomas Smith. (Apr. 1778).

Smith, Samuel, of George Town, South Carolina, bachelor.
Administration to brother and next of kin Robert Smith.
(Mar. 1768).

Smyth, Sarah, of Beaufort, North America, wife of James Smyth.
Administration to only child James Smyth. (Mar. 1791).

Smith, Thomas, of Pennsylvania who died on H.M.S. *Cumberland*.
Probate to Samuel Cherry. (June 1763).

Smith, William, of Dunbar, Scotland, who died in Virginia.
Administration to John Tod, attorney for relict Jane Smith
alias Bulcraig at Dunbar. (Jan. 1738).

Smith, William, of Boston, New England, bachelor. Administration to mother Elizabeth, wife of Daniel Clay. (Sept.
1743).

Smith, William, of Philadelphia but formerly of Royal Irish
Regiment of Foot, bachelor. Administration to brother John
Galt Smith. (May 1774).

Smith, William, formerly of St. Olave, Hart Street, London,
but late of Charles Town, South Carolina, bachelor. Administration to John Shoolbred, attorney for mother Margaret,
wife of William Borland, at Kilmarnock, Scotland. (Dec.
1782).

Smocke, John, of Maryland, widower. Administration to brother
and next of kin Edward Smocke. (Aug. 1711).

Smythies, William, of New York City. Administration to relict
Margaret Smythies. (Mar. 1785).

Sneath, Jacob, of H.M.S. *Pearl*, *Liberty* and *Amphion* who died
in New York Hospital. Probate to Susanna Sharp, widow.
(Aug. 1785).

Snell, Catherine, of St. James, Goosecreek, South Carolina,
spinster. Administration with will to James Crockatt and
William Roos, attornies for Rev. Timothy Millechamp and
Hugh Grange in South Carolina. (Dec. 1743).

Snodgrass, Neal, of Norfolk, Virginia, bachelor. Administration to creditor Robert Gilmour; brother and sisters and
only next of kin Hugh, Ann and Margaret Snodgrass cited
but not appearing. (Apr. 1785).

Solomons, Solomon, of Savannah, Georgia, bachelor. Administration to brother Levy Solomons; father David Solomons
renouncing. (Feb. 1770).

Somers, Charles, of St. Olave, Southwark, Surrey, who died
on merchant ship *Batchelor's Habitation* in Virginia.
Administration to principal creditor John Whibben,
attorney for relict Mary Somers. (Jan. 1702).

Soumaien, Simeon, of Philadelphia, Lieutenant of Captain
Horatio Gates' Indepnedent Company, who died in America.
Probate to relict Aleathea Soumaien. (Dec. 1755).

Southwick, Thomas, of Virginia. Probate to Mary, wife of
Roger Hare. (Dec. 1743).

Sowers, Thomas, of New York City, Captain and Engineer of
H.M. Ordnance. Administration to John Sowers, attorney
for relict Ann Sowers in New York City. (Jan. 1775).

Spalding alias Spaulding, John, of Plainfield, Wyndham Co.,
Connecticut, Captain of 1st Connecticut Regiment of Foot
who died at Havana. Administration to Phineas Lyman,
attorney for relict Lucy Spalding at Plainfield. (Nov.
1764).

Spearing, William, of New York, Lieutenant of Independent
Company who died at Havana. Administration to relict
Ann Spearing. (Aug. 1763).

Speed, Charles, of Deptford, Kent, who died at Rhode Island,
bachelor. Administration to cousin german and next of kin
William West by his solemn declaration. (June 1759).

Spence, Patrick, of Copeley, Westmoreland Co., Virginia,
who died at Allington, Dorset. Probate to Daniel Gundry.
(May 1710).

Spencer, Anne, of St. Bride, London, widow. Administration
to nephew by a brother Paul Batchellor; sister Margaret
Porter, widow, renouncing. (Feb. 1715). Revoked and
granted to daughter Margaret, wife of Thomas Addison of
Virginia, now in England. (July 1715).

Spencer, John, of Savannah, Georgia, bachelor. Administration
to brother and next of kin Henry Spencer. (May 1761).

Spencer, Mottrom, of Earl of Essex Regiment who died at St.
Giles in Fields, Middlesex. Administration with will
(describing testator as of Romini, Westmoreland Co.,
Virginia) to brother William Spencer of Cople, Befordshire.
(May 1703).

Spencer, Nicholas, of Virginia. Administration with will to
John Rust of All Saints, Lombard Street, London, silkman,
attorney for sons Nicholas and John Spencer; other executor William Spencer renouncing. (Jan. 1700).

Spencer, Thomas, bastard son of John Spencer, of Augusta,
Georgia, bachelor. Administration to Henry Spencer for
the benefit of the King. (Dec. 1764).

Spencer, William, of Upper Marlborough, Maryland, bachelor.
Administration to brother and next of kin Joseph Spencer.
(Dec. 1768).

Spendelove, Roger, Major of 43rd Regiment of Foot who died at
Boston. Probate to relict Jane Spendelove. (Aug. 1776).

Spendelow, Charles, of H.M.S. *Gibraltar*, Lieutenant Engineer
of General Braddock's expedition in Virginia, bachelor.
Administration to principal creditor William Wilson; uncle
Rev. Charles Spendelow renouncing. (Jan. 1756).

Spenlove, Ann, of Mount Pleasant, North America, spinster.
Administration to sister Elizabeth Davies, widow. (Sept.
1792).

Sperrmaine, Launce, of ship *Royal William* who died in Virginia,
bachelor. Probate to Elizabeth, wife of David Sperrmaine
with similar powers reserved to said David. (June 1700).

Splatt, Ann - see Brasseur.

Spooner, John, of Boston, Mass. Administration with will to
Sir William Baker, attorney for sons John and William
Spooner in Boston. (June 1764).

Spooner, John, of Boston, New England. Administration with
will to Abraham Dupuis, attorney for Andrew Oliver and
Arnold Welles in Boston. (May 1769).

Spotswood, Alexander, of Orange Co., Virginia, who died at
Annapolis, Maryland, late Major-General and Colonel of
American Regiment. Administration with will to Robert
Cary, attorney for Elliott Bengar and Robert Rose in
Virginia. (Feb. 1742).

Sprague, John, of Boston, Mass. Administration to son
Lawrence Sprague; relict Esther Sprague having died
before administering. (Nov. 1776).

Spratley, Benjamin, formerly of Winslow, Buckinghamshire, but
late of Virginia, bachelor. Administration to brother
Richard Spratley; mother Jane Spratley renouncing.
(Nov. 1783).

Springer, Benjamin, formerly of St. Augustine, North America,
but late of St. Luke, Middlesex. Probate to Richard Dabbs.
(Dec. 1786).

Sprowle, Andrew, formerly of Milton, Scotland, but late of
Gosport, Virginia. Probate to Thomas McCulloch with
similar powers reserved to George Logan, George Surdy and
John Hyndman; executor John Bun renouncing. Sentence
pronounced for validity of codicil and grant of June
1778 made *pendente lite* now revoked. (Mar. 1782).

Squire, Daniel, of New York. Administration with will to
George Moor, father and guardian of executrix Jane Moor.
(Dec. 1786).

Stacy, Samuel, of H.M.S. *Nightingale* who died in New England.
Probate to John Stacy. (Mar. 1716).

Stalker, Peter, of South Carolina, bachelor. Administration
to brother Samuel Stalker; brother John Stalker renouncing. (Feb. 1769).

Stanfield, Thomas, of H.M.S. *Tryton's* Prize who died in New
York. Administration to niece on mother's side Mary
Everatt, spinster. (Nov. 1713).

Stanover alias Stannever, John, of St. Martin in Fields,
Middlesex, and of H.M.S. *Bredah* and *Tryal*, who died in
South Carolina boatswain of H.M.S. *Alborough*. Administration to relict Deborah Stanover. Grant of November 1733
to sister Dorothy Banck now revoked. (Sept. 1734).

Stanton, Jeremiah, of Staten Island, New York. Limited
administration with will to Isaac Lascelles Winn of New
York City, attorney for relict Louisa Teresia Stanton.
(July 1772).

Stanton, John, of Groton, Connecticut, Captain of 1st Connecticut Regiment of Foot who died at Havana. Administration
with will to Phineas Lyman, attorney for relict Prudence
Stanton and son Samuel Stanton in Connecticut. (Jan.1765).

Staple, Peter, of Kittery, York Co., Mass., Lieutenant on
    half pay. Administration to James Fitter, attorney for
    son Peter Staple at Kittery. (Feb. 1769).
Staples, Amos, of H.M. Connecticut Regiment of Foot who died
    at Havana, bachelor. Administration to Phineas Lyman,
    attorney for father Jacob Staples in Connecticut. (Dec.
    1763).
Staples, Isaac, of H.M. Connecticut Regiment of Foot who
    died at Havana, bachelor. Administration to Phineas
    Lyman, attorney for father Jacob Staples in Connecticut.
    (Dec. 1763).
Staples, Robert, master of merchant ship *Eagle* who died in
    South Carolina, bachelor. Administration to principal
    creditors William Mewse and Thomas Harding; father
    Robert Staples renouncing. (Dec. 1719).
Stapylton, Francis Samuel, Captain of 9th Regiment of Foot
    who died at Hubberdown, New York. Administration with
    will to sister Ann, wife of Rev. John Bree; no executor
    named. (Nov. 1779).
Stead, Benjamin, formerly of South Carolina but late of St.
    Marylebone, Middlesex. Probate to son Benjamin Stead
    and daughter Mary Stead with similar powers reserved to
    daughter Elizabeth, wife of Ralph Izard. (June 1776).
Steel, Allen, of Boston, New England, and H.M.S. *Comet Bomb*.
    Probate to Henry Saunders, attorney for relict Deborah
    Steel in Boston. (Dec. 1754).
Steel, John, of St. Philip's, Charles Town, South Carolina,
    who died at Plymouth, Devon. Probate to relict Mary
    Steel. (June 1745).
Stehelin, Thomas, Lieutenant of H.M. Artillery Train who died
    at Boston, bachelor. Administration to father Benjamin
    Stehelin. (Apr. 1777).
Stephen, Alexander, Lieutenant of Sir Geoffery Amherst's
    Royal Americans who died in Virginia. Administration with
    will to John Russell, attorney for brother John Stephen
    in Virginia. (June 1770).
Stephens, James, Captain of Royal Regiment of Artillery who
    died in New York, bachelor. Administration to mother
    Ann Stephens, widow. (Nov. 1768). Revoked on production
    of will and administration with will granted to same;
    no executor named. (May 1769).
Stephens, Newdigate, of Savannah, Georgia. Administration to
    son William Stephens. (July 1772).
Stephens, John, of New York,, Captain of Colonel William
    Gooch's American Regiment, who died in Cuba. Administra-
    tion to Richard Jenneway, attorney for relict Blandina
    alias Belinda Stephens in New York. (Apr. 1743).
Stephens, Richard, of H.M. transport ship *John and Jane* who
    died at New York, bachelor. Administration to mother and
    next of kin Mary, wife of John Stroud. (Feb. 1781).
Stevens, Robert, of St. James on ?Goonowek in South Carolina.
    Probate to John Vicaridge. (Nov. 1722).
Stephenson, Enoch, of New York City. Administration with will
    to Robert Lindsay, attorney for relict Catherine Stephen-
    son, Peter Valet and Joseph Robinson; Pennington
    Stephenson renouncing. (Dec. 1753).
Stevenson, James, of St. Dunstan in West, London, who died at
    Salem, New England. Probate to principal creditor Jocelyn
    Dansey; relict Elizabeth Stevenson renouncing. (July 1728).

Stewart, Alexander, Lieutenant of General James Oglethorpe's
Regiment who died at Frederica, Georgia. Probate to
brother James Stewart with similar powers reserved to
Alexander Heron, George Dunbar, Patrick Sutherland, White
Outerbridge, Dougal Stewart and Patrick Houston. (Apr.
1748).
Stewart, Alexander, sergeant in Captain Sterling's Company of
1st Batallion of 42nd Regiment who died at New York.
Administration to brother William Stewart. (Jan. 1766).
Stewart, Anthony, of London Town, Maryland, widower. Admini-
stration to creditor Thomas Blane; children James, Marga-
ret, Bell, Mary, Jane and Leslie Stewart cited but not
appearing. (Dec. 1791).
Stuart, Charles, of Mobile, West Florida. Probate to Eliza-
beth Hatfield, widow, with similar powers reserved to
Hon. James Bruce, David Hodge and George Troup. (Sept.
1781).
Stuart, Francis, Captain of 26th Regiment of Foot who died at
New York. Administration to relict Mary Stuart. (May
1779).
Stewart, George, of Boston, New England, Captain in American
Regiment who died in West Indies. Administration with will
to Christopher Kilby, attorney for Benjamin Faneuil in
Boston. (Aug. 1744).
Steuart, James, of Woolwich, Kent, who died at Charles Town,
South Carolina. Probate to Mungo Murray the younger with
similar powers reserved to Mungo Murray the elder. (Oct.
1755).
Stuart, Hon. James, Lieutenant-Colonel of 1st Regiment of
Guards who died at Guildford, America, bachelor. Admini-
stration to mother Lady Margaret Blantyre, widow. (Aug.
1781).
Stuart, John, of Pensacola, West Florida. Probate to relict
Sarah Stuart with similar powers reserved to Edward Fenwick,
Alexander Rose and William McKinnon. (July 1783).
Stuart, Ruth, of Boston, New England, widow. Probate to son
Sir John Stuart with similar powers reserved to Rufus
Greene and Mary Johnson, widow. (July 1752).
Stewart, William, of Boston, New England. Administration with
will to John Soden, attorney for Thomas Steel in Boston.
(Feb. 1729).
Stirling, George, of Edinburgh, Scotland, Lieutenant of
General Oglethorpe's Regiment, who died in Georgia. Admini-
stration to Alexander Stirling, attorney for father John
Stirling in Glasgow. (Jan. 1749).
Stoddard, William, of Boston, New England, Lieutenant of H.M.S.
Antelope who died at Flushing, Mylor, Cornwall. Probate
to Henry Pascoe and Norris Bawden. (Nov. 1780).
Stokes, John, of Ottery St. Mary, Devon, who died in Pennsyl-
vania, bachelor. Administration to brother and next of kin
Thomas Stokes. (Sept. 1717).
Stone, John, of merchant ship *Raphannah* who died in Virginia,
bachelor. Administration to William Morris and Susannah
his wife, attornies for mother Susannah Stone at Topsham,
Devon. (Dec. 1737).
Stone, William, of Philadelphia. Administration with will to
William Vaughan, attorney for Samuel Nicholas and Christo-
pher Kuhler in Philadelphia. (July 1788).

111

Storey, George, chief mate of merchant ship *Favourite* who
died at Salem, bachelor. Administration to sister Mary
Storey. (July 1777).

Storrow, Thomas, of Boston, Mass., Lieutenant of 100th Regiment. Administration to David Thomas, attorney for relict
Ann Storrow in Boston. (Aug. 1795).

Stott, Robert, formerly of Charles Town, South Carolina, but
late of Manchester, Lancashire. Probate to sister Ann
Stott. (Nov. 1795).

Stoughton, John, Lieutenant on Independent Company of Foot
who died in New York City. Administration to Edward Paul,
attorney for relict Ruth Stoughton in New York City.
(June 1770).

Strean, John, surgeon's mate of H.M.S. *Russell* who died at
New York, bachelor. Administration to Robert Boyd and
John Bailie, attornies for brother Samuel Strean at
Magharafelt, Ireland; mother Jean Strean, widow,
renouncing. (Aug. 1783).

Stredwick, Samuel - see Strudwick.

Strickland, John, formerly of Camberwell, Surrey, but late of
Baltimore, Maryland. Administration to brother Charles
Strickland; relict Ann, now wife of Thomas Shepherd,
renouncing. (Jan. 1797).

Strudwick alias Stredwick, Samuel, of Wilmington, North Carolina. Probate to relict Martha Strudwick. (Mar. 1797).

Stuart - see Stewart.

Sturdy, Robert, of Virginia, bachelor. Administration to
father Robert Sturdy. (May 1715).

Sturdy, William, of Stafford Co., Virginia. Probate to Robert
Sturdy, father and administrator of Robert Sturdy deceased;
relict Margaret Sturdy having died. (May 1715).

Sturt, Thomas, of Hampton River, Virginia, bachelor. Administration to sister and next of kin Mary, wife of David
Frazier. (Mar. 1765).

Suggitt, Jane, of Northampton Co., Virginia, widow. Administration to mother and next of kin Jane Selby, widow.
(Oct. 1771).

Suggitt, John, of Newcastle upon Tyne but late of Northampton
Co., Virginia. Administration with will to Jane Selby,
widow, mother and administratrix of relict Jane Suggitt.
(Oct. 1771).

Surman, John, of St. Botolph Bishopsgate, London, who died in
Pennsylvania, widower. Administration to principal creditor Ann Thompson. (Feb. 1744).

Susans, John, of H.M.S. *London* who died in Long Island Hospital. Probate to brother William Susans. (Oct. 1783).

Sutherland, Ebenezer, Lieutenant of Marines who died at New
York, bachelor. Administration to Hector Mackay, attorney
for father James Sutherland at Kearquhar, Scotland.
(Aug. 1783).

Sutton, Henry, of Stepney, Middlesex, who died on merchant
ship *William and John* in Virginia. Administration to
relict Elizabeth Sutton. (June 1703).

Swayne, Charles, Ensign of 33rd Regiment who died in New York,
bachelor. Administration to mother Elizabeth Swayne.
(Jan. 1785).

Swaine, John of ship *New Hopewell* who died in Virginia.
Administration to creditor John Neave; relict Elizabeth
Swaine renouncing. (Sept. 1700).

Swan, John, died at sea near New England. Probate to Richard
Heading with similar powers reserved to Margaret Heading.
(Aug. 1701).
Swan, Mary, of South Carolina. Administration to husband
Thomas Swan. (May 1784).
Swayne - see Swaine.
Swift, John the younger, of Philadelphia. Administration to
Hannah Wimbolt, widow, attorney and sister of relict
Elizabeth Swift in Philadelphia. (Jan. 1714).
Swift, Thomas, Lieutenant of Colonel Holt's Marine Regiment
who died in Boston, New England, bachelor. Administration
by decree to principal creditor Robert Hood. (June 1722).
Symmes, Ebenezer, of Boston, Mass. Administration to credi-
tor John Greenwood; relict Ann Symmes and only child
Mary Symmes cited but not appearing. (Dec. 1779).

Taber, Gideon, of Rhode Island who died on H.M.S. *Scarborough*,
bachelor. Administration by his solemn declaration to
Joseph Sherwood, attorney for brother and next of kin
Stephen Taber at Tiverton, Rhode Island. (Dec. 1765).
Tait, James, of H.M.S. *Captain* who died in Boston Hospital,
bachelor. Administration to James Loutted, attorney for
brother Patrick Tait at St. Olla, Orkneys. (Aug. 1774).
Talbot, Henrietta alias Harriet, of Boston, New England,
spinster. Administration to mother and next of kin Mary
Talbot, widow. (Apr. 1799).
Talbot, William Henry, Captain of 17th Regiment of Light
Dragoons who died at New York, bachelor. Administration
to brother Hon. John Chetwynd, Earl Talbot; mother Hon.
Catherine Talbot, widow, having died before administering.
(Feb. 1785).
Tappen alias Toppen, David, of Woodbridge, East Jersey, New
England, and H.M.S. *Vigilant*. Administration to William
Tappen, attorney for relict Mary Tappen at Woodbridge.
(July 1754).
Tarry, Samuel, of Mecklenburgh Co., Virginia. Limited admini-
stration with will to John Tabb of Petersburg, Virginia;
executors Abraham Green renouncing, Edward and Richard
Booker having died, relict having also died, and children
Frances, Mary, Rebecca, George and Edward Tarry cited but
not appearing. (Dec. 1768).
Tasker, Benjamin, of Annapolis, Maryland. Limited administra-
tion with will to Osgood Hanbury and William Anderson of
London, merchants, attornies for relict Ann Tasker. (Dec.
1768, Nov. 1770, Nov. 1772).
Tawse, Thomas, Lieutenant of 71st Regiment of Foot who died
at Savannah, Georgia. Administration with will to Gavin
Young, attorney for Janet, wife of John Stewart, brother
Charles Tawse, and Elizabeth, wife of Archibald Jamieson,
in Scotland. (July 1781).
Taylor, Abraham, formerly of Philadelphia but late of Bath.
Probate to son John Taylor. (Mar. 1772).
Taylor, Bryan, of St. Stephen, Coleman Street, London, who
died in Maryland, bachelor. Probate to brother Freeman
Taylor; executor Philip Smith having died and mother
Mary Taylor, widow, renouncing. (May 1737).

Taylor, Edward the younger, of Charles Town, South Carolina,
and late of River Mississippi, bachelor. Administration
to creditor John Dolland; only child Elizabeth, wife of
said John Dolland, and only next of kin of Edward Taylor
the elder renouncing. (Nov. 1782).

Taylor, Humphrey, of Pennsylvania who died at New York.
Probate to mother Elizabeth Taylor, widow; wife Mary
Taylor having died in testator's lifetime. (Oct. 1716).

Taylor, John, of Savannah, Georgia. Probate to brother William
Taylor. (Oct. 1772).

Taylor, Joseph, of Potuxon, Maryland. Administration to son
Benjamin Taylor; brother Richard Taylor renouncing.
(Oct. 1709).

Tea, Robert, of St. Martin in Fields, Middlesex, who died in
Virginia. Administration to relict Thomazine Tea. (Feb.
1709).

Teagle, John, of Clerkenwell, Middlesex, who died in New
England. Administration to relict Deborah Teagle. (Dec.
1711).

Temple, Sir John, Consul-General to United States of America
who died at New York. Administration with will to Charles
Rivington Broughton, attorney for relict Lady Elizabeth
Temple in New York City. (Feb. 1799). Further grant May
1816.

Temple, Joseph, of King William Co., Virginia. Limited administration with will to son William Temple. (Jan. 1762).

Temple, William, of King William Co., Virginia. Limited
administration with will to John Snow of Bristol, merchant.
(May 1767).

Tenant, Rev. James, of Princess Ann Co., Virginia. Administration with will to Thomas Sandford, attorney for Elizabeth
Conner alias Tenant, wife of Louis Conner and relict of
Anthony Walke, and for Charles Sayer, in Virginia. (Dec.
1729).

Terron, Samuel, formerly of Christ Church, Middlesex, but late
of George Town, North America, bachelor. Administration
to sisters Esther Gabriel, widow, and Judith Cartwright,
widow. (Apr. 1790).

Terry, Zebedee, of Taunton, North America, Captain of late
Royal New England Regiment. Administration to David Thomas,
attorney for relict Hannah Terry at Taunton. (Aug. 1795).

Thelwall, David, Ensign of 34th Regiment who died at Fort
Chartres at Illinois, bachelor. Administration to brother
John Thelwall; mother Mary Thelwall renouncing. (Nov.
1767).

Thiring, Anthony, Lieutenant Paymaster of 21st Regiment of
Foot who died at Mobile, West Florida, bachelor. Administration to creditor Maria Elizabeth, wife of Richard
Spencer; mother Anna Thiring, widow, and brother and
sister Michael Thiring and Juliana, wife of John Frazer,
renouncing. (July 1767).

Thomas, Arthur, of New York City, bachelor. Administration
to Abraham Pastorius, attorney for father Arthur Thomas in
New York. (Feb. 1784).

Thomas, David, of Christ Church, London, who died in Carolina.
Administration to sister Susan, wife of John Staples.
(Jan. 1711).

Thomas, Edward, of H.M.S. *Rose* who died in South Carolina,
bachelor. Administration to creditor George Jacobs;
brother John Thomas renouncing. (May 1738).

Thomas, James, of Philadelphia who died at St. Margaret,
    Lothbury, London. Administration with will to John Askew,
    attorney for Samuel Preston in Philadelphia. (Feb. 1712).
Thomas, Nathaniel Ray, formerly of Marshfield but late of
    Windsor, Mass. Administration with will to Brook Watson,
    attorney for relict Sarah Thomas at Windsor. (Oct. 1789).
Thomlinson - see Tomlinson.
Thomson, Alexander, of Charles Town, South Carolina, who
    died in Jamaica. Administration to relict Mary Thomson.
    (Sept. 1783).
Thomson, Alexander, of New York, bachelor. Administration
    to brother and only next of kin John Thomson by his
    solemn affirmation. (Oct. 1798).
Thomson, Andrew, of Elizabeth City and Co., Virginia, bache-
    lor. Administration to brother Alexander Thomson MD.
    (Apr. 1724).
Thomson, David, of York Town, Virginia, bachelor. Probate to
    Joseph Davidson with similar powers reserved to Joseph
    Anderson. (Dec. 1749).
Thompson, Isaac, Lieutenant of 1st Connecticut Regiment of
    Foot who died at Havana. Administration with will to
    Phineas Lyman, attorney for brother Samuel Thompson at
    New London, Connecticut. (Jan. 1765).
Thomson, James, of H.M.S. *Rose* who died in Carolina, bachelor.
    Probate to William Livingston. (Dec. 1738).
Thompson, John, of Boston, New England, who died on private
    warship *Saltash*. Administration to William Ford, attorney
    for relict Mary Thompson in Boston. (Feb. 1751).
Thompson, Joseph, of Natchez, West Florida. Limited admini-
    stration with will to John Thompson. (Dec. 1781).
Thompson, Thomas, of Carolina, bachelor. Administration to
    brother Edward Thompson. (Nov. 1706).
Thomson, William, Lieutenant of 1st Connecticut Regiment of
    Foot who died at Havana, bachelor. Administration to
    Phineas Lyman, attorney for brother and next of kin Job
    Thomson at Windsor, Hartford Co., Connecticut. (Nov.1764).
Thorogood, Mary - see Wright.
Thorpe, Sarah, of Charles Town, South Carolina. Administra-
    tion to husband Robert Thorpe. (Nov. 1737).
Thorpe, Thomas, of Stepney, Middlesex, who died in Virginia.
    Probate to relict Jane Thorpe. (Jan. 1724).
Thunell, William, of Newport, Rhode Island, and of Lieutenant
    Colonel Christopher Hargill's Company, who died at Havana,
    bachelor. Administration by his solemn declaration to
    Joseph Sherwood, attorney for mother Elizabeth Thunell
    in Bristol Co., Rhode Island. (Dec. 1765).
Thurman, Susanna, of New York City, widow. Probate to John
    Thurman with similar powers reserved to Nicholas Roosevelt
    and Dirck Shuyler. (Jan. 1760).
Tilley, James, of Newport, Rhode Island, and of Lieutenant-
    Colonel Christopher Hargill's Company of Rhode Island
    Regiment of Foot, who died at Havana, bachelor. Admini-
    stration by his solemn declaration to Joseph Sherwood,
    attorney for brother and next of kin William Tilley in
    Newport. (Dec. 1765).
Tilson, John, of Boston, New England, chief mate of merchant
    ship *Blakeney*. Probate to Richard Comport. (Aug. 1757).

Timson, William, of Bruton, York Co., Virginia. Administration with will to Neil Buchanan, executor to brother John
Timson who died before executing; mother Anna Maria Timson
refusing to appear. (June 1736).

Todd, Humphrey, of H.M.S. *Deptford* who died on H.M.S. *Adventure* in Boston, New England. Probate to John Slater with
similar powers reserved to Elianor Slater. (Feb. 1714).

Todd, Samuel, of Londonderry, New Hampshire, commander of
schooner *Rachel*, who died in Jamaica, bachelor. Administration to sister Sarah Todd. (Aug. 1755).

Tolmie, Phebe, formerly of Chelsea, Middlesex, but late of
New York, widow. Administration with will to Samuel
Douglas, attorney for George Douglas the younger and
William Beekman the younger in New York City. (Aug. 1796).

Tomlinson, Edward, of Rotherhithe, Surrey, and of merchant
ship *Rappahannock Merchant*, who died in Virginia, widower.
Probate to daughter Ann Tomlinson. (July 1743).

Tomlinson, John Edge, late of New Bern, North Carolina, who
died at Cardiff, Glamorganshire. Probate to Mary Downs,
widow. (May 1793).

Thomlinson, Robert, of Boston, New England, bachelor. Probate
to brother Richard Thomlinson; no executor named. (Jan.
1741).

Tompkins, Russell, of Jamaica who died in Pennsylvania.
Probate to brother John Tompkins with similar powers
reserved to George Hind. (Jan. 1750).

Topham, Christopher, of South Carolina, bachelor. Administration to mother Anne Topham, widow. (Dec. 1737).

Toppen, David - see Tappen.

Topping, William, of merchant ship *Boughton* who died on merchant ship *New York Postilion* in New York. Probate to
relict Anne Topping. (Jan. 1718).

Towell, Cornelius, of Shadwell, Middlesex, who died on H.M.S.
Triton 's prize in New York. Administration to relict
Margaret Towell. (June 1710).

Towle, George, of merchant ship *Mary* who died at New York,
bachelor. Probate to Matthew Stamford. (Dec. 1757).

Towell, Joseph, of Colonel Phillips' Regiment who died at
Annapolis Royal, bachelor. Administration to principal
creditor Richard Roberts alias Hayward. (Aug. 1725).

Townsend alias Dudgeon, Patrick, of Boston, New England, who
died in West Indies. Probate to William Townsend with
similar powers reserved to Hannah, wife of James Green.
(July 1702).

Towsey, John, of Boston, New England, bachelor. Administration with will to Benjamin Smith, attorney for brother
Thomas Towsey. (Sept. 1709).

Tozer, Joseph, soldier of 40th Regiment who died at Philadelphia, bachelor. Administration to father Henry Tozer.
(Feb. 1781).

Traill, George, assistant surgeon of hospital for sick and
wounded soldiers in North America, bachelor. Administration to James Traill, attorney for father John Traill in
Edinburgh, Scotland. (Oct. 1759).

Traiell, James, of Shadwell, Middlesex, who died on H.M.S.
Shoreham in Virginia. Probate to relict Margaret Traiell.
(June 1718).

Travethan, Mary - see Wright.
Traweek, Robert, of Butomocke, Virginia, widower, who died
on H.M.S. *Plymouth*. Probate to Thomas Bignall, guardian
of son George Traweek. (Aug. 1730).
Treat, John, soldier of H.M. Corps of Rangers who died in Mass.
Administration to William Quarrill, attorney for relict
Abigail Treat at Boston. (Sept. 1765).
Trench, Alexander, of Grandville Co., South Carolina. Probate
to surviving executor Benjamin Whitacre. (Dec. 1733).
Trevillian, Francis, of Dartmouth, Devon, but late of New
York City, widower. Administration to half sister Hannah,
wife of Thomas Pering. (Oct. 1778).
Trohear, Joseph, formerly of Liverpool, Lancashire, but late
of New York, bachelor. Administration to sister and only
next of kin Hannah, wife of James Scott. (Oct. 1781).
Tromball alias Trombel, Robert, of Boston, New England, who
died on ship *Staple Grove*, bachelor. Administration to
principal creditor George Darke. (Mar. 1716).
Try, Ralph, of York Town, Virginia. Probate to relict Frances
Try. (May 1701).
Tubervill, Fortescue, of Middle Temple, London, who died in
Carolina, widower. Administration to Elizabeth Tubervill,
widow, grandmother and guardian of daughter Bridget Tubervill. (Feb. 1711).
Tucker, Elizabeth, of Trenton, New Jersey. Limited administra-
tion with will to James Allan and Thomas Dickason, attor-
nies for David White in Jamaica and Thomas Murgatroyd in
Philadelphia. (Mar. 1790).
Tunstall, formerly Dickins, Grace, of St. Dunstan in East and
after of St. Botolph Aldgate, London, but late of Bladen-
burgh, North America. Administration to James Ayres,
attorney for husband Henry Tunstall at Montgomery Co.,
North America. (Oct. 1788).
Turbill, John, of Middle Temple, London, who died in Carolina.
Administration to brother George Turbill; mother Hannah
Turbill renouncing. (Jan. 1711).
Turner, Barnard, of H.M.S. *Northumberland* who died at Louis-
burgh, North America, bachelor. Probate to Elizabeth Green-
slade, spinster. (Oct. 1758).
Turner, John, of Whitechapel, Middlesex, who died in Maryland,
bachelor. Probate to brother Henry Turner. (Nov. 1724).
Revoked and granted to Thomas Eycott, father and guardian
of executrix Rachel Eycott; testator now described as late
of Badginton, Gloucestershire. (Dec. 1724).
Turner, John, of H.M.S. *Quebec* who died in New York Hospital.
Probate to Elizabeth, wife of John Akurst, formerly Eliza-
beth Burges. (Dec. 1783).
Tute, John, of James River, Virginia. Probate to Thomas Parr
with similar powers reserved to John Comer. (July 1738).
Tyler, Henry, of H.M.S. *Bedford* who died at Staten Island.
Probate to brother William Tyler. (Mar. 1781).
Tynte, Edward, Governor of Carolina. Probate to Frances
Killner. (Oct. 1710).

Uriell, George, of Maryland, master of ship *William*. Probate
to sister Rebecka Iredell, widow. (Dec. 1738).
Usher, Patient, of Philadelphia, widow. Administration to
Elias Bland, attorney for niece and next of kin Margaret,
wife of John Kearsley, formerly Margaret Brand, in Pennsylvania, by solemn affirmation. (Apr. 1749).
Utting, Ashby, of South Carolina, commander of H.M.S. *Ald-
borough*. Probate to relict Amy Utting with similar powers
reserved to Thomas Michells. (Jan. 1747).

Vaber, Hans, of Colonel Holt's Regiment, bachelor. Admini-
stration by decree to principal creditor Robert Hood.
"Pauper." (July 1722).
Van Alstine, Lambert, of Wioming, Pennsylvania, widower.
Administration to John Inglis, attorney for son Isaac Van
Alstine at Fredericksburgh, North America. (Oct. 1790).
Van Camp, Peter, of Half Moon, Albany, North America, widower.
Administration to John Inglis, attorney for son Jacob Van
Camp at Matilda, North America. (Oct. 1790).
Vandrel alias Hookamer, Jacob, of New England who died at
Dover, Kent, bachelor. Administration to cousin and next
of kin Anne Vandrel. (Aug. 1709).
Vandyne, Douw, formerly of Long Island but late of Queen's Co.,
North America, widower. Administration to Brook Watson,
attorney for son Cornelis Vandyne in Queen's Co. (Feb.1789).
Van Horne, Cornelius Garret, of New York City. Administra-
tion with will to John Exley, attorney for son Augustus Van
Horne in New York; executors relict Judith and son Garret
Van Horne having died and Simon Johnson and Peter Jay
renouncing. (Mar. 1770).
Van Swieten, Ouzeel, of New York, bachelor. Limited admini-
stration with will to Jacob *(sic)* Minor Cruger, relict and
executrix of Valentine Cruger. (Jan. 1703). Revoked and
granted to sister Beatrice Ouzeel. (July 1705).
Vans, Samuel, of Bermondsey, Surrey, who died in Boston, New
England, bachelor. Administration to father John Vans.
(Feb. 1709).
Van Veghten alias Van Veightin, John, Major of New York Pro-
vincials who died at Havana. Administration with will to
Thomas Harris, attorney for relict Ann alias Annatje Veghten
in New York. (Apr. 1764).
Vaughan, Martha, (formerly Underwood), of South Carolina,
widow. Administration to brother William Underwood. (May
1754).
Vavasser, Richard, of Philadelphia, bachelor. Administration
to cousin german Lewis John Cole. (July 1778).
Venables, Thomas, of Northern Liberties of Philadelphia.
Administration with will to Daniel Moore, attorney for
relict Rebecca Venables in Philadelphia. (Aug. 1752).
Vernon, Christopher, of Maryland who died at St. Dunstan in
West, London. Probate to Anne Vernon. (Dec. 1724).
Vernon, Thomas, of Savannah, Georgia, bachelor. Administra-
tion to brother and next of kin Henry Vernon. (Mar. & Apr.
1784).

Vion, Peter, of Stratford, New England, bachelor. Admini-
stration to Richard Shuttleworth, guardian of sisters and
only next of kin Mary Ann, Sibell and Christian Vion.
(Feb. 1755).
Von Pfister, Francis Joseph, of Hosack, North America.
Probate to relict Ann, wife of Thomas Bennett. (Oct. 1786).
Voss, John, master of merchant ship *John and Mary* who died
in Boston, New England, widower. Administration to
Christopher Ford, grandfather and guardian of children
Susanna and Ford Voss. (June 1740). Revoked on death of
Christopher Ford and granted to his relict Hannah Ford.
(Apr. 1741).

Waghorne, Ann, of New York who died at sea, widow. Admini-
stration to William Nourse, attorney for brother Richard
Brough in Nottingham. (Feb. 1751).
Walbank, Edward, of Philadelphia. Probate to relict Agnes
Walbank by her solemn declaration. (June 1735).
Waldo alias Walder, Daniel, of Bombay Island, America.
Probate to sister Rebecca Hayes with similar powers
reserved to Elizabeth Brock. (Oct. 1713).
Waldo, Francis (Francois), formerly of Falmouth, Mass., but
late of Brompton, Middlesex. Limited administration with
will to surviving attornies George Erving and John Lane
for executors Samuel and Isaac Winslow in Boston. (July
1786).
Walker, Chapman, of merchant ship *Burrell* who died in Virginia,
bachelor. Administration to father William Walker. (Jan.
1737).
Walker, Flower, of Maryland. Probate to Michael Walker with
similar powers reserved to Thomas Walker and George Dunn.
(Feb. 1709).
Walker, George, of H.M.S. *Pearle* who died in Virginia. Probate
to George Chapman with similar powers reserved to his wife
Hannah Chapman. (Aug. 1719).
Walker, John, of Hanover Co., Virginia, bachelor. Administra-
tion to brother James Walker. (May 1772).
Walker, Robert, of H.M.S. *Charon* who died in Virginia. Probate
to Paul Bartrum. (May 1782).
Walker, Samuel, of merchant ship *Asia*, bachelor. Administration to Joseph Hayward, attorney for brother and next of
kin George Walker of Portsmouth, New England; brother
Nicholas Walker renouncing. (Feb. 1706).
Walker, Thomas, of Boston, Mass., widower. Administration to
daughter Ann Walker. (Dec. 1784).
Wall, John, of H.M.S. *Trident* who died at New York. Probate
to mother Ann Wall, widow. (Jan. 1779).
Wall, John, formerly of St. Michael Royal, London, but late
of Charles Town, South Carolina, bachelor. Administration
to sister Rebecca, wife of Benjamin Blakesley. (June 1786).
Wall, Joseph, of East Caln, Chester Co., Pennsylvania.
Administration by decree to daughter Hannah, wife of
Jonathan Parsons. (Mar. 1752).

Wall, Samuel, formerly of Wetnall, Nottinghamshire, after of Chesterfield, Derbyshire, but late of North America. Probate to Samuel Mettam. (June 1799). Further grant April 1865.

Wallace, formerly Nisbit, Elizabeth, of South Carolina. Administration to husband Thomas Wallace. (Apr. 1762).

Wallace, Hugh, formerly of New York City but late of Waterford, Ireland. Probate to brother Alexander Wallace with similar powers reserved to relict Sarah Wallace, brothers William and Magill Wallace, and to Robert Paul. (June 1788).

Wallace, James, of Ponds Ponds, Georgia, bachelor. Administration to Ralph Gray, husband and administrator to niece and only next of kin Margaret Gray, formerly Wallace, deceased. (Aug. 1798).

Wallace, William Oxford, Lieutenant of Royal Artillery who died in South Carolina, bachelor. Administration to mother Betty Wallace. (Jan. 1790).

Wallis, Josiah, of H.M.S. *Brune* who died in New York Hospital. Administration with will to William Marsh and Henry Creed, attornies for George Meuris at sea. (Oct. 1779).

Walsh, Richard, of Virginia. Administration to relict Mary Walsh. (Apr. 1742).

Walsham, John, of St. Botolph Aldersgate, London, Lieutenant of Colonel Dunbar's Regiment of Foot who died at Albany, bachelor. Administration to brother Robert Walsham; mother Elizabeth Walsham renouncing. (Dec. 1756).

Walters, David, of hospital ship *Smirna Factor*, and late of Charleston. Probate to Thomas Pyke. (Oct. 1703).

Walthoe, Nathaniel, of Williamsburg, Virginia. Probate to Thomas Waller with similar powers reserved to Benjamin Waller. (June 1772).

Walton, Mary, wife of Jacob Walton of New York. Administration to son Henry Walton; said husband having died. (June 1793).

Wansella alias Wansall, Richard, of H.M. Detachment of Foot Guards in South Carolina, bachelor. Administration to brother John Wansall. (Feb. 1783).

Waple, Thomas, of Maryland, bachelor. Probate to Henry Waple and Jonathan Forward. (Apr. 1715).

Ward, Anthony, of Colonel Holt's Regiment, bachelor. Administration by decree to principal creditor Elizabeth Jennings, widow. "Pauper." (July 1722).

Ward, Henry, commissary and paymaster of English Artillery in Pennsylvania who died at Fort Bedford, bachelor. Administration to brother and next of kin Ralph Ward. (June 1771).

Ward, Pearson, of Sunderland, Durham, who died at George Town, South Carolina. Probate to relict Dorothy Ward. (Nov. 1786).

Ward, Samuel Chandler, formerly of Sise Lane, London, but late of New York. Probate to sisters Mary Chandler Ward and Elizabeth Ward. (Dec. 1798).

Warden, William, formerly of Charles Town, South Carolina, but late of Whitechapel, Middlesex. Probate to William Leagoe with similar powers reserved to Stephen Coleman. (Nov. 1746).

Wardrop, John, formerly of Calvert Co., Maryland, but late
    of All Hallows Staining, London. Probate to James Russell.
    (July 1767).
Waring, late Lloyd, Sarah, of St. James, Goose Creek, South
    Carolina, widow. Administration with will to Sarah
    Nickleson, widow, attorney for Benjamin Waring, Elizabeth
    Akin, Peter Taylor, George Austin and Robert Hume in South
    Carolina. (July 1760).
Warner, Nathaniel, late of Boston, New England, who died in
    Stepney, Middlesex. Probate to William Rogers and William
    Rogers. (Oct. 1746).
Warren, John, Captain of Independent Company who died at
    Albany, New York. Administration to relict Elizabeth
    Warren. (June 1722).
Washington, Laurence, of Washington, Westmoreland Co., Vir-
    ginia. Probate to Mildred Gale alias Washington, wife of
    George Gale. (Dec. 1700).
Wasson, William, of Dublin, Ireland, who died in Virginia.
    Administration to principal creditor James MacCartney;
    relict cited but not appearing. (Apr. 1733).
Waters, Richard, of Somerset Co., Maryland. Administration
    with will to Jonathan Scarth, attorney for relict Eliza-
    beth Waters and William Waters in Maryland. (Nov. 1722).
Waters, Richard, of Maryland, widower. Administration to
    Anthony Bacon, attorney for mother Elizabeth Waters, widow,
    in Maryland. (Mar. 1748).
Waters, William, of Northampton Co., Virginia. Probate to
    William Waters. (Oct. 1722). Revoked on death of relict
    ----- Burton, formerly Waters, and administration granted
    to Anthony Bacon, attorney for son William Waters in
    Williamsburg, Virginia. (Oct. 1757). Revoked on death
    of son William Waters and granted to Anthony Bacon, attor-
    ney for grandson William Waters at Williamsburg; daughter
    Margaret Kincade, formerly Preeson, only next of kin,
    having died. (Oct. 1757).
Watkins, Charles, of South Carolina, who died on merchant ship
    Dolphin at sea, bachelor. Probate to brother William
    Watkins. (Oct. 1742).
Watson, Francis, of merchant ship *Little Betsy* who died at
    York River, Virginia, bachelor. Administration to Mary
    Vaughan alias Watson, wife of John Vaughan. (June 1713).
Watson, Henry, of St. George's parish, Prince George Co.,
    Maryland. Probate to son John Watson; executors relict
    Lucy Watson and Peter Wright having died, Peter Sykes
    renouncing and John Belt the younger cited but not
    appearing. (Nov. 1767).
Watson, John, of Maryland, bachelor. Probate to Christopher
    Marshall. (June 1746).
Watson, John, of News River, North Carolina, bachelor. Admi-
    nistration to father Thomas Watson. (May 1759).
Watson, John, of Rhode Island but late of Fishlake, Yorkshire.
    Administration to relict Ruth, now wife of George Paul.
    (Apr. 1789).
Watson, John, Lieutenant of 60th or Royal American Regiment.
    Probate to Ann Weches, spinster. (May 1789).
Watson, Nicholas, formerly of Mortlake, Surrey, but late of
    South Carolina, bachelor. Administration to sister and
    next of kin Sarah Hill, widow. (Mar. 1793).

Watson, William, of Baton Rouge, West Florida. Probate to
David Ross and William Watson with similar powers reserved
to brother Adam Watson. (July 1782).
Watts, Elizabeth, of Maryland, spinster. Administration to
brother Charles Watts. (Feb. 1708).
Watts, John, of Workington, Cumberland, who died in Maryland.
Probate to brother Richard Watts with similar powers
reserved to Joseph Milnor. (Oct. 1736).
Watts, John, formerly of New York but late of St. James,
Westminster, Middlesex. Limited probate to Edmund Antro-
bus and John Antrobus with similar powers reserved to
Thomas Coutts. (Sept. 1789).
Way, Richard, of New England who died on H.M.S. *Namure*.
Probate to John Nightingal alias Nightingirl. (Mar. 1736).
Weatherhead, William, of merchant ship *Boston* who died in New
England, bachelor. Administration to Alice, wife of James
Rogerson at sea, guardian of brother and next of kin Isaac
Weatherhead. (May 1710).
Weaver, Job, of West Greenwich, Kent Co., Rhode Island, and
of Lieutenant-Colonel Christopher Hargill's Company of
Rhode Island Regiment of Foot, who died at Havana, bachelor.
Administration by his solemn declaration to Joseph Sher-
wood, attorney for father Harris Weaver at West Greenwich.
(Dec. 1765).
Weaver, John - see Copson.
Weaver, John, of Bristol who died in Maryland. Administration
with will to sister Mary Weaver; executor John Pikswort
renouncing. (Nov. 1705).
Webb, Giles, of Henrico Co., Virginia. Administration with
will to brother Thomas Webb. (May 1715).
Webb, James, of Fort St. Augustine who died in Georgia,
Deputy Commissary of Musters to H.M. Forces. Administra-
tion to relict Mary Webb. (Nov. 1780).
Webb, Richard, of St. Anne's, North Jamaica, who died at Boston,
New England, bachelor. Administration to brother Thomas
Webb. (Jan. 1731).
Webb, William, of Bristol who died in Maryland. Probate to
relict Sarah Webb. (Oct. 1711).
Webb, William, of South Carolina. Administration to principal
creditor John Owen; relict Sarah Webb having died and
uncle John Webb, guardian of children John and William Webb,
renouncing. (Sept. 1751). Revoked on death of John Owen
and granted to his executor John Strettell by his solemn
affirmation. (Sept. 1759).
Webster, David, gunner's mate of H.M.S. *Squirrel* who died in
Virginia, bachelor. Administration to John Beatson,
attorney for sister and next of kin Margaret Webster at
Pinkie near Musselburgh, Midlothian, Scotland. (Feb. 1767).
Webster, James, of Virginia, bachelor. Administration to
father John Webster. (Nov. 1766).
Weems, formerly Morris, Rachael, of Anne Arundell Co., Maryland. Administration to William Murdock and Horatio
Clagett, attornies for husband William Weems in Anne
Arundell Co. (June 1797).
Wier, Daniel, Commissary-General of the Army in America who
died at New York City. Probate to Jacob Wilkinson with
similar powers reserved to Henry White, Gregory Townsend
and Thomas Aston Coffin. (Feb. 1782).

Welch, Francis, formerly of New York City but late of Knights-
bridge, Westminster, Middlesex. Probate to Richard Neave.
(Mar. 1775).

Wells, Francis, of Bermondsey, Surrey, who died in Virginia.
Administration to relict Mildred Wells. (Nov. 1709).

Westland, John, of H.M.S. *Portsmouth*, bachelor. Administration to John Whiting, attorney for father Nathaniel Westland in West Jersey; previous grant of May 1707 to
principal creditor Thomas Jordan revoked. (Nov. 1710).

Westley, Ambrose, soldier of 65th Regiment of Foot who died
at Charles Town, South Carolina, bachelor. Probate to
mother Mary Westley, widow; no executor named. (Oct.1763).

Wethered, Henry, of Boston, New England, widower. Administration to aunt and next of kin Sophia Lewin, guardian of
children Sarah and Henry Wethered. (Apr. 1763).

Wharton, Richard, of Williamsburgh, Virginia. Probate to
brothers Thomas and John Wharton; relict Ruth Wharton
renouncing. (Apr. 1713).

Wheeler, Joseph, of North Carolina, bachelor. Administration
to sister and only next of kin Frances Norris, widow.
(Sept. 1770). Revoked on death of Frances Norris and
granted to her daughter and executrix Frances Norris.
(Mar. 1778).

Whitaker, Robert, marine of H.M.S. *Chatham* who died at New
York. Administration to relict Ann Whitaker. (Nov. 1783).

Whitborn, John, of West Teighnmouth, Devon, after mate of
merchant ship *Brislington*, but late of South Carolina,
bachelor. Administration with will to brother Peter Whitborn; no executor named. (Apr. 1760).

White, Benjamin, of Boston, New England, master in H.M. Navy
on half pay. Probate to Henry Cort. (Mar. 1774).

White, Elizabeth, wife of Anthony White of New Brunswick,
New Jersey. Probate to John Watts. (Dec. 1785).

White, James, private of 64th Regiment who died at Lancaster,
North America, bachelor. Administration to father Robert
White. (June 1785).

White, John, of Boston, Mass. Administration with will to
Thomas Latham, attorney for Isaac Rand, doctor of physic
at Boston, with similar powers reserved to Greene Amory.
(Jan. 1796).

White, Mary, of New York City, spinster. Administration to
sister Ann Combs, widow; mother Mary White having died
before administering. (Dec, 1790).

White, Robert, of New York, bachelor. Probate to brother
Rev. Nathaniel White. (Nov. 1774).

White, Thomas, of Philadelphia. Administration with will to
Richard Peters, attorney for relict Esther White, son
William White and for Robert Morris in Philadelphia.
(Mar. 1786).

White, Thomas, of Newington, Surrey, but late of Georgia.
Probate to relict Philipi White with similar powers reserved to James Benson. (Feb. 1798).

White, William, of St. Katherine by Tower, London, who died
on merchant ship *Hope* in New England. Administration to
relict Anne White. (Aug. 1722).

White, William, of Charles Town, South Carolina. Probate to
William Smith with similar powers reserved to Robert Shand
and Kenneth Rose. (Jan. 1795).

Whitehall, Robert, of Currituck Co., North Carolina. Administration to William Broden, attorney for son Robert Whitehall in North Carolina; relict Ann Whitehall renouncing. (Mar. 1769).

Whitehead, Rev. John, of South Carolina. Administration to relict Frances Whitehead. (Aug. 1717).

Whitehorne, George, of Boston, New England. Probate to Benjamin Thorp; executor James Warren having died. (Aug. 1722).

Whitehurst alias Whitehust, Thomas, of Brunswick, North Carolina, bachelor. Probate to sister Ann Whitehurst with similar powers reserved to Jacob Lobb. (Oct. 1766).

Whiteman, John, formerly of Ditchling, Sussex, but late of Troy near Albany, North America. Probate to Peter Rowland. (Jan. 1798).

Whitefield, Rev. George, of St. Luke, Middlesex, who died in Georgia, widower. Limited administration with will to Charles Hardy, Daniel West and Robert Keen. (Feb. 1771).

Whitfield, Thomas, of transport ship *Hopewell* who died at York River. Probate to Barbara, wife of James Bonnes, with similar powers reserved to said James. (Sept. 1779).

Whitford, John, of West Greenwich, Kent Co., Rhode Island, and of Lieutenant-Colonel Christopher Hargill's Company of Rhode Island Regiment of Foot, who died at Havana, bachelor. Administration by his solemn declaration to Joseph Sherwood, attorney for uncle and next of kin Edward Casey in Kent Co. (Dec. 1765).

Whitley, Roger, of General Nicholson's Independent Company who died at Fort King George, South Carolina. Probate to William Livingston, attorney for Alexander Nisbett in Edinburgh, Scotland; no executor named. (Dec. 1729).

Whitrowe, Benjamin, of South Carolina, bachelor. Administration to niece Rebecca Whitrowe. (Aug. 1726).

Wickham, Moses, of Southampton, master of H.M.S. *Soulings* who died in New York. Probate to Thomas Orr. (Jan. 1715).

Wier - see Weir.

Wigington, Henry, of South Carolina who died at St. Martin in Fields, Middlesex. Limited administration with will to Robert Horne. (Dec. 1722).

Wigram, William, seaman of H.M.S. *Thames* who died in New York Hospital. Administration to sister and next of kin Betty, wife of William Atherley. (Sept. 1781).

Wilberfoss, William, of Charles Town, South Carolina, bachelor. Administration to father Robert Wilberfoss. (Mar. 1753).

Wileman, Henry, of St. Mary Aldermary, London, widower. Administration to Charles Savage, attorney for children Elizabeth, wife of Henry Gibbs, Magdalen Wileman in Lisbon, Portugal, and Henry Wileman in New York. (Aug. 1714).

Wilkinson, Joseph, of Calvert Co., Maryland. Administration with will to William Tarver, attorney for creditor James Fletcher in South Carolina. (July 1736).

Wilkinson, Wilfred, Lieutenant of 3rd Regiment who died at Charles Town, South Carolina, bachelor. Administration to brother Richard Wilkinson; mother Philadelphia Wilkinson renouncing. (July 1784).

Willabee - see Willoughby.

Willard, Abijah, formerly of Lancaster, Mass., but late of
St. John's, New Brunswick. Administration to George
Erving, son and executor of creditor John Erving; relict
Mary Willard and children Samuel, Elizabeth and Anna
Willard cited but not appearing. (Feb. 1790).

Willett, John, formerly of St. Christopher's, after of New
York, but late of St. Croix, West Indies. Probate to
relict Frances Willett. (Jan. 1767).

Willett, Thomas, of New York City. Probate to son John
Willett with similar powers reserved to relict Elizabeth
Willett, Christopher Billop, Thomas Miller and Joseph
Royal. (Oct. 1768).

Williams, Arthur, Major of 52nd Regiment of Foot who died at
Boston, bachelor. Limited administration with will to
brother Rev. William Williams, sole executor to father
William Williams deceased. (Aug. 1776).

Williams, Elizabeth, of Piscataway, New England, widow.
Administration to cousin and next of kin John Atkins.
(Apr. 1716).

Williams, Henry, of Shepton Mallet, Somerset, but late of
Bedford Township, Nassau Island, New York. Probate to
mephew John Williams. (Mar. 1784).

Williams, John, of Deal, Kent, who died on merchant ship
Robert and John in Virginia. Administration to principal
creditor John Musgrave; relict Margaret Williams renouncing. (Jan. 1714).

Williams, John, of H.M.S. *Nightingale* and late of privateer
Hornet of New York who died in hospital in France, bachelor. Probate to mother Ann Williams, widow. (Oct. 1758).

Williams, Jonathan, of West Chester City, widower. Administration to nephews and next of kin Robert and Joseph
Griffiths. (Mar. 1783).

Williams, Richard, of Pensacola, West Florida, sergeant of
35th Regiment of Foot who died on H.M.S. *Integrity*.
Administration to relict Margaret Hannah Williams. (Dec.
1765).

Williams, Thomas, of Bermondsey, Surrey, who died on H.M.S.
Scarborough in Carolina. Administration to relict Jane
Williams pending production of will. (Apr. 1727).

Williams, Thomas Charles, of New York City. Probate to
relict Sarah Williams and brother John Williams with similar powers reserved to Samuel Shomacken. (Oct. 1784).

Williams, William, formerly of Wood Street, London, but late
of New Orleans in Florida and City of Bath. Probate to
relict Mary Williams, John Stephenson and John Miller.
(Aug. 1790). Revoked and granted to Stephenson and Miller.
(Nov. 1792).

Williamson, Thomas, seaman of H.M.S. *Carisfoot* who died in
Charles Town Hospital. Probate to sister Hannah, wife of
John Wilson, with similar powers reserved to sister Ann
Williamson and Martha Palfrey, spinster. (Dec. 1782).

Williamson, William, of Charles Town, South Carolina. Probate
to Robert Halcrow. (Dec. 1770).

Willing, Charles, of Philadelphia. Probate to relict Ann
Willing and to Thomas Willing. (Jan. 1756).

Willobey alias Willoughby, Thomas, of merchant ship *Prince
Amelia* who died on Potuxon River, America, bachelor.
Administration to principal creditor John Norwood. (Feb.
1721).

Willabee, William, of merchant ship *Williamsburg* who died in
Virginia, bachelor. Administration to sister Elizabeth
Willabee. (Aug. 1723).
Wills, George, of New England who died on H.M.S. *Dragon*.
Administration to Alexander Wath, attorney for relict
Mary Wills in New England. (Jan. 1742).
Wills, John, of H.M.S. *Happy* who died in South Carolina,
bachelor. Administration to William Vaughan, attorney
for creditor James Fletcher in South Carolina. (June 1734).
Wilmot, Henry, of New York, bachelor. Administration to half
brother George Wilmot; mother Mary Wilmot, widow, renoun-
cing. (Jan. 1777).
Wilmshurst, John, of Charles Town, South Carolina. Probate
to daughter Elizabeth, wife of John Dugleby. (July 1774).
Wilson, Alexander, formerly of New York City but late of
Bombay, who died in service of East India Company Batallion.
Administration to sister and only next of kin Elizabeth,
wife of James Boggs, at Stone Araben, New York. (Apr.
1788).
Wilson, John, of merchant ship *Olive Branch* who died in Vir-
ginia. Administration to sister Elizabeth Hilgrove, widow.
(Jan. 1700).
Wilson, John, of South Carolina. Limited administration with
will to Thomas Irving, attorney for daughter Catherine
Martha Wilson. (Mar. 1792).
Wilson, Thomas, of H.M.S. *Raisonable* who died at Rhode Island.
Probate to Samuel Farguson. (Jan. 1781).
Winfield, Thomas, of Virginia. Probate to John Orton.
(Mar. 1722).
Winne - see Wynne.
Winslow, Hannah, of Rhode Island, spinster. Administration
to sister and next of kin Elizabeth, wife of John Winslow.
(Mar. 1797).
Winslow, Isaac, of New York City. Probate to nephew Isaac
Winslow with similar powers reserved to nephews Jonathan
Clarke and Isaac Winslow Clarke. (Oct. 1780).
Winslow, John, of Hingham, Mass., reduced Captain of Colonel
William Shirley's 1st Regiment of Foot. Administration
to Elisha Hutchinson, attorney for only children Pelham
and Isaac Winslow now in Mass. or Nova Scotia; relict
renouncing. (June 1776).
Winslow, Joshua, of Boston, Mass. Administration to relict
Hannah Winslow. (Mar. 1781).
Winslow, Mary, of Boston, Mass., widow. Administration to
Jonathan Simpson, attorney for brother Jonathan Simpson
the younger at Cambridge, North America. (Sept. 1787).
Winter, John, of Charles Town, South Carolina, Lieutenant on
half pay of H.M. Navy, bachelor. Administration to father
Nathaniel Winter. (June 1781).
Wise, John, of New York, formerly of H.M.S. *Kingston* who died
on H.M.S. *Elizabeth*. Administration to William Bryant,
attorney for relict Alice Wise in New York. (Feb. 1749).
Withall, Samuel, of H.M.S. *Spyboate* who died in Virginia.
Administration to relict Jane Withall. (July 1701).
Withers, Hazard, of Oswego Fort, America. Administration to
sister and next of kin Sarah Williams, widow. (Nov. 1763).
Wood, James, of Woolwich, Kent, who died in Maryland, bachelor.
Probate to mother Mary, wife of Thomas Harrell. (Apr. 1750).

Wood, Thomas, of Brook Thorpe, Gloucestershire, who died in
Maryland. Administration to brother and next of kin
Rowland Wood. "Pauper." (Jan. 1712).

Wood, William, of H.M.S. *Nottingham*, widower. Administration
to daughter Hannah, wife of John Bemond, in Virginia.
(Jan. 1729).

Wood, William, of merchant ship *Prince George* who died at
James Town, Virginia, bachelor. Administration to aunt
and next of kin Mary Jemmison, widow. (Apr. 1770).

Woodall, William, of H.M.S. *Beaver* who died at Boston, New
England, bachelor. Administration to sister and next of
kin Olive, wife of James Parker. (Feb. 1772).

Woodbridge, Ruth, of Barbados who died at Boston, New England,
widow. Administration with will to Edward Clark Parish,
attorney for Nathaniel Haggatt in Barbados. (Feb. 1750).

Woodhead, Matthew, of Wapping, Middlesex, who died in New
England, bachelor. Administration to sister and next of
kin Anne, wife of John Hopkins. (Jan. 1720).

Woodrow, Joseph, of New York, bachelor. Administration to
maternal aunt Sarah Taunton, widow. (Jan. 1706).

Woods, Joseph, formerly of Philadelphia but late of Wash-
brook, Suffolk. Probate to father John Woods with similar
powers reserved to brother John Woods. (July 1793).

Woodside, James, of Pemaquid, Mass., late Lieutenant of
Colonel Gooch's Regiment of Foot in West Indies. Administration to Samuel Wragg, attorney for relict Jane Woodside in Boston. (Apr. 1746).

Woodville, John, of Dominica who died in Philadelphia.
Probate to William Thornton, Henry Poole and Benjamin
Eyre. (Apr. 1776).

Woodward, Samuel, of Cape Fear, Carolina. Administration to
Christopher Nicholson, attorney for nephew Benjamin Woodward in Kells, Co. Meath, Ireland. (Apr. 1751).

Wooldridge, Maria Henrietta, of St. Augustine, East Florida.
Administration to Arthur Gordon, attorney for husband
Thomas Wooldridge at St. Augustine. (Apr. 1770).

Wormington, John, formerly of Philadelphia but late of New
York City. Administration to Benjamin John Johnson,
attorney for relict Anna Wormington in New York. (Jan.
1793).

Worthington, John, of Ann Arundel Co., Maryland. Administration with will to James Russell, attorney for sons John
and Charles Worthington in Maryland. (June 1769).

Worthington, William, of Ann Arundel Co., Maryland. Limited
administration with will to Silvanus Grove of London,
merchant, attorney for John Davis. (Sept. 1771).

Wortley, John, of Portsmouth, New England, bachelor. Administration to nephew by a sister and next of kin Peter
Birkhead. (Dec. 1712).

Wragg, Samuel, formerly of Holborn, Middlesex, and after of
Charles Town, South Carolina. Probate to son William
Wragg and Robert Henshaw. (Jan. 1750). Limited admini-
stration with will and codicil as above. (Jan. 1751).
Revoked and limited administration of will and codicial
granted to daughters Mary and Judith Wragg. (July 1754).

Wragg, William, of Charles Town, South Carolina, who died
a passenger on merchant ship *Caesar*. Limited administration with will to George Curling of Whitechapel, Middlesex, attorney for relict Henrietta Wragg in Charles Town.
(Apr. 1779). Further grant September 1807.

127

Wraxall, Peter, of New York City, Captain of Independent
    Company of New York. Probate to relict Elizabeth Wraxall.
    (Feb. 1762).
Wright, Benjamin, of merchant ship *Levite* who died in Virgi-
    nia. Administration with will to John Hunt, attorney
    for Robert Jones at sea; no executor named. (Jan. 1707).
Wright, John, of Maryland, bachelor. Administration to
    brother Thomas Wright. (Jan. 1703).
Wright, John, of South Carolina, bachelor. Administration
    to cousin german and next of kin William Miles. (July 1791).
    Further grant July 1828.
Wright, Mary, wife of Stephen Wright, formerly Mary Thorogood,
    formerly Mary Travethan, of Virginia. Administration to
    Daniel Highmore, attorney for son Stephen Wright in Vir-
    ginia. (Aug. 1754).
Wright, Moses, of Boston, New England, who died on H.M.S.
    Victory. Probate to sister Ann, wife of ----- Dougless
    alias Duglass. (Nov. 1744).
Wright, William, of Annapolis Royal. Probate to relict
    Sarah Wright. (Feb. 1719).
Wrisburg, Daniel, Lieutenant on half pay of 47th Regiment
    of Foot who died in New Jersey, bachelor. Administration
    to sister Johanna Lucia Henriette, wife of Michael Christop
    Hinrickson. (July 1778).
Wyatt, Thomas, of Boreham, Essex, who died in Maryland.
    Probate to brother Samuel Wyatt by his solemn affirmation.
    (Nov. 1756).
Winne, John, of merchant ship *Nancy* who died in Virginia,
    bachelor. Administration to brother William Winne; mother
    Rebecca, wife of James Ryall, renouncing. (Oct. 1753).

Yallowley, Joshua, formerly of East Florida but late of New
    Providence, Bahamas, bachelor. Administration to John
    Fairlamb, attorney for mother Elizabeth Yallowley at
    Hexham, Northumberland. (Mar. 1787).
Yeaveley, Thomas, surgeon of 70th Regiment of Foot who died
    in New York, bachelor. Administration to sister Susanna
    Yeaveley. (Apr. 1767).
Yesline, Jonas, of H.M.S. *Seaford*, bachelor. Administration
    with will to Margaret, wife of John Cudlipp on H.M.S.
    Blandford in South Carolina, attorney for Mary Scott,
    widow. (Oct. 1723).
Yonge, Philip, formerly Surveyor-General of Georgia who died
    in Savannah. Administration to William Yonge, attorney
    for relict Christian, now wife of James Fleeming at
    Wilmington, North Carolina. (Sept. 1793).
Yorston, David, formerly of Well Alley, St. George, Middlesex,
    but late of Charleston, North America. Administration to
    niece and only next of kin Christiana Enson. (May 1791).
Youle, George, carpenter of merchant ship *Concord* in trans-
    port service at New York. Administration to sister Kathe-
    rine Youle. (Mar. 1778).
Young, Edward, of merchant ship *Daniel and Anna* who died in
    Maryland, bachelor. Probate to William Speven with similar
    powers reserved to his wife Lydia Speven. (July 1734).

Young, Nathaniel, of Carolina. Probate to Mary Dearing, widow. (Apr. 1706).
Young, Samuel, of merchant ship *Quare* who died in Virginia. Administration to relict Jane Young. (Aug. 1718).
Young, Stephen, of merchant ship *Dartmouth*, bachelor. Administration to Priscilla, wife and attorney of brother and next of kin Richard Young in New England. "Pauper." (Dec. 1714).
Young, Theophilus, Lieutenant of 45th Regiment of Foot who died at Louisburgh. Probate to father Thomas Young. (Dec. 1758).
Younge, William, of Kinovessing, Pennsylvania. Probate to relict Martha Younge with similar powers reserved to John Leech and Jacob Holman. (Nov. 1787).

Index of Executors, Administrators, Attorneys, etc.

Bolton, Thomas 51
Bond, James 78
    Phineas 64
    Susan 78
Bonham, Samuel 82
Bonnes, Barbara 124
    James 124
Bonnetheare, Peter 75
Booker, Edward 113
    Richard 113
Borland, Margaret 107
    William 107
Bosom, Thomas 82
Bottomley, Benjamin 76
    Betty 76
Boucher, Paul 95
Boughton, John 36
Boush, Mary 101
    Maximilian 101
Bowdoin, William 93,94
Boyd, Robert 112
    William 65
Boys, Richard 57
Brace, John 38
Bracebridge, Jonathan
    105
Bradford, John 21,56
Bradly, Margaret 35
Bradley, William 1
Braidfitt, Lily 31
Brand, Margaret 118
Brattle, Martha 2
    William 2
Bree, Ann 110
    Rev.John 110
Brent, James 66
Brice, Edward 12,31
Brinley, Edward 28
    George 28
Bristowe, Benjamin 71
Brocall, Elizabeth 16
Brock, Elizabeth 119
    William 53
Brocklebank, Christopher
    10
Broden, William 124
Bromfield, Henry 22
Bromwich, Margaret 30
Bronaugh, William 33
Broom, John 40
Broughton, Charles R 114
    Mary 95
    Sampson 95
Brown(e), Anne 44
    Charles 12
    David 36
    Eleanor 2
    Eliz. 36,91
    Hester 3
    John 39
    Lillas 4
    Mary 40,100
    Metatiah 93
    Sophia S 12
    Susanna J 64
    Thomas 46
    Wm. 23,44,71
Bruce, Hannah 62
    Hon.James 111
    John 66
    Robert 62
    Robert G 40
    William 74*

Bruere, Goalston 12
Bryan, John 13
    Jonathan 56
Bryant, William 3,9,13,
    28,57,103,126
Bryson, John 27
Buchanan, George 69
    Margaret 69
    Neil 116
Bulcraig, Jane 107
Bun, John 109
Burch, William 88
Burges, Elizabeth 117
Burgess, William 70
Burks, Elizabeth 35
Burley, Susannah 64
Burnet, George 84
Burr, Aaron 85
Burrell, John 59
Burrington, Robert 56
Burroughs, John 45
Burrows, Samson 70
    William 47
Burton, Frances 79
    Richard 84
    Robert 39
Butcher, Maria 70
Butler, Caleb 42
    Judith 92
    Samuel 28
    William 65
Byard, Stephen 26

Cadman, Sarah 105
Cage, Sekeford 35
Calcraft, John 13
Caldewood, Lucy 20
Callaghan, James 35
Callahan, John 24
Cameron, Ann 74
    Even 74
Campbell, Agnes 72
    Colin 72
    Duncan 47,73,74
    Isabella 29
    Robert 56
    Wm. 56,72
Cane, Abigail 99
    Francis 99
    John 119
Canick, James 73
Card, Thomas 17
Carleton, Dennis 84
Carling, John 59
Carmichael, Walter 58
Carrack, James 90
Carsan, James 76
Carson, Robert 15
Carter, Bashan 83
    Jane 83
    Robert 107
    Thomas 72
Cartwright, Judith 114
Carver, Marmaduke 80
Cary, Archibald 95
    Robert 46,109
Casey, Edward 124
    James 65
Cassels, James 6
Castle, Edmund 25

Catherwood, John 22
Chabot, George 42
Chads, Henry 26
    Susanna 26
Chalmers, Rev.John 82
    Dr.Lionel 55
Chamberlain, Middleton 83
Chambers, Elizabeth 87
Chancelor, David 51
    William 83
Channon, James 4
    Rebecca 4
Chapman, George 119
    Hannah 119
    John 23
    William 42
Chardin, George 69
Chare, Africa 34
Charnock, John 67
Cherry, Samuel 107
Cheshire, Elizabeth 21
Chew, Joseph 62
Chilcott, Rev.William 107
Chipman, Elizabeth 93
    William 10,93
Chope, Richard 79
Christin, Francis H 71
Clagett, Horatio 81*,122
Clapham, John 5
    Jonas 5
Claphin, John 48
Clarendon, Henry, Earl of
    60
Clarke, George 6
    Isaac W 126
    Jonathan 126
    Joseph 96,103
    Margaret 69
Clarkson, David 33
Claus, Daniel 62
Clavering, Sir Thomas 50
Clay, Daniel 107
    Elizabeth 63,107
    Joseph 99
    Richard 85
Cloke, Hannah 50
    Richard 50
Clopper, Cornelius 16,92
Coatsworth, Caleb 84
    Catharine 33
    Susan 84
Cock, Ann 60
    William 60
Cockburn, John 13
Cockshutt, Thomas 63
Codrington, Edward 67
Coffin, Thomas A 122
Coggin, Anne 76
    Edward 76
Cohner, Deborah 101
    Jonathan 101
Colborne, Benjamin 59
Coldham, John 61
Cole, Anne 55
    Benjamin 55
    John 55
    Lewis J 118
Coleman, Stephen 120
Coles, John 11,64,77
    Thomas 13
Colegate, David 12
Collett, John 36
    Mary 36

131

137

*Indicates more than one entry of the name on the page.